# NATIVE DANCER

## The Grey Ghost

OTHER BOOKS BY JOHN EISENBERG

*The Longest Shot:*
*Lil E. Tee and the Kentucky Derby*

*Cotton Bowl Days:*
*Growing Up wih Dallas and the Cowboys in the 1960s*

*From 33rd Street to Camden Yards:*
*An Oral History of the Baltimore Orioles*

# NATIVE DANCER

## The Grey Ghost

HERO OF
A GOLDEN AGE

# John Eisenberg

**WARNER BOOKS**

An AOL Time Warner Company

Warner Books, Inc., 1271 Avenue of the Americas, New York, NY 10020
Visit our Web site at www.twbookmark.com.

An AOL Time Warner Company

Printed in the United States of America
First Printing: May 2003
10  9  8  7  6  5  4  3  2  1

**The Library of Congress Cataloging-in-Publication Data**

Eisenberg, John.
    Native Dancer, the Grey Ghost : hero of a golden age / John Eisenberg.
        p. cm.
    ISBN 0-446-53070-0
        1. Native Dancer (Race horse)  2. Race horses—United States—Biography.
    I. Title.

SF355.N38 E48 2003
798.4—dc21                                                          2002191028

*Design by Meryl Sussman Levavi/Digitext*

# AUTHOR'S NOTE

This book could not have been written without the recollections of various trainers, jockeys, farm owners, racing officials, fans, exercise riders, veterinarians, relatives of the principal figures, and members of the racing media. A list of those quoted in the text:

Appley, Claude "Apples"—longtime Vanderbilt employee who worked as farmhand, groom, exercise rider, and stable manager beginning in 1933; wife Mary also is quoted.

Atkinson, Ted—Hall of Fame jockey who rode for Greentree Stable; won 3,795 races in a twenty-one-year career.

Boniface, William—*Baltimore Sun* racing writer from 1948 to 1981.

Capps, Tim—Maryland-based author, historian, and racing executive who has worked for the Jockey Club, Maryland Horse Breeders' Association, and Maryland Jockey Club.

Caras, Costy—son of Jamaica, New York, restaurant owner and protégé of New York track announcer Fred Caposella; was longtime track announcer at Charles Town track in West Virginia; began career working for *Daily Racing Form.*

Curry, Frank—nephew of Eric Guerin.

Derr, John—longtime CBS radio and TV sports commentator and executive.

Deubler, Judy Ohl—young racing fan in the 1950s.

Dorfman, Leonard—longtime trainer who has worked the backstretch of California tracks since the 1930s.

Florio, Clem—New York–area boxer and horseplayer in the 1940s and 1950s; later, racing journalist and track oddsmaker in Maryland.

Gilcoyne, Tom—historian at National Museum of Racing's Hall of Fame in Saratoga; has followed the sport since the 1920s.

Harthill, Alex—Churchill Downs–based veterinarian for a half century.

Jerkens, Allen—New York–based trainer elected to Hall of Fame in 1975.

Kelly, Joe—longtime racing writer in Maryland; was vice president of Maryland Horseman's Association in the early 1950s.

Kercheval, Ralph—former college and pro football star; managed Sagamore Farm from 1948 to 1958; his wife, Blanche, is also quoted.

Koppett, Leonard—author and sportswriter in New York and San Francisco Bay Area since the 1940s.

Leblanc, Charles Ray—Eric Guerin's first cousin; was jockey and later steward in Illinois and New Orleans.

Passmore, Billy—young jockey in early 1950s; became steward in Maryland.

Pate, Lulu Vanderbilt—daughter of Alfred Vanderbilt's brother, George.

Pedersen, Pete—veteran racing official; has worked as steward, race-caller, steward's aide, newspaper handicapper, paddock judge, placing judge, and patrol judge at West Coast tracks.

Prince, Harold—Tony Award–winning theater producer-director known for successful musicals.

Roberts, Tommy—TV broadcaster and executive who has worked on many racing ventures since the 1950s.

Robinson, Jack—longtime veterinarian in California.

Roche, Clyde—Alfred Vanderbilt's oldest lifelong friend.

Scott, Daniel W.—owner of Kentucky farm where Native Dancer was foaled in 1950.

Scott, Daniel W., III—son of Kentucky farm owner.

Sharp, Bayard—du Pont family heir and Vanderbilt friend who backed a racing stable and owned a horse farm in Delaware.

Shoemaker, Bill—Hall of Fame jockey; began career in California in 1949 and won 8,833 races.

Tannenbaum, Joe—racing writer at *Miami Daily News* in the 1950s, then longtime director of publicity at Gulfstream Park.

Trotter, Tommy—respected racing official; has held many posts throughout the country since the 1940s.

Vanderbilt, Alfred, III—eldest son of Native Dancer's owner; mother is Jeanne; rode horses as a child and still rides for pleasure; took up writing and music and has had a long career in public relations.

Vanderbilt, Heidi—daughter of Alfred and Jeanne Vanderbilt; rode show horses as a child; owns horse farm today.

Vanderbilt, Jeanne—Alfred Vanderbilt's second wife, married to him from 1946 to 1956; resides in Paris today.

Winfrey, Carey—Bill Winfrey's eldest son; editor in chief of *Smithsonian* magazine today.

Winfrey, Elaine—Bill Winfrey's second wife, married to him from 1952 until his death in 1994.

# INTRODUCTION

The train pulled into Cincinnati's Union Station early one morning in late April 1953. No passengers got on, no passengers got off, no one even paid attention until a station mechanic on a routine check idly slid open a car door and stepped back in amazement at the scene he had uncovered. A muscular grey horse stood on a bed of straw in the far corner of the car, next to a black man wearing a hat.

"Is that . . . is that the Grey Ghost himself?" the mechanic stammered.

"It sure enough is," the black man replied with a smile.

The mechanic opened his mouth without emitting a sound, stunned at his discovery. Then he began to shout: "Hey, everyone, over here! You can't miss this!"

Within moments a mob of commuters, laborers, and onlookers had gathered on the platform, straining for a glimpse of the train's famous passenger—a celebrity who would be hailed by *TV Guide* at the end of 1953 as one of America's three most popular figures, along with entertainer Arthur Godfrey and host Ed Sullivan. His stopover in Cincinnati, lasting all of five minutes, was deemed newsworthy enough for a story in the local paper the next day. Fathers eating breakfast read the story and said to their families, "I wish I'd missed my train and gotten stuck at the station."

It was an epic time for mythmaking in America. In the aftermath of a depression and war, at the dawn of the television age, the country was moving to the suburbs and learning to commune over heroes hatched in living rooms on flickering, black-and-white TV sets. Out of the mists of the early 1950s rose a star as bright as any, a thoroughbred champion with blue-blood roots, a knack for drama, and a name that would gain a permanent place in the nation's vocabulary: Native Dancer.

Bred, owned, and championed by Alfred Gwynne Vanderbilt, the sporting scion of one of the country's most celebrated families, Native Dancer would finish first in twenty-one of twenty-two races in his career (the one loss was by a nose), securing a place among horse racing's legends. Although his story was suffused with the sweet whiff of the underdog—his canny young trainer, Bill Winfrey, was raised on the dust and straw of Depression-era racing, and his jockey, Eric Guerin, was a blacksmith's son raised poor in Louisiana's rural backwaters—at its essence, Native Dancer's reign was about power, glory, and class at the pinnacle of American society. He was a product of rarefied lineage and the finest farms and barns, blessed with physical and mental endowments his bloodlines couldn't explain, an odds-on favorite every time he raced. At a time when Americans saw their country as wealthy and invincible, Vanderbilt and his horse constituted a national self-portrait.

The horse's brief stop in Cincinnati was on the last leg of his trek from New York, where he was stabled, to Louisville's Churchill Downs, where he would run for racing's ultimate glory in the Kentucky Derby on the first Saturday in May 1953. The nation was waiting for what it foresaw as a coronation, captivated by the colt's undefeated record and agonizing habit of seemingly waiting too long before making his move. Prior racing legends such as Man O' War and Seabiscuit had inspired public fervor, and the soaring arc of Native Dancer's renown was similar and even higher in some ways. He was racing's first matinee idol, his triumphs witnessed by millions on coast-to-coast TV broadcasts. His popularity was evidence of the growing power of the new medium; New York sportswriter Jimmy

Cannon would later write that "Native Dancer probably sold as many Zeniths as Milton Berle."

His appeal was as simple as the times. Television cast a black-and-white picture. Native Dancer's coat was grey. Anyone could pick him out and cheer him down the stretch as he sprinted with his head slung low, veering through traffic until he was alone in front. And cheer him they did: in bars, airports, train stations, living rooms, department stores—anywhere that people gathered and gawked in front of TV sets, still awestruck by the ability to see what they previously had only been able to hear.

The sight of Vanderbilt leading his horse into the winner's circle became a Saturday afternoon TV staple and turned Native Dancer into a star without peer. Thousands of fans crowded around the walking rings and saddling stalls before he raced, anxious just to glimpse the granite monster weighing more than 1,200 pounds, yet possessing a burst of acceleration and a finishing kick that left hardened horsemen groping for adjectives. "He was in the company of the gods, inspiring a reverence felt only for other immortals such as Babe Ruth and Jim Thorpe," racing author Bernard Livingston wrote years later. "It became routine for bettors not to cash their winning tickets, instead pocketing them as souvenirs. A small piece of Native Dancer was more important than any monies won."

America in 1953 was a cocky sprawl just beginning an unwitting transition from the unified glory of World War II to the splintered days of Vietnam and the sixties. The cold war with the Soviet Union was escalating as American soldiers fought grimly in Korea and bomb shelters were erected across America amid growing concern that communists had infiltrated the country's political and cultural institutions. Seeking to soothe their jangled nerves, Americans had elected Dwight Eisenhower, a paternal army general, as their president. It was the last decade without cynicism, with lives slower, choices fewer, and joys less complicated than what lay ahead. Racing was the playground of the thrill seekers. The sport was in a gritty golden age, perched atop the nation's sports scene. Every week 700,000 people spent at least a day at one of the country's 130 tracks.

Native Dancer was the perfect horse for the moment. Before the din and anarchy of the sixties, symbols of power were still beloved and embraced; institutions were to be admired, not challenged. The sports world was brimming with them. Baseball's New York Yankees were in the midst of a run of five straight World Series titles. Notre Dame's football team was a constant in the top five of the college polls. Calumet Farm, racing's dominant stable, had won the Kentucky Derby five times since 1941. Golfer Ben Hogan had come back from a crippling car crash to win a string of major championships. It was an age of winners, and America itself was the biggest, bulging with prosperity. Native Dancer, a champion horse belonging to one of the nation's wealthiest families, fit seamlessly into the landscape.

A half century later, he was judged one of the greatest horses of the twentieth century by several panels of experts. But judging him solely on his record and winning times misses the essence of his career. He was racing's original pop star, the equine Elvis Presley, an iconic marker of an easier but unsettled time and place. When American racing was at its best in the early 1950s, its best was an indelibly charismatic horse known as the Grey Ghost. "It was a good time to be alive and a great time to be a racing fan," said Joe Hirsch, the long-time *Daily Racing Form* columnist. "When Native Dancer came along, he was more than just a horse. He was a happening."

# NATIVE DANCER

## The Grey Ghost

# ONE

He was a sprinkle of light on a dark canvas, the only grey horse in a dizzy tumble of bays, blacks, and chestnuts coming down the stretch. The 40,000 fans crowded into Belmont Park on September 27, 1952, could easily pick him out and see he was in trouble, trapped between and behind other horses with the finish line fast approaching. Only days earlier, a columnist for the *New York Morning Telegraph,* a newspaper that focused on horse racing, had wondered in print, "Is Native Dancer Invincible?" With two furlongs left in the Futurity Stakes, one of American racing's most important events for two-year-olds, the horse's aura of invincibility was being challenged as never before.

He had reached the finish line well ahead of his rivals in his prior seven races at New York tracks in 1952, his renown building with every success. The sportswriters at New York's seven daily newspapers had hailed him from the beginning as a young horse to watch, and he had yet to disappoint. Muscular and riveting, with a gargantuan stride and an unyielding will, he had ambled along in the middle of the pack in every race, constrained by his jockey, Eric Guerin, until he was told it was time to sprint to the finish line; then, in a transformation as stunning as it was consistent, he lowered his head, lengthened his stride, accelerated past his rivals, and left them behind, usually in just a few moments. He had won such races as the Youth-

ful Stakes, Saratoga Special, and Hopeful Stakes, and now New York's
hard-boiled racetrack crowd had turned out to see if he could win a
race that often determined the best two-year-old in America.

It was a typical racing crowd, composed mostly of men dressed
in coats and hats, with a smattering of women and no children. Belmont's grandstand, opened in 1905, seated just 17,500, so every inch
of the aisles, aprons, and terraces was filled. The crowd was sweaty
and testy, knowing and charged-up. Racing was at a spectacular
zenith of popularity across the country, with stables such as Calumet
Farm and jockeys such as Eddie Arcaro as familiar to sports fans as
baseball star Mickey Mantle and heavyweight champion Rocky Marciano, and major tracks routinely attracting 50,000 fans for important
races. The hordes had come to Belmont for one reason on this sunlit
September Saturday: to bet on Native Dancer in the Futurity, a mad
dash of six and a half furlongs down the Widener Straight Course, a
straightaway chute cutting diagonally across Belmont's main track.

The air had been electric in the saddling paddock before the
race. Hundreds of fans surrounded the Dancer and shouted encouragement to the familiar trinity of men responsible for the horse: Alfred Gwynne Vanderbilt, the handsome millionaire who had bred the
Dancer and now campaigned him; Bill Winfrey, the youthful trainer
who had yet to make a false move with the horse; and Eric Guerin, the
twenty-eight-year-old Cajun jockey who rode all of Vanderbilt's top
horses under a contract arrangement. Long lines at the betting windows snaked through the crowd as the Dancer's odds dropped in the
tense minutes before the race. He was 7–20 by post time, his allure so
powerful that the Big Apple wise guys accustomed to angling for the
slightest edge had just shrugged and given in to getting thirty-five
cents on the dollar.

The other nine horses in the field were supposedly some of the
nation's best two-year-olds, but they had received scant attention from
the fans. They were just the supporting cast in this star vehicle. The
second choice, Tiger Skin, owned by Jock Whitney's Greentree Stable, had provided a modest challenge to the Dancer in the Hopeful
weeks earlier at Saratoga before fading in the stretch. A colt named
Tahitian King had already lost three times to the Dancer but was

being ridden now by Arcaro, the king of America's jockeys. Little Request was a California speedster expected to set a fast early pace. Dark Star was the best of Harry Guggenheim's Cain Hoy Stable. None were given much of a chance of beating the Dancer.

Winfrey offered Guerin a leg up with the advice he always gave: "Just ride him with confidence." Wearing a white cap and Vanderbilt's silks of cerise and white diamonds with cerise and white sleeves, the jockey jogged the horse down the chute along with the rest of the field. One by one, the horses were loaded into the starting gate as early evening enveloped the track and a slanting sun cast lengthening shadows. After a brief pause, the gate doors opened and the horses came charging out. A roar went up from the crowd. Was there a better sports moment than a fast horse's reach for greatness?

Seen from the grandstand, horses on the Widener course started as tiny, vague shapes in the distance and grew larger and clearer to the fans only as they neared the finish line in front of the grandstand. The crowd relied on track announcer Fred Caposella's distinctive nasal call, listening for any mention of the Dancer. Guerin settled the horse five lengths behind Little Request as the Californian set the anticipated fast pace, covering the first half mile in 46⅘ seconds.

Races on the Widener course were often won by top jockeys, their skills especially valuable on the seldom-used track. Any jockey could tell when he had covered a half mile or was turning for home on the main oval, but those markers were harder to judge on a straightaway. Jockeys with less ability or poorer instincts often moved at the wrong time, and in a short race for young horses, that was usually fatal. "Jockeyship often took effect on the chute," recalled Hall of Fame trainer Allen Jerkens, who began his career in New York in 1950. "You had to be pretty darn good to win the Futurity."

Guerin had won it on Blue Peter in 1948, and after navigating an easy half mile on the Dancer, he inched the horse out of the pack and toward the front. It was time to make the winning move the crowd had expected. But just as the Dancer's ears went back, Arcaro, a jockey so adept at measuring pace and timing moves he was nicknamed the Master, struck boldly. He drove Tahitian King, a 10–1 shot, through a hole on the far rail, past Little Request and into the lead. The crowd screamed with surprise as Caposella's pitch rose and Little Request, suddenly fading, blocked the Dancer's path and stalled the favorite in the pack. The big grey had never experienced anything like this.

If any jockey could take a lesser horse and steal the Futurity, it was Arcaro. At age thirty-six, he was still in the prime of a career that had included five Kentucky Derby victories and dozens of other triumphs in major races such as the Futurity, which he had won three times. He was at his best in the big events, and his move on Tahitian King was a classic. Knowing he wasn't on a horse that could beat the Dancer in a stretch duel, he had preemptively grabbed the lead, hoping the favorite might get blocked long enough to cause problems. The plan had worked, and Arcaro, sensing a possible upset, asked Tahitian King for a finishing kick.

That the Dancer was behind so late in a race wasn't unusual. He had trailed in all of his races until making a late move, then often, curiously, loafed to the finish line once he had established his superiority, almost as if he wanted the others to catch him. After months of observation, Winfrey had deduced that the horse preferred the company of others when he raced; running alone and in front bored him, it seemed. Winfrey had thus conditioned him to race behind the front-runners, in traffic, until it almost seemed too late, accelerating just in time to win at the end, leaving little time for loafing.

But if it was normal that he was behind Tahitian King with a quarter mile left in the Futurity, it wasn't normal that horses were in front of him and on either side, leaving him without a running lane. Guerin knew he had to react quickly. A successful rider on the New York circuit, known for his cool head and steady hand, he recognized that the race was on the verge of getting away. He hesitated, hoping the pack around him would begin to break up, and knowing he was in trouble if it didn't. Magically, it did: Little Request dropped toward the rear, fading fast, and a sliver of daylight opened to Guerin's right. He steered the Dancer into the opening, loosened his grip on the reins, and shouted at the horse. Back went the Dancer's ears and out went his stride, his reach so extended that, it was said later, you could see the bottoms of his hooves at midstride.

In the career of every top athlete, equine or otherwise, there is a moment when it becomes clear this is no ordinary competitor. For Native Dancer, that moment came in the final two hundred yards of the Futurity. Once he had found running room and accelerated, he drew even with Tahitian King so quickly that Arcaro had no chance to react. It almost resembled a deft magician's trick: he was pursuing Tahitian King one second, eyeball-to-eyeball the next. Cheers soared into the air, and just as quickly, the Dancer wrested away the lead and took aim at the finish. He had gone from fourth to first in five remarkable steps without Guerin even drawing his stick.

A combination of factors would send the horse's popularity soaring in the coming months: his prodigious talent; his come-from-behind style, which exhausted his fans but left them wanting to see more; the timing of his arrival, at the dawn of the TV age; and the sheer humanness he exuded with his limpid eyes and charisma. But of all the factors, none were more important than, simply, his color. His grey coat stood apart in any equine crowd, discernible not only to fans at the track but also to those watching on TV.

A fast grey was a phenomenon. Only one of every one hundred thoroughbreds was grey in 1953, and through the years, other than a stallion named Mahmoud that C. V. Whitney had imported from England and a colt named First Fiddle that had won some races during World War II, greys had not distinguished themselves in American racing. Many horsemen had long considered them unlucky, lacking stamina, or even diseased, as the legendary Italian breeder Federico Tesio had written. "It wasn't prejudice so much as a sense of caution and reservation," longtime *Daily Racing Form* columnist Joe Hirsch recalled years later. "Greys just were different. It was a sense of racism, I suppose."

Greys would have disappeared entirely from racetracks around the world in the late 1800s if not for a French stallion named Le Sancy, the single horse from which all modern grey pedigrees are traced. Le Sancy's son, Le Samaritain, won the French St. Léger, a major race, and sired a colt named Roi Herode. After a respectable racing career, Roi Herode retired in Ireland and sired a brilliant colt named The Tetrarch, a light grey with white patches dotting his coat. Nicknamed the Spotted Wonder, he won all seven of his races as a two-year-old in England in 1913, then was injured and retired to stud, where he sired a speedy filly named Mumtaz Mahal and many other winners.

The Tetrarch restored enough faith in greys to keep the line alive in England and America, yet many owners, breeders, and horsemen still avoided them, and racing secretaries were still writing "grey only" races into their condition books as late as the 1940s, believing the curios would draw women to the track. Even in the early 1950s, many horsemen still saw them as sissified novelties and claimed, only half jokingly, that if you came across a grey or a horse with three or four white legs, you might as well cut off its head and feed it to the crows.

There was no substance to the notion that greys were genetically inferior, of course. Coloring had no effect on a horse's ability to race. The grey tint in the Dancer and others was attributable to a lack of pigmentation in some hairs, leaving the coat a blend of dark and light hairs that appeared grey from a distance. Many greys were born dark and died white, and spent much of their lives in a state of transformation from one extreme to the other. The Dancer, colored chocolate brown at birth, was now a rich dark grey with patterns of light rings just visible in his coat. His sire, Polynesian, was a bay, but the genes of his dam, Geisha, had dominated his coloring. Geisha was a grey great-great-granddaughter of Roi Herode and a daughter and granddaughter of greys. Now her son was a grey, becoming more famous every day.

Those who still doubted him because of his color had no argument left after his move to the front in the Futurity. Many in the crowd had thought he was beaten, but he had broken free from the pack with a breathtaking burst, and now, with seventy-five yards to go, embarked on the triumphant sprint many had envisioned. He drove forward in a grinding gear, for once not easing up with the lead as his slanting shadow bobbed farther ahead of the others. His rivals were left behind, their inferiority underlined. The Dancer was two and a quarter lengths ahead of Tahitian King at the finish line, and nine lengths ahead of every other horse except the distant third-place finisher, Dark Star.

There was a cheer, and then another, even louder, when the win-ning time was posted. The Dancer had run the race in 1:14⅗, as fast as any horse anywhere had ever covered six and a half furlongs on a straightaway course. He had tied a world record! A two-year-old named Porter's Mite had set the record on the Widener course fifteen years earlier, carrying three fewer pounds than the Dancer. "I'm sure he would have broken the record if we hadn't been fighting a head-wind the whole way," Guerin told reporters. The jockey had won a Kentucky Derby and stood in hundreds of winner's circles, but clearly he was moved by what he had just experienced. "I don't believe," he said, "that I have ever ridden a better horse."

More cheers rained down as Lester Murray, the Dancer's el-derly black groom, attached the shank and held him in the winner's enclosure at the foot of the grandstand. Vanderbilt and Winfrey posed for win pictures as reporters surrounded Arcaro, who could only shake his head. "I wish the race had been six furlongs instead of six and a half," the Master muttered. "I thought I had it won until that grey horse just smothered us."

It was a busy sports Saturday in New York and across the country, with Notre Dame playing Pennsylvania in college football before a na-tional TV audience and 75,000 fans in Philadelphia, the pro football sea-son kicking off, and tickets selling for the World Series between the Yankees and Brooklyn Dodgers beginning the next week. Baseball was dominating the talk on the streets of New York. There wasn't much room in the papers for big news from Belmont. But Native Dancer had given the sports editors no choice. As Joe H. Palmer, the esteemed rac-ing writer for the *New York Herald Tribune,* wrote in his column the next day, the grey colt had "just plain murdered the field in the Futurity," rais-ing glorious echoes of past champions such as Count Fleet, Citation, and Man O' War. America's next great horse had arrived, and he was a grey, of all things, a pale specter sprinting through the stretch. People were calling him the Grey Ghost, his coloring and shadowy dominance stir-ring imaginations. If his victory in the Futurity didn't warrant a bold headline at the top of the sports page, what did?

# TWO

Twenty minutes after the Futurity, with the crowd still buzzing about the Dancer's charge, the colt headed back to Barn 20 on the backstretch at Belmont, where Vanderbilt's horses in training were permanently stabled. Harold Walker, the stable's mammoth night watchman, held the lead shank as the Dancer pranced through the track's treelined barn community. Lester Murray brought up the rear. Clothed in the white coat and broad-brimmed hat he always wore to the races, the groom gripped the Dancer's tail tightly with both hands and chattered nonstop. "You done good, you bum, you done real good," Murray huffed at the horse as they moved along.

None of the men who worked for Vanderbilt could remember where Murray had come from, but they also couldn't remember the barn without him. With his round head perched on his round body as he waddled across the straw, forever spinning a yarn, he was a sixty-three-year-old lifelong horseman, steeped in the backyard remedies and unerring instincts of racing's old school. His wisdom was incalculable, his devotion to his horses immutable. No one loved the Dancer more. Murray and the Grey Ghost spent hours together in the stall every day, Murray wrapping and unwrapping bandages, passing out dandelions as treats, and engaging in nonstop conversation, his rumbling voice pitched in the melodious, intimate tone a mother might use when alone in a room with a child. He sprawled on the floor as he worked, often dozed in the straw when finished, and when it was time to rise, grabbed the Dancer's tail and held on for leverage as he hauled himself up. The horse never responded angrily to the tugs, seemingly understanding that he was helping his friend. On some level, it could safely be said, the Dancer and his groom were in love.

Murray handled the groom's chores by himself on most days, but the colt was such a handful, so immense and unpredictable, that Winfrey had assigned the responsibility of the lead shank to Walker on race days. Murray's aging grip just wasn't enough, especially with the swirl of people and noise around the horse seemingly increasing with every victory. What if the Dancer abruptly reared, as he occasionally did during morning workouts? Murray alone wouldn't be able to keep him under control.

There was no reason for concern once the entourage reached Barn 20 after the Futurity, so Walker handed the shank to Murray and the groom led the Dancer around and around the long indoor enclosure, cooling out from the race. Once his breathing eased, the horse was bathed and deposited in stall 6, his kingly lair. Murray took off his coat and hat and went to work, removing the tight racing bandages on the horse's legs and replacing them with looser stall bandages. "You just want to eat," the groom groused good-naturedly. "You hungry, you are."

The barn was immaculate and efficient, radiating the crisp glow of a wealthy family's country home. Two dozen well-bred Vanderbilt horses were on the premises, operating on a tight schedule of training, racing, feeding, and sleep. Their stalls were piled deep with hay. Pampered black cats dashed about wearing collars with cerise and white diamond stitching. During morning workout hours, the exercise riders were dressed in uniforms of boots, jodhpurs, and cerise and white sweaters, and the grooms bustled through their chores with precision.

The family ambience wasn't happenstance. At a time when many of racing's top stables belonged to society families such as the Wideners and Whitneys, a job with Vanderbilt was a job to keep. Most of the staff, like Murray, had worked in the barn for years, becoming as associated with Vanderbilt as his colors and silks in the insular backstretch world. There were exercise riders such as Bernie Everson, who rode the Dancer every morning, and Claude "Apples" Appley, who had worked for Vanderbilt since the Depression; grooms such as Walker and Murray; and J. C. Mergler, the stable foreman who paid the feed man and made sure Vanderbilt's high standards were met. They had hummed along for years, a racing family, working together through Vanderbilt's prosperous times in the sport, and also his many disappointments.

A handful of top horses such as Bed o' Roses, Next Move, Loser Weeper, and Cousin had passed through their hands in the past few years as Vanderbilt's stable experienced a renaissance after falling off badly during the war. Now there was Native Dancer, the best yet. Physically, he was awesome. Though still a gawky equine teenager as a two-year-old with growing to do, he was already fearsome at 16.1 hands tall (5'6") and 1,100 pounds, with rippling muscles, firm withers, and brawn over his kidneys and in his hindquarters and back, where horses were seldom so defined. He was a fullback in football, a cleanup hitter in baseball, a muscle-bound intimidator who could throw one punch and knock you cold. He loomed over his opposition in his post parades, yet where some horses his size were too bulky to race effectively, the Dancer was coordinated and graceful, a heavyweight as nimble as a lightweight, never taking an awkward step.

Everything about him was outsized. Great whooshes of air passed through his nostrils as he charged down the track, hammering the ground with every step and violently throwing his front legs out and down, as if the goal was to see how far he could reach or how much dust he could raise. Early in 1953, *Life* magazine measured his stride at twenty-nine feet, one foot longer than Man O' War's and seven feet beyond the average for a thoroughbred. The effort required to propel his massive frame should have exhausted him, but he was never out of breath at the end of training or a race. Seemingly blessed with lungs the size of circus balloons, he had a limitless capacity for work.

Even his flaws were amplified: his ankles were pocked by bulbous, fleshy lumps that horrified most horsemen, many of whom be-

lieved the defect would prevent him from surviving the rigors of training and racing. Winfrey downplayed the issue, dismissing reporters
when they suggested the ankles might become problematic. Privately, he was at times concerned: a horse that pounded the ground
so hard was always susceptible to ankle problems. But the matter
hadn't yet caused him to miss a race, and Winfrey and Vanderbilt
were optimistic.

Through the years, other equine champions had entranced the
public by winning despite shortcomings or infirmities. Exterminator,
winner of fifty races from 1917 to 1925, was nicknamed Old Bones.
Seabiscuit, hero of the Great Depression, was undersized and had a
troublesome right foreleg. Assault, a Triple Crown winner in 1946,
limped when he walked and had such nicknames as Cripple and Club
Foot. But the Grey Ghost generated no such disbelief. No one who
watched him race wondered how or why he was winning. He exuded
exactly what the public thought a champion should exude. His muscles were intimidating, his coordination fascinating. His walk was
proud, his trot graceful, his sprint the stuff of poetry. When he walked
down the track, people on the fence just looked at him and sighed.

He was such a robust, healthy individual that he didn't require
the hormone injections, vitamins, penicillin, and heat treatments so
many other horses needed; his doctoring consisted of little more than
dabs of liniment rubbed on his ankles. His appetite was vast; when
you put food in front of him, it was gone: two quarts of oats at 11 A.M.,
four quarts at four in the afternoon, four quarts at 1 A.M. and so much
mixed clover in between meals that his hayrack needed filling twice a
day. "The clover has those sweet buds and he's like a child with a
Tootsie Roll or something; he stuffs himself with it," Winfrey explained to writer John McNulty in a 1953 *New Yorker* article. The
clover was replaced with straight timothy four days before a race,
Winfrey told McNulty, because it wasn't as sweet and "he's more sen-
sible about it."

The pros in Barn 20 loved him. With his 8–0 record after the
Futurity, he was a star shooting across racing's constellation, wiring
the barn with the electricity a good horse produces. But although his
success reflected well on the barn's horsemanship, he wasn't treated

with deference. Visitors to the barn were shocked to see Winfrey give the horse a harsh slap across the bridge of his nose to get his attention, or Murray tug on his tail as he rose from the straw. That was how they handled the Dancer, as a wise older brother might treat an immature but gifted younger sibling: with tough, heartfelt love. Such treatment was necessary. The horse was unpredictable, at times a ham who pricked his ears for photographers and made funny faces for strangers; but also occasionally lashed out without warning. When visitors to the barn or horsemen he didn't know or trust tried to pet him or work with him, he nipped at their fingers and sometimes even chased them out of his stall. Years later, he chomped a finger off a groom's hand. You didn't want any novice dealing with him. He could be just plain dangerous.

Yet, remarkably, he seemed to know the difference between whom he could bully and whom he should respect. He played endlessly with his favorite black cats and never gave Murray or Winfrey any trouble, but a police dog who entered his stall one morning was sent flying into a wall. Visitors to the barn were warned to keep their distance, but Vanderbilt's young children could yank on his tail without fear. "One time Dad ushered Heidi and myself into his stall and let us pull on his tail—hard—while Lester stood at his head. An incredible scenario," Alfred Vanderbilt III recalled. "Dad told us: 'Don't worry. He won't kick anyone, and he won't kick you.' We ran up and down both his sides in the stall, making a terrible racket. All he did was calmly look back over his shoulder at us. It was magic."

His comportment on the job was what mattered, of course, and there, he was a pleasure. He had sailed through his schooling in the fundamentals that troubled many other young horses, adapting easily to riding under tack, breaking from the starting gate, and "rating" behind other horses early in a race to save energy for the stretch. Although he occasionally dipped his shoulder without warning and dumped Everson—just to let everyone know he could, it seemed—he was adaptable and businesslike in his training and racing, seemingly endeavoring to get the job done without wasting anyone else's time— or more importantly, his own. Winfrey had suggested to reporters that he could "train himself," and horsemen familiar with the colt understood. "He would look right at you with those big, bright, shining eyes, and you could almost see the wheels turning. I swear that horse could think," recalled Dan W. Scott, the Kentucky farm owner who foaled the Dancer in 1950.

Everson, who rode him almost every morning, marveled at his intelligence and natural curiosity. Trees and birds distracted him, and other horses could make him forget what he was doing. After observing steeplechase horses training in the infield one day, he abruptly jumped across shadows on the track a few days later, obviously impressed by what he had seen. His fascination with other horses, Winfrey believed, was the reason he wanted to race mostly in the middle of the pack until the home stretch, instead of in front.

Yet as much as he preferred the pack, he was, in the end, fiercely competitive. Many thoroughbreds circled a track without seriously attempting to finish ahead of other horses, either not comprehending that the object was to finish first or not caring. Conversely, a rare few cared desperately, their innate competitiveness evident even in training. Native Dancer was an extreme case. Once his dash through the stretch began, his determination to finish first—his will to win—engulfed him. He often stared at his rivals as he passed them, his neck swiveling until it almost was wrenched. Some attributed this maddening habit to his inexperience, others saw it as evidence of an understanding that only a few champions had exhibited—the knowledge that his decisive move to the front had dealt his opponents a devastating psychological blow, underlining their inferiority and crumbling their desire to compete.

"He would come from way off the pace and just blow them away," Dan W. Scott said. "This was a horse that loved to run, loved to compete. And when you have a horse that is a competitor every time, there's your champion. When War Admiral won the Belmont in 1937, he got stepped on and lost a lot of blood during the race, but he led the whole way. That's a champion. Native Dancer was the same kind of horse. Nowadays, they have these monitors that measure a horse's heart. Gosh, I would love to have monitored Native Dancer's heart."

While it was a stretch to suggest that any horse understood his lot in the racing world, the Dancer seemed to understand he was a winner, plucked from the masses and elevated to a pinnacle. He strutted through his days with a haughty swagger, oozing superiority. And nothing was more cocksure than his come-from-behind racing style, which, unmistakably, had come from within the horse, not from his trainer.

"A good horse always figures out the racing game sooner or later, and the style to which he is comfortable is the style he'll race in," Joe Hirsch said. "That was certainly the case with this horse. Winfrey had to go along with him. It wasn't the easiest style, and it forced the horse to work harder, but the horse was up to the task and it suited Winfrey."

The great Exterminator had won many of his races similarly, making his move in the stretch on his own, without regard for the jockey's suggestions, and winning narrowly, without exerting an ounce of extra effort. He had taught his jockeys how to win, it was said, and Guerin, who rode the Dancer, believed the big grey possessed the same sagacity. "He has all the instincts and reactions of a human being," Guerin told *Life* magazine, "and sometimes I think he has more real sense of how to run a race than I do."

He was a prodigy, a youngster already exhibiting qualities of greatness. He was also, unmistakably, a star, blessed with an ineffable magnetism. Fans who came to see him invariably left the track talking only of him, as if no other horses had raced. He grabbed their eyes and held them, his spectral dashes through the stretch as riveting as the sight of Joe DiMaggio angling gracefully across the outfield grass in pursuit of a fly ball. People loved his eager white face bobbing up and down as he charged from the gate like the young colt he still was, flecks of foam gathering at the corners of his mouth. They loved the way he almost seemed to look for them in the stands, his eyes wandering until he really grabbed the bit and got serious. They loved the way he always knew where he was on the track, and what he was doing. They loved his amazing, athletic moves around the turns. They loved and understood his inherent laziness, his sweet tooth, his childish habit of playfully terrorizing those around him. It was all too human.

Lester Murray had worked with horses for years, rubbing them and talking to them and watching them run, good ones and bad ones, characters and dullards, and he had never encountered such a blend of talent and individuality. The old groom didn't like to let on, but the grey colt amazed him. He had never seen a horse that came from behind with such power and purpose in the stretch, almost making it seem as if the other horses were suddenly standing still. And he was a smart one, too, as observant and shrewd as any horse Murray had come across. Like a lot of people who had spent their lives at the track, the groom halfway believed in the inexplicable, and he was waiting for the day when the Dancer started talking back to him.

Kneeling in the straw after the Futurity, Murray slowly removed safety pins from the row he had pinned to his pants and used them to fasten stall bandages to the Grey Ghost's priceless legs. Dusk enveloped the barn and the Dancer whickered loudly.

"You want food," Murray said to the horse.

There was no doubt; the Dancer's afternoon meal was delayed until early evening on race days. Winfrey did not want to fill him up.

Four quarts of oats were dumped into the cerise and white feed bucket. The Dancer dug in ferociously.

The New York newspapermen who covered the racing scene had discovered Murray as a wellspring of material—"he's the hottest-gittin' horse I ever saw," he had told one reporter about the Dancer—and several stood outside the stall now, watching him work and asking for his unique insights into what made the grey colt tick.

Murray whistled.

"That's how I get him to make water," he said.

They continued to watch the horse attack his food.

"He knows me like a book, and I knows him," Murray said idly, eyeing the colt with a fatherly pride.

When the bucket was empty, Murray picked it up and whacked the Dancer on the ass. The horse didn't budge.

"He's a big bum," Murray said to the reporters, "and what I think he like is, he like standing in that winner's circle and having his picture took."

# THREE

On the day after the Futurity, Alfred Vanderbilt rose early at Broadhollow, the 110-acre estate on Long Island where he lived with his wife Jeanne and their children, Heidi and young Alfred. He had slept little after a postrace celebration in Manhattan with Jeanne and friends at Le Pavillon, his favorite restaurant, but he was a racing man, and no matter what happened the night before, a racing man always began his day while the rest of the world slept.

He was headed to Belmont to spend the morning watching Native Dancer and his other horses train, and also to enjoy reviewing the Grey Ghost's victory with Bill Winfrey. Vanderbilt's valet, Louis Cheri, was up to make sure he departed on time, and a driver was also up, offering to drive him to Belmont, but as usual, Vanderbilt slipped behind the wheel of his Mercedes and pulled away. Other men in his social circle preferred being driven, but Vanderbilt loved to drive. Moreover, he was uncomfortable putting on certain airs, especially around the track.

His day always began with a commute to the barn to see his horses, no matter if he was in Southern California, where he spent part of every winter; Florida, where he owned real estate; outside Baltimore, at Sagamore Farm, his horse farm; or in New York. He cherished racing's eternal morning routine, sipping coffee and trading opinions with horsemen amid the shadowy light and acrid smells of training hours. The afternoons, with their color and noise and racing thrills, appealed to the public, and Vanderbilt certainly enjoyed them, but he truly relished the quiet mornings when real horse people conducted the real business of horses.

He was, in theory, out of his element on the backstretch, too lordly to commune with grooms, feed men, and exercise riders. His ancestry included two of the sovereign figures of America's industrial age: his mother's father, Isaac Emerson, the "millionaire chemist" from Baltimore who had amassed a fortune manufacturing and selling Bromo-Seltzer, the upset-stomach remedy; and his great-great-grandfather, Cornelius Vanderbilt, the legendary Commodore, who borrowed a hundred dollars from his mother, built an empire of ferries, steamships, and railways, and left a $100 million estate, the largest ever probated in the United States, when he died in 1877. Their wealth was so profound it could still endow a man's life generations later: Alfred Vanderbilt's inheritances had included more than $10 million, a horse farm, and a racing stable. It wasn't as much as the reported $40 million his cousin and Long Island neighbor John Hay "Jock" Whitney had inherited ("I wish I had his money," Vanderbilt would later sigh, famously, about Whitney), but it was enough to ensure that Vanderbilt could do as he pleased in life.

An independent thinker who had excelled as a racetrack operator in his twenties, he could have produced Broadway shows, directed a business conglomerate, or run for office—typical Vanderbilt endeavors—and whatever he chose, he surely would have flourished. But he wanted horse racing. Immersed in the sport since childhood, he had already lived a full, varied racing life. He had bred expensive horses, operated a top racing stable, even mucked a few stalls. He had been in charge of the daily operation of two tracks, owned a majority interest of stock in one, served as president of the Thoroughbred Racing Associations, and experienced racing's highest honor, election to the Jockey Club, the sport's august ruling body, at age twenty-seven. As if all that weren't enough, he had hosted CBS's TV broadcast of several major races, including the 1947 Belmont Stakes, and, legend had it, ghostwritten his share of newspaper columns after one of his friends in the racing press had passed out at the typewriter after a long day at the bar.

The suggestion that he was too aristocratic for the backstretch would have dismayed him. He had unceasing respect for racing's foot soldiers and their ritualistic tasks that underwrote his sport. He was a horseman himself, capable, knowledgeable, and instinctive; he had even overseen his horses' training at times before hiring Bill Winfrey to run his stable in 1949.

Lanky and pallid, Vanderbilt radiated the aura of a debonair schoolboy with impish gaps in his front teeth, dark hair that fell across his forehead in a boyish widow's peak, and tailored suits that drooped on his thin frame. He joked about his looks, but he had dated starlets such as Ginger Rogers before marrying, and Jeanne, as a schoolgirl, had pinned up pictures of him in her room when friends were pinning up pictures of Cary Grant.

"It was common to say he was our unofficial crown prince," said theater producer-director Harold Prince, who met Vanderbilt in the early 1950s and became a close friend. "He was so glamorous, so attractive. Women surely liked him, but so did men. And he was worth liking. He was easy and relaxed and very smart and very inquisitive, very independent. When I first met him, I thought, 'This is the crown prince who I used to see pictures of at the Stork Club with Ginger Rogers and other lovely ladies,' and you saw his fedora and you saw how he looked, and it was almost Fred Astaire. He wasn't really like Astaire, but there was a kind of imperial grace about him."

Among the wealthy men who invested in racing, only Vanderbilt came to the barn every morning, monitoring his horses and conversing with the grooms and jockeys, dropping the impeccable English he had learned at St. Paul's and Yale for the rugged patois of the track. "I just can't do that," said Jock Whitney, who co-owned Greentree, another top stable, with his sister. The ease came naturally to Vanderbilt. For all his advantages, he had a knack for relating to—and looking out for—the common man. His friend Oscar Levant, the piano-playing wit, once told a reporter that Vanderbilt related better to the poor than to the wealthy because nannies and nurses had raised him.

"As privileged as he was, and as much as he lived in luxury, he didn't give a damn about that," recalled Clyde Roche, Vanderbilt's oldest lifelong friend. "He was totally indifferent to that sort of thing, perfectly comfortable in any setting. He didn't want to be driven anywhere. One time I had aspirations to write something, and he said, 'We'll go for a long drive and talk it out.' We drove from Long Island all the way up to the White Mountains in New England, stayed overnight at some hotel, and then Alfred said, 'Well, let's go home now,' and we drove back. The trip was made solely for the purpose of him getting to drive."

Racing was far from his only interest. He loved opera, theater, music, and books. His close friends included George Abbott, the legendary theater director and producer known as Mr. Broadway, and Levant, an eccentric who virtually lived at Broadhollow. A nimble pianist himself, Vanderbilt owned a massive record collection and was deemed as knowledgeable about music as a professional. He and Levant could spend hours scouring Lower Manhattan's used record shops for dusty gems. "Alfred had a wonderful ear," Roche said. "Oscar and his friends thought the song 'You Are From Another World' would be the biggest hit, but Alfred listened to it once and said no, and he was right."

His more serious pursuits included raising money for veterans around the world and publishing a popular magazine for school-age readers. He also published a series of annual books on racing. Although he had no interest in riding horses or touring his barns with carrots, intent on making equine friends, he was an avid outdoorsman who loved to fish, sail, play tennis, and fly planes. "He probably would say, looking back, that he should have had a business or an occupation, but I don't know of anyone who had more fun as he went through life," his son Alfred Vanderbilt III said.

His manner was reserved, and even cautious around strangers. "I hesitate to use the word 'distance,' but you didn't encroach," Prince said. "He was very friendly, very informal, there were lots of laughs, lots of everything, but there was a polite distance. It was part of his upbringing." He had reason to be concerned. In 1951, a fifteen-year-old boy saw his picture in the paper and sent him a note threatening to kill him if he didn't hand over $10,000; police arrested the boy with a toy gun at the scheduled "drop-off."

"His name was an iconic name, and I think it's only natural that you develop some defenses," Alfred Vanderbilt III said. "He would get letters from people asking for money and help doing this and that. One time he got a letter addressed to 'Alfred Vanderbilt, United States of America.' That really tickled him."

Born to prominence, he was famous for who he was, like members of Britain's royal family or, later, the Kennedy children. The *New Yorker, Time* magazine, and the *Saturday Evening Post* had profiled him, intrigued by racing's wealthy boy wonder as he matured into adulthood as a font of courtly contradictions: privileged but unspoiled, reserved in public but offhand around the track, a racing man who never drank and seldom gambled. Joe Palmer had titled his 1952 study "The Riddle of Alfred Vanderbilt," astutely writing that Vanderbilt let you know him only as well as he wanted you to know him.

Only those who knew him best knew of his most distinguishing characteristic: a devilish dry wit. He had once handed a sandwich, flashlight, and wrist compass to Ted Atkinson before the jockey rode a Vanderbilt-owned long shot in the Saratoga Cup. "It may be dark before you get back," Vanderbilt explained. Many of his horses' names had arch explanations or featured a wry twist on the names of the sire and dam. When he married Jeanne, who was from a prominent family but Irish Catholic, he was dropped from the Social Register, the vanguard of old-school society. He responded by naming a colt Social Outcast. The sire's name? Shut Out.

To Vanderbilt, naming horses was a keen test of mental powers, and in time, he would be recognized as perhaps the best there ever was. His greatest hits included Splitting Headache (sired by a stallion named The Axe out of a mare named Top o' The Morning), Ogle (by Oh Say out of Low Cut), and Dirty Old Man (by Tom Fool out of Last Leg). The name "Native Dancer" came from the caption of a picture he had taken of dancers in New Guinea, where he served in the navy during World War II. The names of the horse's sire and dam, Polynesian and Geisha, had him thinking of the South Pacific.

As broad as his interests were, racing was the only constant in his life, the common denominator connecting his days. "The track was what he loved the most; he resisted making a total commitment to anything else," Roche said. That passion, like his wealth, was inherited, passed down on both sides of his family. Vanderbilts had been linked with horses going back to the Commodore's days, and the Emersons—his grandfather, Isaac, and his mother, Margaret— had provided him with the tools of the trade: a horse farm and the origins of a racing stable.

His father, Alfred Vanderbilt Sr., was the wealthiest man in America at the turn of the century. Lean and graceful, he was a spectacular horseman, "one of the most prominent in America," according to the *New York Times* in 1911. He bred top horses at his farm in Newport, Rhode Island, and won blue ribbons at important horse shows in America and England, showcasing a team of greys. His specialty was coaching, a once-popular sport in which horse teams covered long distances led by whip-toting drivers in carriages. It was losing its public as automobiles clogged the roads, but Alfred Sr. did his best to keep it alive. He drove around New York in his red and white coach, set a land-speed record on the New York-to-Philadelphia route in 1901, then shipped seventy horses to England and set another record traveling from London to Brighton as thousands of cheering Britons lined the streets.

Alfred Sr. and Margaret Emerson were married to other people when they met in 1908 at the Plaza Hotel in New York, where Alfred Sr. had a permanent suite. Margaret's husband was the doctor on her father's yacht, but he was also an alcoholic who beat her, and she divorced him, claiming cruelty. (He knocked her out and put her on an eighth-floor window ledge at the Plaza one night; fortunately, the night air revived her and she rolled back inside instead of off the edge.) Alfred Sr.'s marriage also ended in scandal after his affair with Agnes O'Brien Ruiz, the wife of Cuba's attaché in Washington; his divorce cost him a reported $10 million. Ruiz committed suicide when Alfred Sr. took up with Margaret, but the scandal eventually subsided and Alfred Sr. and Margaret were married in 1911.

Margaret, heiress to the vast Bromo-Seltzer fortune, was a strong, restless woman. Dark-haired, opinionated, and self-sufficient, she rode expertly, beat all comers at croquet, won skeet-shooting contests on the Riviera, and had circled the world on her father's yacht several times. Fond of horses, she was a perfect match for Alfred Sr. They quickly had two sons: Alfred Jr., born near London in 1912, and George, born two years later. Their life seemed idyllic.

On May 1, 1915, in New York, Alfred Sr. boarded the *Lusitania*, a luxurious British steamship, bound for a meeting of the International Horse Show Association in England. He was looking forward to a week of caviar, cocktails, and conversation on board, and like most of the almost two thousand passengers, had paid little attention to a warning from the German government: "Travelers are reminded that a state of war exists between Germany and her allies and Great Britain and her allies; that the zone of war includes the waters adjacent to the British Isles; and that . . . vessels flying the flag of Great Britain, or any of her allies, are liable to destruction in those waters."

Days later, the *Lusitania* steered right through the "zone of war" off the Irish coast instead of charting a more evasive route, and a German U-boat captain fired a torpedo that hit the *Lusitania* and sank it. More than seven hundred passengers survived, but Alfred Sr. drowned after handing his life vest to a woman and suggesting that the men endeavor to "save the children," an act that, the *New York Times* wrote, "gave expression to the whole modern idea of civilization."

It was a noble death, but it tore a devastating hole in the ornate tapestry of the Vanderbilt dynasty. The family fortune soon began to shrink, carved up by a wicked scythe of taxes, marriages, children, divorces, the end of the railroad monopoly, and the failure of future generations to continue making money.

Alfred Vanderbilt Jr. was two years old when the *Lusitania* went down. Although his father's will generously stipulated that he receive $5.87 million in government bonds, with the principal and accumulated interest to be paid in four installments as he grew into adulthood, he had lost his father. "His childhood was a lonesome one," the Associated Press reported in a 1936 profile of Vanderbilt. "Surrounded by luxury in houses full of servants, he had little company.

His health was always delicate, and usually there was a nurse hovering with physicians making frequent calls."

Margaret remarried in 1918 to Raymond Baker, the head of the United States Mint. (She was now known as Margaret Emerson McKim Vanderbilt Baker and maintained a residence in Nevada for facilitating divorces.) Her boys, growing up without their own father, increasingly turned to her father as a paternal influence. Captain Emerson, as he was known, was a mustachioed yachtsman and world traveler with a $20 million estate. Margaret was the love of his life—his yacht was named after her—and he doted on her children.

On a trip to Baltimore in 1923, Margaret took Alfred to see the Preakness Stakes, one of the biggest events in racing. They watched the races from the Old Clubhouse, the Victorian manor overlooking the head of the stretch, and Alfred, at age ten, cashed a winning bet on the Preakness. His horse, Tall Timber, finished fifth but was coupled with the winner. "The excitement of being allowed to eat a hot dog with mustard, most of which ended up on my lapels, was forgotten when I saw the horses and the bright silks of the jockeys coming down the stretch. I never got over that feeling," Vanderbilt wrote years later in a *Daily Racing Form* essay.

Margaret had never seen Alfred so excited, and within months, she had bought a steeplechase horse, partly to appease him. After winning several races with the horse, she decided to follow the lead of other society families and back a full-fledged racing stable. She hired a broad-shouldered, no-nonsense trainer, Joseph "Bud" Stotler, who made some purchases at the Saratoga sales. She named her outfit Sagamore Stable—a sagamore was an Indian tribal chief—and Margaret's sprawling wooded retreat in the Adirondack Mountains, which she had inherited from Alfred Sr., was named Sagamore Lodge. Her silks were cerise and white in a pattern of blocks; Alfred Sr.'s coaching colors had been red and white, and cerise is a vivid purplish red.

Sagamore Stable experienced instant success when a two-year-old colt named Rock Man won the Incentive Stakes and Nursery Stakes at Pimlico in 1925. As a three-year-old the next spring, he had the lead in the Preakness after a half mile and trailed only one colt entering the stretch before fading. Disregarded at 42–1 odds in the Kentucky Derby five days later (before World War II, the Derby was sometimes run after the Preakness), Rock Man pressed the leaders up the backside and into the homestretch before tiring. He finished eight lengths behind the winner but stuck his neck out for third.

Another Sagamore colt, Lord Chaucer, showed even more promise as a two-year-old in 1926, winning the Hopeful Stakes at Saratoga. Pointed for the classics the next spring, he was running third and taking the measure of the leaders on the turn of the Pimlico Futurity when he collided with a rival and tumbled to the dirt. His leg broken, he was humanely put to death.

The stable thrived, recording forty-six wins and more than $125,000 in earnings in 1926 and 1927. Three years after its inception, Sagamore was one of racing's top fifty outfits. Sensing his daughter's excitement, Emerson came up with an idea. Long entranced by the rolling limestone hills north of Baltimore, where he owned a summer estate, he purchased a 250-acre tract from a farmer and gave it to Margaret with plans to turn it into a horse farm for her stable. He would spend $500,000 on indoor and outdoor training tracks, a barn with fifty stalls, two paddocks, and housing for workers. Privately, he hoped the farm—to be named, naturally, Sagamore Farm, after the racing stable—would lure his daughter to Maryland more often.

Within months, the farm was bustling with grooms and exercise riders as the barns, paddocks, and racing strips were built. Another three-year-old ran well for Sagamore in 1928, a colt named Don Q. who finished well out of the money as one of eighteen starters in the Preakness, then ran seventh among twenty-two starters in the Kentucky Derby. By the end of the year, Margaret's horses had won twenty-one races and she had divorced Raymond Baker and within twenty-four days married her fourth husband, Charles Minot Amory, a Harvard graduate from Boston society.

The stable's rise matched young Vanderbilt's growing interest in racing. He followed his mother's horses in the newspapers and, school vacations permitting, by her side, and traveled with her every August to Saratoga, where he spent mornings at the barn, afternoons at the races, and evenings at dinner with racing's upper crust. He sat for hours with Colonel E. R. Bradley, the master of Idle Hour Farm, learning from one of the nation's eminent breeders and horse owners; Bradley later sent him racing books and magazines, solicited his opinions on equine matters, and offered a free stud service to his first mare. Bud Stotler also spent many hours with the young man, answering his many questions around the barn and during the races.

During the school year, Vanderbilt arranged to receive the *Daily Racing Form* at St. Paul's, the boarding school he attended in Concord, New Hampshire; the paper came in the mail in an unmarked envelope to prevent the deans from suspecting his mind might not be on his studies. He read it under his bedcovers, by flashlight, after lights were out; his mind was, indeed, distracted. He ran an annual betting book on the Kentucky Derby, cashing in big in 1929 when none of his classmates backed the long-shot winner, Clyde Van Dusen.

In the late 1920s, Margaret let him make some breeding decisions and pick out several yearlings and follow them as if they were his own. One won a stakes race at Aqueduct, and when another won at Saratoga in 1928, the local newspaper labeled Vanderbilt, fifteen, as "the youngest owner on the American turf." That he would follow his mother's lead and have his own racing stable was already apparent.

He used his allowance money to buy his first horse in August 1931, just before starting at Yale. He slipped away with Stotler one night at Saratoga, went to the yearling sales, and came home with a smallish chestnut filly that had cost $250. The filly, which he named Sue Jones—a dull name not up to the high standard of cleverness he later set—joined Margaret's stable and debuted on June 16, 1932, at Aqueduct, finishing third. The *Blood-Horse,* a prominent racing industry journal, noted the debut of young Vanderbilt's silks, which incorporated the same cerise and white colors as Margaret's, only in a pattern of diamonds instead of blocks.

Plainly more interested in racing than literature or economics, Vanderbilt lasted just three semesters at Yale before dropping out. "I believed I had discovered what I wanted in life, and I was right: I wanted racetrack," he later told interviewers. Conveniently, Margaret was tiring of the expense of keeping the farm and stable running, especially after her father died in 1931. Emerson's will stipulated that

Margaret pass the farm on to Alfred when she died, but she decided to step up the timetable and give it to him when he turned twenty-one.

It is doubtful anyone in America celebrated a more bountiful or conspicuous birthday in 1933. At the lowest ebb of the Great Depression, Vanderbilt received from his mother Sagamore Farm and a racing stable, a burnt-gold Rolls-Royce, and the lifelong services of valet Louis Cheri. From his father's estate, he received more than $2 million, with three similar payments scheduled for his twenty-fifth, thirtieth, and thirty-fifth birthdays. The *New York Times* noted in an article that another Vanderbilt scion had "reached his majority"— turned twenty-one—and was planning to devote his money and time to racing thoroughbreds.

"I went to the races with Margaret once at Hialeah, and she enjoyed it immensely, but Alfred wanted it to be his own show, and she graciously gave him the stable," his friend Clyde Roche said. "For her, it was a circle of people who knew each other and enjoyed the racing setting, but I don't think she had a devotion to it. Alfred certainly did."

Looking for horses to improve the stable, which had sagged, Vanderbilt focused on a big, heavy-looking two-year-old named Discovery. Sired by Display, a Preakness winner nicknamed the Iron Horse, Discovery was owned by Walter J. Salmon, a New York financier who, looking to cut costs, had leased the horse to Adolphe Pons, a horseman whose father had immigrated from France and become associated with the Belmont family. Salmon wanted Pons to sell Discovery.

Stotler began negotiating a price after seeing Discovery win a race, and Vanderbilt, thinking the deal was done, put his silks in his car and drove to Saratoga, expecting Discovery to run for him in the Hopeful Stakes. Instead, Salmon and Pons elected to let the horse run in Pons's colors once more, then called off the deal when Discovery ran third, raising his value. After several more months of negotiations, Vanderbilt offered $25,000 and left on a four-month hunting expedition in Africa. He had been at sea for a day when he received a simply worded telegram from Stotler: "Discovery yours." It would be the most important equine purchase of his life.

In Africa, Vanderbilt bagged a lion and several elephants, was chased by a rhinoceros, fished with Ernest Hemingway, and met Beryl Markham, the female aviator. Upon returning, he jumped excitedly into the business of running a farm and a stable. His hunger for knowledge was so intense that Stotler utilized him as an assistant trainer even though he was the boss, dispatching him to small tracks to run minor horses, a seemingly thankless job Vanderbilt relished. He ran the stalls and established a rapport with the other men on the backstretch, asking for no favors and insisting that he be called Alfred or Al.

Discovery ran well enough in the spring of 1934 that Vanderbilt took him to Louisville for the Kentucky Derby. Sent to the post at 12–1 odds, he took a three-length lead into the stretch as jockey Johnny Bejshak furiously worked him. Pandemonium reigned in Vanderbilt's private box. Although Cavalcade rallied to win, Discovery finished second, and Vanderbilt never forgot the sensation of holding a lead so late in America's greatest race. Discovery eventually recorded several major wins that year, but he was known more for losing a series of races to Cavalcade.

Racing as a four-year-old in 1935, Discovery had lost five in a row in the spring and was being dismissed as a disappointment when "all of a sudden, he got good," Vanderbilt recalled in a *Thoroughbred Times* interview in 1993. He won eight straight stakes races in seven weeks in New York, Chicago, Boston, and Detroit, setting several track records while enduring an exhausting schedule of train rides. By the end of the year, the horse known as the Big Train had traveled nine thousand miles and won eleven stakes races at eight tracks, with handicappers asking him to carry as much as 139 pounds. It was a remarkable performance, and Vanderbilt was acclaimed for his willingness to run the horse anywhere against anyone under any conditions.

Vanderbilt's stable finished 1935 with more than $300,000 in earnings, tops in the nation, and thirty-seven stakes wins, the most by any stable in twenty-five years. Less than two years after taking over, Vanderbilt was at the top of the game along with Belair Stud, C. V. Whitney, Brookmeade Stable, and the rest of racing's ruling class. He purchased a neighboring farm to double the size of Sagamore Farm and spent lavishly to turn it into a showcase. "When he came in for a visit, we all lined up, like a military greeting," Claude Appley recalled. "He knew the breeding of every horse in the field, and we had a lot of horses. He was an encyclopedia."

It was inevitable that he would become more involved in the racing industry. Vanderbilts seldom lingered on any sideline for long, and anyone with his enthusiasm and financial wherewithal belonged in racing's hierarchy. The success of his stable led the Maryland Jockey Club, which operated Pimlico, to give him a seat on its board of directors in 1936. Soon, when the board was deciding whether to take out a liquor license—snobbish Pimlico had previously abhorred the idea—Vanderbilt, a nondrinker, cast the tie-breaking vote in favor of alcohol, believing it would draw more fans to the track. Pimlico's vice president resigned, and a longtime secretary announced that his stock in the track was for sale. "I'll buy it!" Vanderbilt roared. Before long, he had purchased a controlling interest of Pimlico stock and was running the track as its president.

As his vote for liquor indicated, Vanderbilt had strong and unconventional ideas about tracks and racing. He was, at twenty-five, a maverick, even though he was a member of high society. He believed that racing had been run for the sake of its wealthy old guard for far too long and that the interests of the average fan had been ignored. There was too much emphasis on betting, he felt, and not enough on making the race-day experience interesting for the customers. In general, he believed, an infusion of spirit and innovation was needed.

"He was, as we'd say today, a guy who thought 'outside the box,'" said Tim Capps, a Maryland-based racing author, historian, and executive. "He was an iconoclast. Didn't fit the genre of the 'old money' crowd. He operated outside the framework of what people thought third- or fourth-generation money ought to be like. He had a sense of what the fans wanted. He understood the value of promotion. He was willing to take chances."

At Pimlico, which had been losing money and fans, he increased purse sizes and inaugurated new races such as the Pimlico Special, intending to attract better horses and give fans at least one stakes race every day. He installed a public-address system, teletimers, cameras, and a starting gate with closed doors, the first on the East Coast.

Most famously, he spent $58,000 to remove the hill in the infield that
had given the track its nickname, Old Hilltop. Some saw the mound
as historic, and many old-timers were aghast, but fans had complained that they couldn't see their horses run, and away it went. "He
was the only guy who wanted to protect the public to the extent he
did," longtime California steward Pete Pederson said.

A hands-on boss, he demanded high standards from his employees and made sure those standards were met. "He would get up
one day and not shave, not wear a tie, wear a sport shirt, and go to the
track unrecognized," Alfred Vanderbilt III said. "The next day, there
would be hell to pay. He knew which pari-mutuel clerks had been
rude, what was and wasn't getting done, and what needed to be
done."

Pimlico experienced a rebirth, drawing better horses and larger
crowds. "It was my theory that if the product was right, everything
else would take care of itself, and that was how it worked out: attendance picked up, business picked up, the net profit picked up and the
prestige picked up," Vanderbilt told *Sports Illustrated* in 1963. Impressed with his progressive management, as well as his commitment
to racing, the Jockey Club made him its youngest-ever member in
1937, when he was twenty-five.

The Associated Press had labeled him "one of the most eligible
bachelors between Bar Harbor and Palm Beach" in 1936 and asked in
a headline, "How Long Till Vanderbilt Weds? Society Wondering." He
had courted a coterie of women in society, the theater, and the movies.
Then he began dating Manuela Hudson early in 1938. She was the
daughter of a San Francisco attorney and the niece of Charles
Howard, who owned Seabiscuit, the most popular horse in America.
Vanderbilt and Manuela met at Santa Anita, married in the summer of
1938, had a daughter named Wendy, bought a thirty-room house in
New York, built another home overlooking Sagamore Farm—then divorced in the early 1940s.

The brief marriage did help Vanderbilt pull off his greatest
achievement at Pimlico. The best horses of 1938 were Seabiscuit, by
then a rags-to-riches hero, and War Admiral, winner of the Triple
Crown the year before. Tracks across the country were competing to

hold a match race between the two, and Vanderbilt cleverly worked his way into the mix. Assured of Howard's favor, having married into the family, he sweet-talked War Admiral's owner, Sam Riddle, suggesting that War Admiral could beat Seabiscuit. Ultimately, he secured the race with a $15,000 offer, far less than other tracks such as Belmont had been offering. Seabiscuit defeated War Admiral before 40,000 fans at Pimlico and a radio audience estimated at 40 million.

Pimlico was bathed in glory, and when Joseph Widener retired as president of Belmont in 1939, Belmont's principal stockholder, C. V. Whitney, hired Vanderbilt to revitalize the prestigious New York track in the same manner. Many had thought Widener's nephew, George Widener, another industry leader, would get the job, but Whitney was himself a bit of a maverick, and Vanderbilt was hired. Given a mandate to make Belmont more attractive to the general public instead of just to bettors and the upper crust, Vanderbilt performed his magic with purse sizes, new races, and more standing room, and Belmont flourished.

When World War II broke out, Vanderbilt was stirred by a distant voice. "The idea of meeting your obligations in life came to him from what he knew about his father giving up his life jacket to a woman on the *Lusitania;* I think Alfred regarded that as the standard of conduct," Clyde Roche recalled. The navy tried to give him a cushy recruiting job, but he joined the PT-boat service and led more than three dozen patrols in New Guinea in 1943 and 1944.

"They'd take the boats along the coastline at night, turn down the engine, and float with the current in the dark until they heard the Japanese talking, at which point they'd fire, start the engine, and get out of there," Roche said. "When I asked Alfred later if they destroyed a lot of Japanese installations, he said, in typical fashion, 'Who knows? But if we didn't, we wasted a lot of ammo.'"

His wartime experience was hardly typical. "He used to say he was the only guy in the army who had Ginger Rogers's home phone number," Alfred Vanderbilt III said. When Dan Topping and Del Webb were negotiating to buy baseball's New York Yankees in 1944, they reached Vanderbilt by phone in the South Pacific and asked if he wanted to join their group. "You know, I'm kind of busy," Vanderbilt replied.

When a Japanese pilot caught his boat in the open and began firing one afternoon, Vanderbilt, alternately driving and firing back, made a series of sharp turns to keep from getting hit and finally blasted the Japanese plane. He earned a Silver Star for bravery and later downplayed the honor, claiming it was awarded mostly because his squadron leader thought medals were good for morale. "He insisted that what he'd done wasn't a big deal, but it was," Roche said.

His time on the front lines ended when he developed a fungus growth in his foot in 1944 and was sent to the hospital for a month. Certified as unfit for tropical duty, he spent six months on a cruiser in the Aleutians and was studying at a combat intelligence school in Honolulu when the war ended. He came home at age thirty-three to find he no longer had a job. Belmont had given the job of running the track to George Widener, and Widener never gave it back; the racing world would always suspect that Belmont's board of directors was more comfortable with Widener's traditional vision than with the maverick Vanderbilt's. Although Vanderbilt always joked that he should sue to get his job back under the terms of the G.I. Bill, he was hurt.

More somber and contemplative after the war, he told Joe Palmer he wouldn't make any decisions for six months, then made a major one, marrying for the second time in 1946. Jeanne Murray had been a model and actress—she was one of the nurses in the movie *Mr. Roberts*—and now worked in the publicity office of the Stork Club, the popular nightclub. She had long harbored a crush on Vanderbilt from seeing him in newsreels and in the newspapers, and then her dream came true. "I was in the Stork Club one night and a man came over and said, 'Alfred Vanderbilt is here and would like to meet you,'" Jeanne recalled. "He took me to see *On the Town* on one of our first dates. We were married three months later."

They started a family—Heidi was born in 1948, Alfred III a year later—and moved to Broadhollow, a starry couple operating at the epicenter of society. "They were both bright and loved getting together with people and being around people," Alfred Vanderbilt III said. "He had this innate sense of knowing how to make sure that his horses were talked about and he was talked about, and here was this woman who knew exactly all of the same stuff. She wasn't so interested in horses, but she loved the celebrity and moved in it well. They had a Jack and Jackie thing going before the Kennedys, that 'couple charisma.'"

Their friends were Bill and Babe Paley, Jock and Betsey Whitney, and Tex McCrary and Jinx Falkenburg—other prominent couples that had married around the same time and lived near each other on Long Island. Known in the New York papers as the Smart Set, they turned heads when they made their entrances at restaurants or parties amid a tumult of laughter. Bill Paley was the president of CBS, his wife a glamorous style-setter. Jock Whitney was an early venture capitalist, and like Vanderbilt, a racing enthusiast and heir to a family fortune. Falkenburg, a pinup girl and B-movie star in the 1940s, now hosted a popular morning radio talk show in New York. Her husband, an influential pioneer in public relations, was her cohost.

Vanderbilt's mother, Margaret, also lived nearby on Long Island. She had given up on marriage after four tries but remained as strong-willed as ever, favoring wide slacks and long cigarette holders. "She was a powerhouse," Jeanne Vanderbilt recalled. Her impact on her elder son was profound. She gathered people from the arts, politics, and business every summer at Sagamore Lodge in the Adirondack Mountains, where she "camped" with cooks, maids, and fine linens and china. Howard Hughes and Madame Chiang Kai-shek were among those who had visited—the Madame had come with her own silk sheets—and frequent guests included composer Richard Rodgers, actor Gary Cooper, General George C. Marshall, and the Paleys and Guggenheims. Vanderbilt and Jeanne instituted a similar tradition at Broadhollow, lording over starry weekends of dining, games, and conversation. An invitation to spend a weekend with the Vanderbilts was coveted.

"The first time I went, I drove out and parked my car and was taken to my room, and I looked out the window and two people were already washing my car. I'd been there two minutes!" Harold Prince recalled. "It was a window to a way of life that didn't exist much longer. There was a clock on your door that you set to tell [the servants] when they should wake you up. Louis, who ran the house, was remarkable: quiet, gracious, and incredibly efficient. You went outside and there was a long lawn sloping down to the swimming pool. You swam or played tennis. Dinner was magnificent. You played games after dinner. And so many fascinating people were there."

Recalled Clyde Roche, "I once had a friend who arrived for a weekend and put her bag down, and we sat and talked. When we went upstairs, she came and knocked on my door and said, 'This is so embarrassing, but I don't know what's happened to my bag.' I said, 'Have you looked in your closet?' She was so amazed. Everything had been taken out, pressed, and put in drawers."

Broadhollow was, in a sense, a modern Shangri-La. George Abbott directed the children's puppet shows. General Marshall, who was overseeing the rebuilding of Europe after World War II, would arrive in a helicopter. The entire casts of Broadway shows would come for brunch and play softball. Hounds chased foxes across the lawn on Saturday mornings. Vanderbilt was the centerpiece, orchestrating the games and serving as the arbiter of taste and humor. By the fall of 1952, he seemed to have it all. He was married to a beautiful woman and had a young family, traveled in glamorous circles, and backed one of racing's most successful stables.

The reality beneath that glittering outer layer was more sobering. His marriage to Jeanne was troubled; it would end in divorce in 1956. "Alfred's mother was married four times, and I think he was influenced by that," Jeanne recalled. "He had that reserve, didn't show a lot of emotion, and I was from a big loud Irish Catholic family. That was appealing to him, and I think he tried, but there was this big wall he just couldn't break through."

Moreover, he was less confident than he had been when he was younger, according to Jeanne. "Stanton Graffis asked us to go to Spain with him when he was the ambassador there [in 1951–52], but Alfred wouldn't go," she said. "I think he was scared [of the responsibility]. He had such great intelligence and common sense; that's one of the things I liked about him—no nonsense, no bullshit, just smart—but his self-confidence was sagging. When he was younger and running Pimlico and Belmont, he was tremendous. He had so much drive, so many ideas, so much caring. He was so good at it. I think he lost heart when they didn't want him to run Belmont anymore. I think that setback really knocked him off his feet."

Whatever the source of his malaise—his brushes with death in the war, his "setback" at Belmont, his marriage—it was eased by his racing stable, which had struggled during the war but was thriving again, with Bed o' Roses, Next Move, and Loser Weeper winning races and thrusting Vanderbilt into the spotlight. Even in that success, however, there was a caveat—a Vanderbilt horse hadn't run in the Kentucky Derby since Discovery in 1934. For all that Vanderbilt had accomplished in racing, he had barely competed in America's greatest race.

He badly wanted a second chance, having never forgotten the elation he felt when Discovery turned for home with the lead at Churchill Downs, but he had started to wonder if that time would ever come. Now Native Dancer had arrived, and his optimism was soaring as he drove through the dark on his way to Belmont on the morning after the Futurity. The Grey Ghost certainly looked like the kind of horse that could deliver the Derby glory he desired. Maybe, just maybe, his time had come. If he was, in fact, experiencing a crisis of confidence, and stumbling in marriage, a horse was the perfect antidote. He was, after all, a racing man, and all any racing man asked for, other than God's grace, was one great champion to cheer down the stretch.

# FOUR

It seemed almost impossible, given his commitment to his stable, that Vanderbilt had gone nearly two decades without running a horse in the Kentucky Derby. But despite spending hundreds of thousands of dollars and breeding his mares to expensive stallions since the early years of Franklin Roosevelt's presidency, he had not come close to producing another three-year-old worthy of running at Churchill Downs on the first Saturday in May. Discovery, now a twenty-one-year-old stallion at Sagamore Farm, was still his only Derby horse.

How had this happened? Part of the problem was the youthful enthusiasm Vanderbilt had exhibited after taking over the stable in 1933. Naively, he had bought far too many horses, ending up with eighty-six in training—far more than Bud Stotler, or any trainer, could handle. Most successful stables kept about twenty-five in training at any time. Vanderbilt had thirty-eight two-year-olds alone in 1936; one of them, a black colt named Airflame, set a world record in a three-furlong dash and was pointed for the 1937 Derby but failed to make it. The overpopulation caused serious problems. Five years after leading the nation in wins, with eighty-eight, and earnings, with $303,000, in 1935, Vanderbilt won just thirteen races and $38,000 in 1940.

Another problem was a change in trainers hastened when Stotler was involved in a serious car accident while driving to a race in Havre de Grace, Maryland, in April 1939. Struck from behind in a thick morning fog, the trainer's car careened across the road and caught fire. It was initially thought Stotler wasn't seriously injured. He tumbled out of the flaming wreck, asked if anyone had seen his hat, and hitched a ride to the track to speak to his jockey about the upcoming race. Tests taken later that day, however, revealed fractured vertebrae and other injuries that would force him to recuperate for months.

When his parting with Vanderbilt was announced eight months later, the Associated Press reported that Stotler, who had trained for Vanderbilt and Margaret Emerson since 1925, was resigning because the stable was shrinking and Vanderbilt wanted to train some of the horses himself, which was true. "He was there every morning, and although he was never officially put down as the trainer, he was training the horses," recalled William Boniface, a racing writer for the *Baltimore Sun.* Claude Appley said years later that another factor was paramount in Stotler's departure, claiming Vanderbilt fired his mentor after discovering that the small cash bonuses, called stakes, that the help was supposed to earn when a Vanderbilt horse won a race weren't being paid.

"Stotler got sacked over Airflame," Appley recalled. "The horse went to Havre de Grace and won. A boy called Ernie James was galloping him, and when they got back to the barn, Mr. V. said, 'Well, Ernie, did you get staked?' Ernie was about half lit up and said, 'I ain't seen no stake around here.' Vanderbilt said, 'What do you mean? You get a stake for this horse winning.' Ernie said, 'I ain't never seen it.' And Mr. V. sacked Stotler. Well, first [Stotler] had the accident. Then, after the accident, he got sacked. I don't know where the stakes were going, but they weren't coming to the boys."

Whatever its rationale, Stotler's departure didn't help the stable. With Vanderbilt increasingly distracted by his duties at Pimlico and Belmont and his failing first marriage, he had little time to concentrate on conditioning and racing his horses. He eventually hired another trainer, a low-key veteran named Lee McCoy, but the stable continued to slump in the early 1940s, then was drastically pared when Vanderbilt joined the navy. He ordered many of his race-age horses sold, keeping only Discovery, now a stallion, several mares, and a few youngsters. The stable won just eight races in 1943 and ten in 1945. Vanderbilt later regretted that he wasn't around to preside over the sale: among those sold was Miss Disco, a daughter of Discovery that later foaled Bold Ruler, winner of the 1957 Preakness and sire of Secretariat.

Although a combination of factors had conspired to keep the stable from producing another Derby horse, the most important was Vanderbilt's mediocre record as a breeder through the late 1940s. He had faithfully bred up to two dozen horses a year at Sagamore Farm, with Discovery as his centerpiece sire, and while his record wasn't disastrous, he hadn't bred many top horses. A son of Discovery named New World had defeated Whirlaway as a two-year-old in 1940, then missed 1941 with an injury as Whirlaway swept to a Triple Crown. That was Vanderbilt's closest Derby call since Discovery, and it wasn't very close.

By the late 1940s, Vanderbilt was upset. He hadn't bred one of the more than two hundred horses in American racing history that had earned at least $100,000; by contrast, William Woodward had bred eleven, H. P. Whitney ten, and E. R. Bradley nine. Vanderbilt usually placed somewhere in the bottom of the top twenty of the annual breeders' standings—based on the combined earnings of the Vanderbilt-breds that raced for him and those he had sold to others to race—and he knew he should be doing better with all the effort and money he was investing.

"Well, Alfred," Vanderbilt's friends often told him, "at least you had Discovery."

That comment, intended as solace, irritated Vanderbilt as much as his continuing inability to breed a Derby contender. Owners of his standing didn't race just to win—that was crass—and certainly didn't need the money. Their goal was to win with horses they had bred. "My father firmly believed that improving the breed was the overarching obligation of the racing establishment," Alfred Vanderbilt III said, "and that the whole point of winning a race was that it showed your breeding was sound." Vanderbilt's was disappointing.

He finally made a change in 1948, handing the decision-making in his breeding business over to Ralph Kercheval, a husky, handsome Kentuckian. After starring at football for the University of Kentucky in the early 1930s, Kercheval had played running back and cornerback and handled the kicking and punting for the National Football League's Brooklyn Dodgers for seven years, taking time off every fall from a full-time job with the Whitney stable. Sportswriter Grantland Rice had once called him football's best punter—an eighty-six-yarder he booted in 1935 stood as the NFL's longest for more than a decade—and his credentials as a horseman were just as strong. He had assisted top trainers such as Silent Tom Smith and Woody Stephens and directed the Frank Frankel stable. During the war, he was stationed at an army remount depot in Nebraska, training horses used in cavalry and artillery units.

Officially, Kercheval, at thirty-five, was hired to manage Sagamore Farm and oversee Vanderbilt's breeding operation. "I'm trying to start a new program, one of more winners," Vanderbilt explained to reporters. Unofficially, Kercheval's job was to get Vanderbilt back to the Kentucky Derby. Vanderbilt had spoken about Discovery and the big race at Churchill Downs so passionately during their interview that Kercheval, upon accepting the job, had pledged, "I'll breed you a Derby horse in five years or I'll quit."

Kercheval moved to Sagamore and immediately made major changes. Vanderbilt had previously bred his mares mostly just to Discovery and other stallions in Maryland. That, Kercheval felt, was the primary problem. Although Discovery produced quality broodmares, he wasn't consistently passing his power and stamina down to the horses he directly sired. And while some of the other stallions in Maryland were capable enough, they weren't in the same league as Kentucky's powerful array.

"I was fairly blunt with Alfred," Kercheval recalled. "I told him if he wanted to start breeding better horses, he needed to take his best mares down to Kentucky and start breeding them to the outstanding sires there. He said to me, 'You're running it,' obviously realizing that if he wanted to make any changes, he could. He was a really good horseman, extremely knowledgeable; he knew what he was doing. But he pretty much let me do what I thought was right. I don't think he cared for the way things were going, and he'd brought me in to make them better. So I gave him what I had in mind, and he looked it over and didn't change too many things. You couldn't ask for a better boss. We were the same age, just two months apart, and we got along, had respect for each other's opinions horsewise. We sort of hit it off."

Polynesian was the prototypal Kentucky stallion Kercheval wanted Vanderbilt to use. The horse had won the Preakness and Withers Stakes and set two track records as a three-year-old in 1945 and had won seven major handicap races as a four-year-old. His trainer, a steeplechase expert named Morris Dixon, had kept him out of the Belmont Stakes and other longer races, doubting his ability to win at those distances, but there was no doubting his breathtaking speed. "I had always thought Polynesian had a great deal of brilliance, and that he was even a much better horse than he had an opportunity to show," Kercheval recalled. "I felt he could have raced well at those longer distances. And I felt he had a terrific chance as a sire."

He was also an equine Cinderella. Raised on a formula of cow's milk fed from a bucket after his mother died, he had begun his racing career with three losses as a two-year-old, then contracted a rare form of blood poisoning that caused stiffness in his legs and loins. His future in doubt, he was carried to a van and driven to Dixon's farm in Pennsylvania to convalesce. For ten days, he stood almost motionless under a tree in a paddock as grooms dragged him to and from his stall. Then he was attacked one morning by hornets; Dixon said later that his ten-year-old son was playing in the paddock and probably shook the tree, angering the hornets. Stung repeatedly, Polynesian embarked on a wild-eyed twenty-minute dash. Once he was corralled, magically he was cured. Either his condition had run its course, or as some old-timers believed, the hornet stings had served as the unlikeliest of remedies. Either way, he was a cranky handful upon returning to the races, often refusing to train on certain tracks in the morning, but he blazed through his afternoons, totaling twenty-seven wins in fifty-eight starts before being retired. Alfred Vanderbilt said of him years later, "Some people are born to greatness, some have greatness thrust upon them. Other, apparently, have to be stung into it."

He had gone to stud in 1948 at Gallaher Farm on Russell Cave

Pike in Lexington, Kentucky, and just months later, by chance, Vanderbilt, organizing the new Kentucky branch of his breeding operation, began boarding his mares right across the street at Dan W. Scott's farm. (Kercheval had recommended Scott; they had gone to high school and college together.) When Kercheval and Vanderbilt were deciding how to breed their Kentucky mares in 1949 to produce foals in 1950, they reserved three "seasons" to Polynesian, meaning that three of their mares would be bred to him that spring. The fact that Polynesian was across the street was a factor in the decision to make Geisha one of the three mares. Geisha, then a compact six-year-old roan, detested being loaded into a van. "The steps of vans were quite high off the ground in those days, and a horse could develop a real horror of having to get in," Scott recalled. "Geisha was practically impossible to load. But we didn't have to load her to get her bred to Polynesian. All we had to do was walk her across a road with very little traffic. It was just simpler and it made sense, especially since the pedigrees were an interesting mesh, anyway."

Years later, Kercheval smiled when it was suggested that Geisha's reluctance to load was a factor in the fateful decision to breed her to Polynesian. "I would never put off something I wanted to do on account of something like that," Kercheval said. "By my way of thinking, I could load any horse. You could always find a way."

The "mesh" of pedigrees was more important, Kercheval said. "Despite Geisha's poor record and productivity to that point, her family was the kind that could produce something good," he said. Her grandfather John P. Grier was one of Man O' War's toughest rivals. Her grandmother La Chica was a blind mare who had produced a champion two-year-old. She had a full sister who was a stakes winner on the steeplechase circuit. And of course, her sire was Discovery. "The key was Discovery," Kercheval said. "I had always felt Discovery was probably the greatest horse I ever saw. His history of weight and distances matched with Polynesian's speed was a good match."

The philosophy of the breeding industry was "breed the best to the best and hope for the best": deal in the highest available stock to improve your chances of breeding a winner, but never forget that it was an imperfect science. Vanderbilt's philosophy was only slightly different: "breed the best to a Discovery mare and hope for the best," he often said. In that spirit, Geisha was led across Russell Cave Pike on May 8, 1949, bred to Polynesian in the hallway of the barn at Gallaher Farm, and led back: a morning walk, briefly interrupted.

Vanderbilt was later hailed for having the insight to breed Polynesian to Geisha. Typically, he was careful not to boast, pointing out that if he accepted the credit for breeding a horse so gifted, he should also accept the blame for having bred so many horses that, he said, "couldn't get out of their own way." (Along the same lines, when asked if there had been reason to believe Geisha might be better as a broodmare than she was on the track, he replied, "It's hard to say; I trained her myself.")

In reality, Vanderbilt and Kercheval together made the decision to breed Polynesian to Geisha. "I would say both were driving the car," Dan W. Scott said. Kercheval's wife, Blanche, recalled years later, "Alfred told Ralph several times 'I'm getting all the credit for this horse, but I wouldn't have him if it hadn't been for you.'"

Vanderbilt's stable embarked on a resounding comeback in 1949, coinciding with the hiring of Bill Winfrey as a trainer. Vanderbilt had used Lee McCoy since the early 1940s and occasionally trained some of the horses himself, but just as he had felt the need to overhaul his breeding operation, he also felt it was time to put a better trainer in charge. Winfrey's touch was so galvanizing that Vanderbilt soon began referring to the years before 1949 as B.W.: before Winfrey.

The stable's comeback had started, ironically, with breeding decisions Vanderbilt made at his lowest ebb of frustration, shortly before he hired Kercheval. Bed o' Roses, a filly foaled in 1947 out of a Discovery mare, swept the East's four richest races for two-year fillies in 1949, earning $199,200, the third-highest total ever for a two-year-old, male or female. She was so feminine and attractive that Eric Guerin, her regular jockey, said of her years later, "If she could have cooked and cleaned, I would have married her." Also in 1949, Loser Weeper, a four-year-old chestnut sired by Discovery, won the Metropolitan Handicap. Next Move, another filly foaled in 1947, won eleven races and was voted the champion of her class of 1950.

Suddenly, Vanderbilt was back, his stable's lean war years a distant memory. The stable soared from thirty-three wins in 1948 to sixty-eight in 1950 as earnings jumped from $162,000 in 1948 to $584,000, the third-highest total in the nation, in 1950. And Vanderbilt had bred the horses winning the big money, restoring his faith in his abilities as a breeder. Still, his ultimate goal wasn't to win races for fillies such as the Demoiselle Stakes and Matron Stakes, lucrative though they were. True greatness was conferred in the Triple Crown, and Vanderbilt was continuing to fail there, again not even entering a horse in the Kentucky Derby as Calumet Farm's Ponder won in 1949 and the King Ranch's Middleground won in 1950.

Five weeks before Middleground's victory, Dan W. Scott awoke at 2 A.M. on March 27, 1950, to the sound of a branch scratching across his bedroom window—a sign from his night watchman, Lloyd Craig, that another equine life was about to begin. It was the prime of the foaling season at Scott's 280-acre commercial farm, and with no phones or radios available to pass along news, Scott had instructed Craig just to awaken him with a branch whenever a mare sank to the ground and began to deliver at night.

The thirty-four-year-old farm owner scrambled out of bed, threw open the second-story window, and peered down at Craig, who simply said, "Geisha's down." Scott wasn't surprised. Geisha was long overdue, having been scheduled to deliver her foal by Polynesian on February 28. The extended pregnancy wasn't a concern, though. To the contrary, Scott was pleased. A meticulous record keeper, he had noted that eighteen of the twenty-five stakes winners foaled at his farm had come late. A foal's lungs and breathing apparatus developed in the final weeks of the mare's pregnancy, and Scott suspected that horses who were delivered late could breathe better and were better equipped to handle duress on the track.

Otherwise, there was little reason to expect the foal Geisha was ready to drop into the world to possess uncommon qualities. Geisha had won only one of eleven starts in her racing career and birthed a single, unremarkable foal since being retired. "Alfred didn't think that much of Geisha; at the time she was no big deal to Alfred," Scott recalled. And her foal was part of just the second crop that Polynesian had sired, so it was still too soon to know whether he was a stallion who would pass along his greatness.

Geisha's foal certainly wasn't the most anticipated of the twenty-six that would constitute Vanderbilt's foal crop of 1950. Seven of his mares were in foal to Discovery that spring. Good Thing, the dam of Bed o' Roses, was in foal to Polynesian. Other Kentucky sires such as Amphitheater and Questionnaire had been mated with Vanderbilt's best mares. Maybe one of those would develop into the Triple Crown star Vanderbilt wanted.

A routine delivery unfolded that night in front of Scott, a college-educated second-generation farm owner, as comfortable delivering a foal as he was dealing with society clients such as the Wanamakers, Whitneys, and Vanderbilts; and Craig, the black night watchman Scott would later recall as "someone I treasured, the kind of horse-man they don't make anymore." In a dark barn behind Scott's house—Scott believed mares were more relaxed giving birth in the dark—a chocolate-brown male emerged in perfect condition at 2:10 A.M., the head positioned properly, all limbs functioning.

The foal blossomed quickly in the coming weeks. Geisha was a strong milk producer. The farm had good grass. Scott turned out his horses as the weather warmed, letting the foals stay out at night.

"Native Dancer was a big, rough foal that wanted to play all the time," Scott recalled. "I once had a fraternity brother, a great big man with great big hands, and he would shake your hand and not realize he was breaking your hand. Native Dancer was like that as a baby. He'd entice the other foals away from their mothers, and they'd play, and there'd be some big ruckus over something he had started, and someone would get hurt, but never him. He was very healthy; you didn't have to do anything other than make sure he wasn't too full of himself. He was just the most exuberant foal you could imagine, a joy to be around. No one had any idea he was going to be a Native Dancer, of course. You can't watch horses run in a field and decide. The track is an entirely different ball game. People ask me, 'Did you recognize a champion?' I said, 'No, but I recognized a wonderful animal.'"

Through the spring, Vanderbilt's other mares in Kentucky also delivered; there were eleven foals in all by the end of the season. They returned to Sagamore Farm after their mothers had been bred back to various stallions. Geisha and her baby were loaded onto a van on June 28, 1950—Geisha did load, however reluctantly—and returned to Maryland, where Vanderbilt's other mares had delivered. In all, nine colts and seventeen fillies constituted his foal crop for the year: a rollicking mass of infinite possibilities.

They spent the next eighteen months at Sagamore, by now a 950-acre spread regarded as Maryland's finest horse farm. Incorporating twenty buildings and seventy full-time employees in three divisions—breeding operations, training operations, and maintenance—the farm had immaculate barns, fences and paddocks, an outdoor racing strip, and a quarter-mile indoor track for winter gallops; a kitchen, chef, dining room, and dormitory housing for the staff; and a large house for Kercheval and his wife.

From the beginning, even when he was just another yearling in the field, Native Dancer stood apart. "He was a very nice individual as a youngster, did things easily, had nice balance and a powerful physique," Kercheval recalled. "There was never a doubt about his athletic qualities, and he was handsome from the word go, a very nice-looking foal without the crooked legs a lot of them have."

Several other horses in the crop also showed promise through their breaking, development, and early light training. The best was Crash Dive, a speedy colt sired by Devil Diver, a popular Kentucky stallion. Find, a son of Discovery, also showed promise, as did the colt named Social Outcast. In the fall of 1951, they were put through quarter-mile trials one morning, taking their first quantifiable steps as racehorses. The annual event lured Vanderbilt from Long Island, anxious to see the first crop of youngsters he had bred with Kercheval. There was a buzz in the air as Vanderbilt, Kercheval, and Winfrey strode to the two-story tower by the finish line of Sagamore's training track. The yearlings galloped around the track and were timed over the final two furlongs as their balance and fluidity were studied. A stopwatch served as the final arbiter.

A lot was at stake. The stable's annual trek to California was looming, and Winfrey needed to know which of the pending two-year-olds to take. He liked to run the early bloomers in the three-furlong dashes for juveniles at Santa Anita and leave his youngsters with more far-reaching potential at home; they were better served, he felt, by receiving several more months of schooling at Sagamore and then starting their racing careers in the spring in New York, where the racing was better.

That morning, it wasn't hard to separate the horses with potential from those destined to accomplish little. Social Outcast looked sharp; he would go to California. Find also ran well. But the best of the crop were Crash Dive and Native Dancer. Working together with Appley riding Crash Dive and Bernie Everson on Native Dancer, the pair circled the track and blazed to the finish line. They were at the head of the class.

It was up to Winfrey to choose which to take to California; taking both and having them compete against each other seemed pointless. The trainer deliberated briefly and decided to leave Crash Dive on the farm and take Native Dancer to the West Coast. "I thought Crash Dive was probably the better of the two, not necessarily on ability; he just seemed at the time like the better-bred horse," Winfrey told the *Blood-Horse* in 1985. "If I'd had to make a choice, at that point, of buying one or the other, and the price was the same, I probably would have taken Crash Dive."

As it happened, Crash Dive suffered a rash of slender "quarter cracks" on his heel bones that kept him from racing at all as a two-year-old. He returned to win some races later in his career but never realized the potential he showed on the farm.

Native Dancer went in the other direction, dazzling backstretch clockers at Santa Anita. With Vanderbilt watching on Christmas Eve morning in 1951, the colt effortlessly covered two furlongs in twenty-three seconds, a remarkable effort for a yearling.

"That'll do," Vanderbilt deadpanned.

Would it ever.

# FIVE

The Dancer worked so impressively as a yearling and early two-year-old at Santa Anita that Winfrey decided the colt was too talented to race in the gimmicky three-furlong dashes that were so popular in California. The horse just trained in California, then was shipped back East with the rest of Vanderbilt's stable in March. His racing career began in April 1952 on a chilly afternoon at Jamaica, the egg-shaped track in Queens, New York. More than 40,000 fans were there for the Wood Memorial, a key stakes race for the East's best three-year-olds. The Dancer was entered in the second race, a five-furlong dash, and he made sure he was noticed.

His eye-popping workout times had been published in the racing papers, and word had spread that Vanderbilt had a speedy two-year-old. Reaching the post as a 7–5 favorite, he broke alertly, waited briefly behind two horses, and overtook them easily when Eric Guerin asked him to run in the stretch. He crossed the finish line almost five lengths in front. "Jumped a mud puddle at the sixteenth pole and still won easy: very impressive," recalled jockey Bill Shoemaker, who was at Jamaica that day.

Winfrey and Vanderbilt brought him back just four days later in the Youthful Stakes, another five-furlong race. Twelve other horses were entered, turning the event into a wild scramble of inexperienced horseflesh. Guerin kept the Dancer, a 9–10 favorite, near the front and out of trouble. A colt named Retrouve had the lead heading into the turn, but Guerin was just waiting to move. He let the Dancer loose turning for home, and the colt zoomed past Retrouve, pulled away, and won by six lengths. James Roach, the racing writer for the *New York Times,* was so impressed he announced that evening in the press box that he didn't believe Vanderbilt's colt would lose a race all year, and anyone who wanted to take him up on that proposition could do so.

Within days, it was announced the colt would be sidelined for several months. Vanderbilt's veterinarian, Dr. William Wright, had detected bucked shins—tiny fractures in the cannon bones of the forelegs, a common, minor ailment for young horses, cured only by time off. The Dancer would miss three months and several important races before returning in August at Saratoga, but that was fine with Winfrey. The East's two-year-olds usually sorted themselves out at Saratoga.

Within days of the announcement about the Dancer, Vanderbilt experienced his greatest Kentucky Derby frustration with a horse named Cousin, a talented but troubled colt.

Vanderbilt had bought Cousin for $20,000 as a yearling in 1950, thinking that if he couldn't breed a Derby winner, maybe he could buy one. Cousin lost his first start as a two-year-old in 1951, then won three in a row and was shipped to Saratoga, where he won the Flash Stakes, Saratoga Special, and Hopeful Stakes within four weeks. "What a horse he could have been if he'd gotten straightened out," Appley recalled. "But he was crazy from the word go. After I galloped him the first time, I came home and told my wife, 'I got on the damnedest horse today.'"

While dominating at Saratoga, Cousin refused to train on the main racing strip. "He'd get to the track and fall over like he'd been shot and refuse to get up," Appley recalled. Jock Whitney offered Vanderbilt the use of Greentree's private training track in Saratoga, and Cousin resumed training. Whatever aversion the horse felt for the main track didn't extend to the afternoons: in the Hopeful, he defeated Tom Fool, Greentree's best two-year-old and later a handicap champion.

"Cousin was a nut, but he could run," recalled Bayard Sharp, Vanderbilt's friend and fellow Jockey Club member. "We were all helping Alfred with the horse at Saratoga. Alfred came to me and said, 'I have this nut and he hates my lead pony and I can't get him to the track to work. Maybe we can fool him. Would you lend me your lead pony?' So I did. And it didn't help. Cousin kicked the hell out of my lead pony and never got to the track. But then we got to the Hopeful, and here we've all helped Alfred with the horse, lent him lead ponies and whatnot, and Cousin goes and beats us all."

To most observers, the victory marked Cousin as a contender for the 1952 Kentucky Derby, but within the stable, concerns about his behavior overshadowed the achievement. He had thrown Guerin before the start, almost lain down in the starting gate, and then again refused to train on the main track after the race. "They brought in a vet," Appley recalled, "and the vet said, 'This horse is plum crazy.'"

Winfrey somehow got him through two more races in the fall of 1951, but he ran seventh in the Anticipation Stakes and eighth in the Futurity after curiously breaking into the air coming out of the starting gate. Vanderbilt and Winfrey hoped he would mature over the winter and come back more willing in the spring, but he was even more difficult, occasionally consenting to light training but otherwise refusing to follow orders. He produced a third-place finish in two starts at Jamaica in April 1952, and Winfrey went ahead and shipped him to Churchill Downs with contingencies. If the colt trained agreeably, he would run in the Derby, ending Vanderbilt's streak at eighteen years without a Derby horse. But if he caused problems in training, he would run in the Derby Trial, a smaller prep race run at Churchill Downs four days before the big race, and Winfrey and Vanderbilt would then reassess.

A disaster unfolded. Cousin refused to train at Churchill and put on a monumental show of stubbornness one morning in front of hundreds of disbelieving railbirds. Winfrey waved a bullwhip, took the colt to the paddock, walked him around the track both ways, and brought in an older horse to try to convince him to run, all to no avail. Finally, after an hour of balking, Cousin extended himself mildly on a single trip around the track, then returned to the barn. Reporter

Jerry McNerney of the *Louisville Courier-Journal* wrote the next day that Cousin had "behaved as if he were related to the mule family."

Winfrey knew how badly Vanderbilt wanted to run in the Derby, but he also knew he couldn't enter such a contrary horse in such an important race without knowing if a genuine effort would ensue. Thus, Cousin was entered in the Derby Trial, his last chance to prove himself.

Vanderbilt, in the midst of his term as the president of the Thoroughbred Racing Associations, spent the morning of the Trial at the barn, chatting with reporters and track officials.

"What are you going to do with that crazy horse?" asked Churchill's track director, Tom Young.

Vanderbilt laughed. "You mean, what is Cousin going to do with *us?*"

That afternoon, the colt balked at entering the starting gate, broke sixth in a field of eight, and quickly lost interest, finishing last, more than forty lengths behind the winner. Vanderbilt left town. Cousin was out of the Derby. "If the horse had run as fast as Alfred did in running to catch his train after the race, we'd have won by seven lengths," Winfrey told reporters. Cousin was removed from training, sold, and sent to Europe, where he raced with success on a steeplechase circuit before being killed in a race.

The Dancer was convalescing in New York as Cousin unraveled in Louisville. The grey colt returned on schedule two months later, having given his sore shins time to heal. He resumed training in July at Belmont and was shipped to Saratoga.

Saratoga Springs had been a summer place unlike any other for decades, thriving on illegal gambling as bribed politicians looked the other way and bookmakers worked out of bars, the backs of stores, and glittering nightclub-casinos on the nearby lakefront. "You talk about a live town," recalled Tommy Trotter, a New York racing official in the early fifties. "There were nightclubs going, celebrities from Hollywood, just a fun town. I'd be eating breakfast at a little grill across from the track at seven in the morning, and here would come the showgirls, coming in from doing the shows, along with guys with their tuxedos still on. It was absolutely wide open, all high-class, just top racing and shows at night and gambling."

But dramatic changes were afoot in 1952. An anticrime panel led by Tennessee Senator Estes Kefauver had discouraged organized crime with televised hearings in which sweating mobsters were grilled. Saratoga's bookies were gone, its casinos shuttered; racing's Gomorrah had reluctantly discovered religion. The members of horse racing's high society, who regarded Saratoga's meeting as their annual convention, still spent their days at the track dressed in jackets, hats, and other formal wear, rooting for their horses from private boxes; then gathered at night for elegant dinners, yearling sales, and big-band parties lasting until dawn. The Spa, as the town was known, was still a seersucker jacket in the sun and a dance in the dark. But the grand hotels were closing, and high rollers were no longer promenading down Broadway.

The start of the racing meeting was met with relief as a sign that not all of the town's traditions were changing; there were still few better settings for racing, few tracks with fans more knowing and caring. The sport's best stables were still present, their horses exercising on steamy mornings and racing through hot afternoons. As always, Vanderbilt's cerise and white colors were hung on the barn nearest the track. He loved August at Saratoga. It was where his society roots and passion for racing blended most seamlessly, and where he had first learned about racing as a boy. Now, as then, he commuted from Sagamore Lodge in the nearby Adirondack Mountains, where he had spent his boyhood summers and where his wife and children were now staying. Vanderbilt spent the weekdays with his family and his weekends at the races and sales amid the racetrack fraternity he considered his second family.

The owner was anxious to see the Dancer back in action, as were Winfrey, Murray, and everyone in the barn. The grey colt had shown potential in his two victories in April, but he had a lot of catching up to do after such a long layoff. Two-year-olds were campaigned as rigorously as possible in the early fifties. This was a custom that horsemen had maintained through the first half of the century, before big money invaded the breeding industry and turned top horses into valuable commodities that needed more conservative handling and preservation for stud duty. Seabiscuit made an astonishing thirty-five starts as a juvenile in 1935, and twenty-three more the next year. Whirlaway raced sixteen times at age two in 1940, one more start than Count Fleet made as a juvenile two years later. Vanderbilt's Bed o' Roses had raced twenty-one times in her championship juvenile campaign of 1949, so, clearly, Winfrey wasn't afraid to push a young horse. The Dancer was painfully raw by those standards, having made just two starts as August began. It was almost as if his career had not even begun.

Winfrey and Vanderbilt planned to change that at Saratoga. The month-long meeting at the historic wooden track on Union Avenue was a hothouse for two-year-old racing, with the best juveniles in the East and Midwest gathering and sparring in a series of stakes. There was the Flash Stakes on the first day of the meeting and the prestigious Hopeful Stakes on the last day, and in between, such races as the Saratoga Special, the Grand Union Hotel Stakes, and the United States Hotel Stakes. Cousin had won three, including the Hopeful a year earlier, and Winfrey and Vanderbilt wanted to push the Dancer even harder and run him in four. It was an audacious blueprint. Years later, any trainer who suggested running an inexperienced juvenile four times in twenty-six days—against top opposition, no less—wouldn't have a job the next day.

It was deemed a routine projection in 1952, however, and the Dancer's busy month started with the Flash on August 4. Skies were sunny in central New York after a morning rain. The usual eclectic blend of society icons, gamblers, and horsemen was on parade among a crowd of 15,000. Jock Whitney and his sister, Mrs. Charles Shipman Payson, the co-owners of Greentree, flew in from Casco Bay, Maine, where they summered, and greeted Vanderbilt in his box overlooking the finish line. Guests staying at the elegant Gideon Putnam Hotel, nestled in the trees near town, came to the track and lingered in front of the betting windows.

The Dancer was made the favorite in the Flash at 4–5 odds, but he was beaten out of the gate and up the backside by Tiger Skin, a Greentree colt who had won his first race, and then was passed on the turn by a long shot named Torch of War. But just as he had in his first two races months earlier, the Dancer accelerated when turning for home, with minimal urging from Guerin, and quickly moved ahead. Torch of War faded and Native Dancer sprinted alone down the stretch, reaching the finish line two and a quarter lengths in front of Tiger Skin.

Winfrey watched the race from Vanderbilt's box and soon found his way to the barn. The grey colt had put on quite a show, beating able, fresher horses as if they, not he, were coming off a layoff. Winfrey elected to give the colt twelve more days off before bringing him back in the Saratoga Special, a six-furlong event known for its unusual financial conditions: the owners put up the $17,000 purse themselves and the winner got it all. That attracted a solid field, including Tahiti, another undefeated son of Polynesian, and Tiger Skin.

The race was run on the day of the Travers Stakes, Saratoga's most important race, but rain fell through the morning and early afternoon, limiting the crowd and leaving the Dancer to negotiate for the first time a track rated "sloppy." He was still the favorite at 7–10, and as usual, he was settled behind the leaders after breaking from the gate, with Guerin positioning him along the rail. Doc Walker, a long shot, set the pace for the first half mile, with Tahiti and Tiger Skin close behind and the Dancer fourth. Coming out of the turn, Guerin swung the colt off the rail and asked him to run. The Dancer blew past Doc Walker and coasted to the finish line three and a half lengths ahead, with Tiger Skin and Tahiti out of the money.

His superiority was indisputable. Joe Palmer wrote in the *New York Herald Tribune* that "as far as Saratoga is concerned, Native Dancer has only one barrier left, Tahitian King." That was yet another undefeated son of Polynesian. The horses met a week later in the Grand Union Hotel Stakes. Eleven horses were entered in the six-furlong race. New York racing secretary John Campbell assigned Native Dancer the top weight, 126 pounds, meaning the horse would carry that much as a handicap, the total including Guerin. "Native Dancer is tops with me," Campbell told reporters. Tahitian King was given the next-highest weight assignment, 122 pounds, along with

Laffango, a colt making his Saratoga debut after winning four straight races in New Jersey.

With three tough horses in the field, six of the other eight entrants were scratched on the day of the race. "They were waiting in line at scratch time this morning, and I didn't blame them for wanting to get out," said John Gaver, the Princeton-educated trainer for Greentree. They were scratching mostly to avoid the Dancer, of course. "If he doesn't win this one, I'm not only going to be surprised, I'm going to be very disappointed," a confident Vanderbilt told reporters shortly before post time.

The horse's reputation was beginning to spread. The largest crowd in Saratoga history—26,232 fans—jammed the track on an afternoon that, Joe Palmer wrote, "was cool enough for a lady to wear a mink if she had one, and warm enough that if she didn't, she could pretend she had left it at home." All eyes were on the Dancer and Tahitian King. The Dancer broke first from the starting gate, then dropped to third along the rail, behind Laffango and Tahitian King, as the pack moved up the backside and into the turn. At his favorite spot—turning for home—the Dancer swept wide of the leaders, passed Tahitian King and Laffango, opened up a lead, and coasted to the finish line three and a half lengths in front. So much for the battle of unbeatens. Tahitian King was no match for the Dancer. The colt had now won five in a row without Guerin even once using the stick to urge an extra effort, and imaginations were beginning to stir. The Associated Press reported that the horse had "run like another Citation, or as some predict, another Man O' War."

It had been a long month; as always in August at Saratoga, the afternoons and evenings were hot, and the mosquitoes were terrible. The Dancer, like many greys, had a sensitive hide, so the buzzing of mosquitoes and flies agitated him. Murray also was annoyed.

"You just like me, you bum," the groom grumbled as he pinned bandages to the Dancer's legs after a morning workout. "That buzz makin' me sweat. That buzz terrible."

Finally, J.C. Mergler, the barn foreman, brought a fan into the Dancer's stall to cool the horse, and also constructed a mesh screen that went over the front of the stall and kept bugs away. Of course, it wasn't entirely clear if the fan and screen were there more to protect Murray or the horse.

One more race remained on the Dancer's Saratoga docket: the Hopeful Stakes, the culmination of the Spa's juvenile season. Having already beaten all rivals on the grounds, the Dancer was virtually conceded the victory and was sent to the post at 1–4 odds. Another record crowd of almost 25,000 fans, the largest closing-day crowd in Saratoga's history, came to watch, certain they would see the Grey Ghost complete his sweep of four stakes wins in twenty-six days. To their surprise, they saw him tested for the first time.

Tiger Skin had already lost twice to the Dancer, but Teddy Atkinson, the fine contract rider for Greentree, had noted the grey's custom of accelerating in the turn and charging from behind down the stretch, and he altered his tactics accordingly. This time, when Guerin and the Dancer swept wide and began their familiar charge from sixth place—a little farther back than usual—Atkinson squeezed Tiger Skin between the long shots that had set the early pace and he took the lead at the top of the stretch. For a moment, he opened daylight on the rest of the pack as the Dancer briefly stalled; he had gotten the jump on the grey. Guerin went to the whip for the first time in the Dancer's career, striking him twice on the right flank. That was all that was needed: the Dancer came on steadily, caught Tiger Skin at the eighth pole, and pulled away. He eased up once he had the lead but still won by two lengths. Dismounting, Guerin spoke to Atkinson within earshot of reporters. "You have to ride him to really see how good he is," Guerin said with a smile.

The Dancer's subsequent victories in the Futurity and a preceding tune-up ran his record to 8–0 by the end of September. He had accomplished enough to warrant taking the rest of the year off. His superiority among his two-year-old class was established. His undefeated record, earnings of $191,970—$27,000 shy of the all-time record for a two-year-old—and world record at six and a half straight furlongs argued for his inclusion on the list of American racing's greatest juveniles. There was more to lose than gain, it seemed, by having him make another start and risk his place in history.

But as Vanderbilt and Winfrey discussed their plans, thoughts of history ran second to concerns for the future. Two-year-olds were always raced with an eye to their three-year-old seasons, and the Dancer was no different. In fact, his success had only heightened interest in his prospects for the Kentucky Derby and the rest of the Triple Crown the next spring. Did he have the tools to win all three races, the surest pathway to American racing glory? The question was still unanswered, despite all the Dancer had accomplished. He had never raced around two turns or farther than six and a half furlongs, and the spring "classics" for three-year-olds were much longer, the Derby at a mile and a quarter, the Preakness Stakes at a mile and three-sixteenths, and the Belmont Stakes at a withering mile and a half. Though the Grey Ghost's dominance at shorter distances was established, his capacity for carrying his weight over longer distances—the mark of a champion—remained uncertain, especially since Polynesian, too, had excelled at shorter distances and wasn't yet considered a safe bet to sire horses with stamina.

Horsemen typically began testing their two-year-olds at longer distances in the fall, inaugurating the process of sorting out the contenders and pretenders for the Kentucky Derby. Winfrey and Vanderbilt weighed several options and entered the Dancer in the East View Stakes, at a mile and one-sixteenth, on October 22 at Jamaica. The race lacked the purse and importance of the Hopeful and Futurity, but the racing press wrote that it might reveal more about the Dancer's Triple Crown potential than his prior eight races combined. Was the Grey Ghost a legitimate Derby horse or, like Cousin, just a talented temptation destined to frustrate Vanderbilt? The owner was certainly curious, his memories of the Cousin fiasco still fresh. "You know Cousin was a prime motivation as the Dancer came on," Alfred Vanderbilt III said.

In the twenty-five days between the Futurity and the East View Stakes, Winfrey put the horse through a regimen of longer workouts aimed at building his stamina. Five other horses were entered in the race, including Laffango, winner of the Champagne Stakes, a prestigious race covering a mile, in his last start. Almost 20,000 fans came to Jamaica on a cool, cloudy weekday afternoon to see the Dancer's attempt to prove he had stamina as well as speed. All other activity at the track halted as the horses were loaded into the starting gate. The fans buttoned their topcoats and rubbed their hands, anticipating a show in the early autumn chill. "Even the hard-bitten pros felt a twinge of excitement," *Newsweek* reported later.

Laffango took the early lead and held it around the first turn and up the backstretch, with his jockey, Nick Shuk, determinedly slowing the pace, covering the first half mile in 48 seconds. That was fine with Guerin, who kept a tight hold on the Dancer as they rolled along in fourth place, behind several long shots as well as Laffango. The favorite at 1–5 odds, the Dancer started to run on the second turn, easily passed the long shots, and bore down on the leader when turning for home. With Shuk also asking Laffango to run, the possibility of a duel down the stretch briefly loomed. But even with Guerin just waving his stick and tapping it on the Dancer's neck instead of using it, the Dancer's finishing kick was too strong. He caught Laffango with a furlong to go and quickly put daylight between them, opening a two-length lead. He slowed just before reaching the finish line, but was still one and a half lengths ahead at the wire and ten lengths up on the rest of the field. His unbeaten record was intact, his first distance test passed.

He was breathing harder than usual after the race, but Guerin dismissed suggestions that he had been pressed in his first race over a distance. "He had no trouble at all," the jockey said. "He always does just what you ask him to do. He tried to pull himself up before the finish, like he always does, but I kept him going."

The winner's purse of $38,525 pushed the Dancer's earnings for the year to $230,495, a record for a two-year-old. The old record belonged to Top Flight, a filly that had earned $219,000 in 1931. There were no longer any doubts about the Grey Ghost ranking with the finest two-year-olds American racing had seen.

After the race, several newsmen pressed Winfrey about the horse possibly running yet again in 1952, in the Pimlico Futurity. The trainer quickly quashed the idea. Within hours of the East View, he announced the Dancer was done for the year. "Native Dancer has done everything asked of him this year, and he has been asked to do a lot," Winfrey said in a statement that was circulated in the press box.

The fans wouldn't see the horse again until the spring of 1953, when—no doubt about it now—he would loom above the crowd as a heavy favorite to win the Kentucky Derby. At last, it appeared, if all went well over the winter, Vanderbilt would get another chance to win the famous race that had eluded him.

# SIX

Winfrey wasn't sleeping well. Though only thirty-six, he had spent his life around racing, and he knew what he had on his hands. He had never trained a horse as talented as Native Dancer, and neither had his father, George Carey "G.C." Winfrey, a respected horseman who had trained a public stable since World War I. Trainers often toss and turn through the night, their minds cluttered with options and concerns, especially when they have a star horse capable of demolishing fields and spawning headlines. The fear of blundering with such a horse and having to live with regrets is enough to fray any trainer's nerves, and the Dancer was obviously such a horse.

"As the situation developed, my father could scarcely believe it," Carey Winfrey, Bill's son, said years later. "His attitude toward Native Dancer was one of enormous gratitude, that he had been given the gift of this fabulous horse when he was relatively young in the game, at least compared to his father. He approached it with a sense almost of humility, that something so talented could come into his hands, like a gift from the gods. He just felt so lucky."

Born in 1916, Winfrey was originally named William Colin Dickard. His biological father, Claude Dickard, came from a prosperous family that owned a cotton gin in Wills Point, Texas, a small town fifty miles east of Dallas. Claude married a Wills Point woman named

Mary Russell, went to college, and took a job with General Motors in Detroit, but he began drinking and the couple divorced after having two children, Bill and an older sister, Janis. Mary took her children back to Wills Point. Claude committed suicide, putting a rifle to his chest in a hotel room in Dallas and pulling the trigger. "He left a poignant note saying, 'Take good care of my baby boy Bill,'" Carey Winfrey said.

Mary soon found another man in Wills Point. George Carey Winfrey was genial and dependable, and he adopted Mary's children and raised them as his own, doting on the boy, now named William Colin Winfrey. "My grandfather was just a lovely man, wonderful to everyone, totally nonjudgmental, and funny," Carey Winfrey said. "When he was in his prime, he would drive quite fast and accelerate into turns; he was very robust and outgoing. He adopted my father, but he was more of a father than most people are with their real sons. They had a very close relationship. Early on, they went places, just the two of them."

In a 1985 interview with the *Blood-Horse*, Bill Winfrey said, "I had a thing about going out to the track with him in the morning. I didn't want my father to go without me. He'd be out there at the crack of dawn. He was a world champion hot coffee drinker. He'd have his finished, I'd be half done, and he'd say, 'Come on, Bill, let's go.' I loved it. It would be just Pop and me."

George Carey Winfrey had become familiar with horses while working in a livery stable as a youngster in Wills Point before the turn of the century. He dropped out of school to join the racing circuit and came to New York as a groom for Tokalon, winner of the 1906 Brooklyn Handicap. He stayed in the East, worked for top trainers, and finally went out on his own. Thorough, indefatigable, and more interested in horsemanship than self-promotion, he operated a small New York-based stable that featured mostly claiming horses, lower end thoroughbreds available for sale whenever they race. Mary's bracelets and rings were in hock as often as they were on her hands, and there were times when George Carey's gambling successes kept the family afloat. But he was an astute trainer and won his share of races. Known for jogging horses to keep them fit rather than putting them through fast works, he was a favorite of knowing New York bettors. One spring, he won with ten of his first sixteen starters at Jamaica.

"He'd stay in New York all winter, stabled at Jamaica, and you'd go up there in the spring and his horses would be big and fat with long hair, and they didn't look like they were fit, but they could outrun a spotted-ass ape," recalled 1950s jockey Charles Ray Leblanc, Guerin's cousin. "[George Carey] Winfrey was a hell of a trainer. He and Hirsch Jacobs were probably two of the greatest there ever was."

Bill and his sister were inured to the nomadic racing life as Depression-era youngsters, spending winters in New Orleans and summers in New York, Maryland, or wherever their father raced. When Bill was six, he rode a circus pony named Sparkle to a victory in a staged-for-grins race at Hialeah. At ten, he was handing out betting numbers on the backsides of tracks. At fifteen, he dropped out of school while on a winter sojourn to Miami with the stable and became his father's fulltime assistant. He had started at John Adams High School near Aqueduct in New York, but his parents hadn't come south with the proper papers to enroll him in school in Florida, and he convinced them he preferred the racetrack to higher education anyway. Although he was thrilled that his goal of becoming a jockey was near, he later regretted that he had ended his academic career prematurely.

He took out a jockey's license at age sixteen, intent on proving his mettle despite his youth. But he weighed ninety-one pounds when he took out the license in January in Florida, and he was up to one hundred ten pounds by the Saratoga meeting in August. He won just four races in nine months before giving up on the project. "I was long on weight and short on talent; just plain no good as a jockey," he told John McNulty in their *New Yorker* interview in 1953. He became an exercise rider and a groom, and that fall his father gave him a small string of horses to take to Laurel, a track in Maryland. He handled the assignment deftly, and his future as a trainer began taking shape.

Before that happened, though, he left the track for two years in the mid-1930s to work for Eddie Burke, an indomitable bookmaker who had played on pro basketball's original Boston Celtics and married Winfrey's sister, Jan. Bookmaking was still legal in New York—pari-mutuel wagering didn't arrive until 1940—and Winfrey wrote prices and ran information in Burke's betting rings. He was good with numbers, but he had to return to the barn when his father suffered a heart attack in 1937. He ran the stable until his father returned the next year, then started his own public stable in New York.

The young Winfrey lived on the edgy flow of the claiming game, buying cheaper horses right off the track and then—hopefully—raising their value and selling them for a profit after a few wins. Winfrey was twenty-two years old, competing against keen veterans such as Calumet's Plain Ben Jones, but he held his own. It was said you could count on one hand the trainers who had claimed useful horses off Jones over the years, but Winfrey pulled it off when he claimed a filly named One Jest, earning a smiling rebuke from Jones; the Calumet trainer and Winfrey's father were old friends.

He won his first stakes race in 1938 with Postage Due, a horse he had claimed off Vanderbilt, then turned a filly named Dini he had claimed for $2,000 into a top sprinter, winner of twenty-seven races. Raised among old school racetrackers, he was as businesslike and taciturn as he was insightful, preferring to let his horses do his talking. In 1940, he took on several wealthier clients, married a pretty brunette, and soon fathered a son. "He was developing a reputation as a good horseman and a square shooter," Carey Winfrey said.

When World War II broke out, he first tried to join other horsemen in the Beach Patrol, a Coast Guard unit patrolling Florida's beaches on horseback, looking for German submarines. He wound up enlisting in the Marines and becoming a rifle coach.

"Before he went into the service, they were having a party," Carey Winfrey said. "He asked his sister to take a walk around the block. She didn't know if he was going to impart some wisdom or ask her to take care of me or my mother or whatever, but they walked all the way around the block and he didn't say a word. Then, when they got to the end, he said, 'Want to go around again?' She said sure. They went around again and he still didn't say anything. And then he left the next day. To her dying day, she wondered what it was he was trying to say that day."

After serving in the South Pacific on Guam and Truk, he was discharged in 1946, came home, and began rebuilding his public stable. He soon had fifteen horses, including several stakes winners. Then Vanderbilt hired him. "Alfred used to come by when I was running Dini; he'd be there in the paddock, and we'd chat, but I didn't think anything of it," Winfrey told the *Blood-Horse* in 1985.

The wealthy young sportsman and his new trainer had a lot in common. Both had halted their education prematurely to pursue racing. Both were on their second marriage; Winfrey's first had collapsed, the long separations caused by war and racing taking a toll. Both were reserved in public and indifferent about spending their afternoons with society swells in trackside boxes, preferring mornings at the barn. Though raised in different circumstances, "they were kindred spirits," Carey Winfrey said. And as much as both loved racing, they had facile minds and broad interests beyond the game.

"My father felt the greatest mistake his parents made was letting him quit school to become a jockey," Carey Winfrey said. "He felt it totally circumscribed his life and eliminated options. I don't think he went through a day when he didn't contemplate another career. Not that he didn't love what he was doing. He just felt there were so many other things he might have done that he didn't get to do. He went water-skiing one day, then never again. He just wanted to experience things. He talked about being a lineman on a telephone line. He was always fantasizing about other professions."

Elaine Winfrey, to whom Bill was married for forty-two years, until his death in 1994, said, "It was strange, a man so accomplished in one field wanting to do other things. But he was quite intelligent for a man that didn't have a formal education. He took night classes and thought about getting into real estate. He felt it was somehow beneath a man to spend his life training horses."

It wasn't beneath him in the early 1950s. Short, trim, and well dressed, he took Vanderbilt on smiling strolls to winner's circles across the country. "They had a great relationship, the best," Elaine Winfrey said. "Bill respected Alfred, and Alfred respected Bill. Alfred never interfered with what Bill wanted to do. There was no one better to train for. Bill knew it."

Vanderbilt, in turn, introduced Winfrey to Fred Astaire, Gregory Peck, and a high life he had never imagined as a boy. "Bill and Fred Astaire became good friends," Elaine Winfrey said. "We'd go over to his house, and Bill and Fred would play pool and I'd watch a movie in the screening room."

But success never swelled his head. Winfrey was loath to accept applause for his training, preferring to credit his father, his horses, and racing luck. "He never took credit for anything," Carey Winfrey said. "He thought bragging, being boastful, was sinful. He would say, 'Well, you know, it's the luck of the draw' or 'Good horses make a trainer look good.' Who knows how much of it was true? He knew what he was doing. He'd learned a lot from my grandfather and he put it to use. On the other hand, once he was with Alfred, he certainly had the kinds of horses he'd never had before. But regardless, he was modest, always modest. Once we went into a store and the guy behind the counter was going on about what a great trainer Winfrey was and how great Native Dancer was, and my father said, 'Yeah, yeah,' and never identified himself. At some fundamental level, he was insecure or shy or something, because he was always self-deprecating. Just a modest man. He almost made a fetish of being modest."

That was never more evident than when he was interviewed by McNulty for *The New Yorker.* "Tell the truth, a man my age doesn't deserve a horse like this," Winfrey said. "My father is sixty-eight, training horses all his life, and he's never had the luck to handle a horse like this grey. I know many trainers who are seventy, seventy-five, training horses for fifty years or more, working hard, knowing the business much more than I know it, and they never had the luck to get a horse like this grey. Tell the truth, a man of thirty-six doesn't deserve it, that's all."

His respect for the older man who had shown him how to train a horse was enduring. Whenever strangers introduced themselves at Barn 20 and asked for "Mr. Winfrey," Winfrey waved in the direction of George Carey's barn across the backside and said, "I'm Bill Winfrey; my father, over there, he's Mr. Winfrey."

"My father, to his dying day, claimed my grandfather was much the superior horseman, and that was probably the case," Carey Winfrey said. "My grandfather could make bad horses run faster than just about anyone. My father was probably a better manager of the stable and better at the politics and stuff, but as far as a horseman, he always felt my grandfather was the real horseman."

But it was Bill Winfrey, not George Carey, into whose hands Native Dancer had dropped, and now, with an undefeated juvenile season behind them and the Kentucky Derby looming, it was up to the son, not the father, to make sure the horse realized his full potential in front of a nation of racing fans.

"There was a great deal of interest in the horse," Dan W. Scott recalled. "I spent a lot of time with Bill, went to some races with him. He had a great time. He would paint Native Dancer's ankles with iodine just to make people think he was worried about them, when he wasn't. He was having fun. And he did a wonderful job. Native Dancer had all those muscles, and Bill took care of them and made sure they kept growing. The horse was lucky to have such a trainer. But Bill wasn't sleeping well. He was constantly worried about doing the right thing. He'd say to me, 'This horse can train himself, he's that good.' A horse like that is a gift. I knew it. Alfred knew it. Ralph Kercheval knew it. Bill certainly knew it. And Bill didn't want to be the one to mess it up."

# SEVEN

One evening in November 1952, a train pulled away from Baltimore's Pennsylvania Station with twenty-eight horses and an army of grooms attached to the rear in three special cars. The Vanderbilt stable's annual trek to California was under way. Horses such as Indian Land, Half Caste, First Glance, Whiffs, Parlor Pink, Newsmagazine, and Next Move—young and old, male and female—stood in hay-lined stalls, wearing protective leather headgear and swaying with the train as it navigated the curving rails of central Maryland, bound for Chicago and ultimately Los Angeles. Native Dancer, with Lester Murray hovering, was in a car with Social Outcast, his fellow two-year-old. The Dancer's favorite barn pet, an old black cat called Mom, was curled up in a box in the corner. The Dancer occasionally leaned over and nuzzled the cat, who wasn't the least bit afraid.

Vanderbilt had taken a stable of horses west for the winter racing season beginning in the mid-1930s, when he was young and single and gambling had just become legal in California. Santa Anita was a splendid new track, opened on Christmas 1934, and Vanderbilt, like many easterners, had been fascinated by news accounts of horses racing for substantial purses before large, sun-drenched crowds of movie stars. He shipped Discovery out for the Santa Anita Handicap in February 1936, and although Discovery ran poorly, finishing seventh, Vanderbilt, then twenty-three, so enjoyed attending the races and Hollywood parties that he returned in December with twenty-seven horses, Bud Stotler, and his top grooms, jockeys, and exercise riders. He took over a barn just inside the backstretch gate and stayed for the entire winter racing season. His colors were seen each day at the races, and he made the rounds at night with such actresses as Joan Crawford and Ginger Rogers.

In the beginning, the size and scope of his westward trek made headlines. The cost and labor required to ship more than two dozen horses from coast to coast boggled Depression-era minds. Horses had long traveled by train, but not so many at once. It took hours just to get the animals from Sagamore Farm to the Baltimore rail yard and loaded onto the Capitol Limited; then, halfway through the journey, they changed trains to the Chief in Chicago and continued on to the West Coast. Vanderbilt himself made the trip with Stotler, residing in a private car. The massive adventure didn't seem as outlandish to him as it did to others. His father, Alfred Sr., had shipped seventy horses from America to England on a steamship before making a run at the London-to-Brighton coaching record. Compared to that, this was easy.

Vanderbilt was a constant wintertime presence in California's racing and social circles for several years in the late 1930s, cohosting a kitschy roller-skating party with Rogers one year and dominating the three-furlong dashes for two-year-olds with record-setting horses such as Airflame, Balking, Galley Slave, and Impound. "Horse racing was just coming to California, and here comes this young guy, America's most eligible bachelor, handsome, rich as hell, and a lot of fun," Alfred Vanderbilt III said. "All he had to do was see Ginger Rogers or someone at lunch and tell them that he was having a party, and word would spread, and Hollywood would turn out. Henry Fonda, Jimmy Stewart, Claudette Colbert, Clark Gable—everyone wanted to be at Alfred Vanderbilt's party."

He stopped coming when he married and divorced his first wife, took on the job of running Pimlico and Belmont, and joined the navy, then resumed his annual trip when he married Jeanne after the war. Every autumn, he uprooted his stable and shipped two dozen horses west. They raced at Hollywood Park in November and December and shifted to Santa Anita after Christmas, staying until the end of the Santa Anita meeting in March before making the long trek back across the country to Barn 20 at Belmont in time to start the New York racing season in April.

The grooms and exercise riders rented small apartments in Arcadia, near Santa Anita. "We drew rent money from Vanderbilt wherever we went on the road," Claude Appley recalled, "and in California we stayed in a little place on First Avenue in West Arcadia. It was always quite a time out there. Mr. Vanderbilt was friendly with the movie stars, and he'd bring them to the barn in the mornings. Betty Grable came one day. Fred Astaire was around a lot; he liked the races. Mickey Rooney would come out and go up to the track kitchen for breakfast and buy everyone something to eat."

When Vanderbilt and Jeanne made the trip as newlyweds in 1947, they drove across the country by themselves, stopping in motels at night. After that, they flew out every year, and Vanderbilt's driver made the cross-country trip in Vanderbilt's car and met them there. The young couple rented a house in Beverly Hills and brought a staff of butlers and maids from Long Island. "Alfred told me to have [socialite] Slim Hayward find us a place, and I wrote to her saying we needed six maids' rooms," Jeanne recalled. "Slim never got over it. She wrote back, 'Six maids? Are you kidding? There's nothing out here with six maids' rooms.' We finally found a place that was suitable."

Billy Passmore, a young jockey from Maryland, came out with the stable in 1949. "Vanderbilt was kind of taking care of me," said Passmore, who was Bernie Everson's nephew and later became a racing steward in Maryland. "He'd come and pick me up and bring me over to the house to swim, or take me out somewhere. We went through MGM Studios when Mervyn LeRoy was the president. He and Vanderbilt were friends, and I got the royal tour. I met Peter Lawford and Clark Gable and Liz Taylor when she was just a kid."

Vanderbilt and Jeanne spent their days at the track and their evenings at parties and dinners. "At Santa Anita, people would spend the day in our box or just drift by to talk," Jeanne recalled. "The movie people loved the racing scene. The crowds were big. Alfred's horses were running and winning. Merle Oberon would come with us for the day and bring these delicious tea sandwiches—made by her French chef, of course. In the evenings, we would be invited to someone's house to eat and watch movies. That was exciting, seeing the movies before they came out. The Astaires had us over. Gary Cooper and his wife. Sam Goldwyn and Frances. We'd go to the Goldwyns for a movie, and Frances would be on the sofa with a box of chocolates when the lights went out, and the box would be empty when the lights came back on, but she never gained a pound! Someone later told me that she only ate dark chocolates which had no fat."

Clyde Roche said, "Alfred moved in the top Hollywood circles, all the big producers and big stars. He enjoyed that circle and the show business ambience, and they enjoyed him, respected his judgment and wanted his approval."

Jeanne eventually tired of overseeing the house and talked Vanderbilt into moving into a bungalow at the Beverly Hills Hotel in the early 1950s. "That was better. We'd have a nanny and maybe one maid, and we had the kids with us, and it was just much easier," Jeanne recalled. "Phyllis Astaire [Fred's wife] helped move us out of the house and into the hotel. She came by with a station wagon with sheets laid out in the back, and we piled a bunch of stuff in there."

Santa Anita's racing meeting was a splendid affair by the early 1950s. Many of the nation's top stables sent their trainers and some of their best horses, with the emphasis on the two-year-old and handicap divisions. Calumet Farm, the reigning superstable, sent trainer Jimmy Jones, winner of five Kentucky Derbys, and signed Eddie Arcaro to ride its best horses. "You either went to Florida or New Orleans or came out here in the winter, and the big money was out here," recalled Leonard Dorfman, a longtime California trainer.

Each racing day was an event, with huge crowds filling the terraces and grandstand. Los Angeles was swelling exponentially with people and money, but it was still a frontier outpost in the sports world, without major league baseball or pro basketball, and the recognition as a major-league racing circuit was welcomed.

"Racing was the only game in town," said Dr. Jack Robinson, a veterinarian on the California circuit in those days. "There were no Lakers, no Dodgers; the Rams were new. When one of the big strings of horses from the East arrived on the train, there'd be a story and a picture on the front page of the *Los Angeles Times* sports section. That was news."

The Hollywood crowd was deeply involved in the racing scene. Bing Crosby opened Del Mar, near San Diego—"where the surf meets the turf," he crooned in a hit song—and helped turn its summer meeting into a feast for stargazers. Many stars either owned horses or frequently came to the races as fans. Dorothy Lamour, W. C. Fields, Edgar Bergen, Don Ameche, Ava Gardner, Red Skelton, Desi Arnaz, Betty Grable, Mickey Rooney, and Jimmy Durante were among those who could be seen. Durante was at Del Mar so often that the track named its turf course after him.

"The people who ran the tracks were intelligent enough to connect to the film industry," longtime California steward Pete Pedersen said. "Santa Anita had Lou Mayer and Cary Grant. When Mayer died, people didn't say, 'Too bad about Louie Mayer.' They said, 'Who's going to get his box at Santa Anita?' Those were the glory years. Racing was the social thing to do, the sport for people with money."

Recalled jockey Bill Shoemaker, who was an apprentice in California in 1949, "Those were the best days of racing; the best ever, really, with all the people and noise and enthusiasm. You could draw 70,000 for a major handicap race. There were no other teams and sports competing for attention, and no off-track betting yet, so everyone came to the track."

Vanderbilt's stable was active, racing its best at Hollywood Park and Santa Anita. Bed o' Roses raced for the first time as a two-year-old at Santa Anita in 1949. Next Move ran fourth in the Hollywood Gold Cup in 1950, competing against males at the end of her championship three-year-old season. She then lost the Santa Anita Handicap by a neck in March 1951.

As usual, Vanderbilt didn't just race his horses: he became a prominent figure in the local racing hierarchy, never taking a title but always volunteering opinions. In January 1952, he gave a controversial speech at a Los Angeles football writers' luncheon, stating that

jockeys were "getting away with rough riding" throughout California
and tougher policing was needed, and also that the racing strip at
Santa Anita was "too fast and dangerous." California's stewards and
track operators ripped back, suggesting that if Vanderbilt was so dis-
pleased, he could take his horses and opinions back to New York.

Tempers had cooled by the fall of 1952 when it was time to head
west again. Vanderbilt and Winfrey decided Native Dancer should
make the trip, even though the horse wouldn't race again until the
spring in New York. The Dancer was unbeaten and the Kentucky
Derby was coming up, and Winfrey and Vanderbilt didn't want the
horse out of their sight, especially with a minor but important proce-
dure scheduled to be performed on the Dancer's ankles. Vanderbilt's
vet, Dr. William Wright, had spotted osselets—small areas of swelling
and leakage—in one fetlock, or ankle, several days after the East
View Stakes in October. It was a common problem, and Winfrey and
Vanderbilt had elected to use a common treatment and "fire" all four
ankles. The Dancer would be given a local anesthetic and a tranquil-
izer as the ankles were painted with iodine, and then a hot iron would
be applied, leaving a checkerboard pattern and a solid, sealed mass
where there had been swelling and leakage. Basically, the osselets
would be seared away, bolstering the tendons and reducing the
chance of a breakdown.

Winfrey and Vanderbilt decided to have the ankles fired in California, with veterinarian Dr. John Peters handling the iron. "It was the
right thing to do and the only thing to do," said Dr. Alex Harthill, the
famed Churchill Downs veterinarian, who was working at Santa Anita
that winter. But the move was not without risk. The Dancer would be
sidelined for six weeks while his ankles recovered, and he couldn't resume serious training until February. He would have only three
months of conditioning before the Kentucky Derby, with his first race
just weeks before it. Winfrey would suddenly be operating with little
margin for error.

Vanderbilt's horses arrived in California in mid-November, and
according to Harthill, while Next Move and the others resumed training and were pointed for the races, the Dancer was put on another
train and sent to Brown Shasta Farm, a hilly spread in Northern Cal-

ifornia, at the foot of Mount Shasta. Howard Oots, a Kentucky breeder and horseman, owned the farm and was friendly with Vanderbilt, and it seemed like a terrific place to give the Dancer a brief vacation after his long racing campaign. "He was up there in that beautiful country, happy as hell, running up and down those hills," Harthill recalled.

His ankles were fired on December 1. "There had been some weakness," Winfrey explained to reporters "and if anything went wrong after a race or two as a three-year-old, it would have been too late to do anything about it except lay him up and miss goodness knows how many valuable engagements."

He convalesced at Santa Anita, where Harold Walker led him to the walking ring every morning and stood with him in the sunshine. "The horse would stand there in the middle of the ring—what a big, good-looking sucker he was," Leonard Dorfman recalled. "They didn't fire him very deep. It was just a precautionary thing. Winfrey thought the ankles were a little poochy. It wasn't serious. He came back quick."

Being out of heavy training didn't prevent the Grey Ghost from making headlines. He was named America's Horse of the Year in a poll of thirty-seven racing secretaries from Thoroughbred Racing Associations tracks, becoming the first two-year-old to win the annual balloting. He also won the annual Horse of the Year poll run by *Turf and Sport Digest,* which surveyed the opinions of 176 racing writers and commentators. (One Count, winner of the Belmont and Travers in 1952, won a third election in which twenty-five handicappers and newspapermen were polled.) Most significant, he was assigned 130 pounds, seven more than any other two-year-old, in the Experimental Free Handicap, a prestigious Jockey Club ranking in which racing secretary John B. Campbell handicapped all of the nation's top two-year-olds in a hypothetical race at one and one-sixteenth miles on dirt. Tahitian King and Laffango received the second-highest assignments, 123 pounds.

The horse made headlines in other ways, too. After a jog in the rain at Santa Anita on January 29, he broke free from Harold Walker and Lester Murray, dumped Bernie Everson, bounced off the rail, and cavorted around the paddock for five minutes before being caught. The Associated Press reported that he "jumped benches and plowed through flower beds, narrowly avoiding fences and stands," and finally got one leg tangled in his reins, enabling Winfrey to catch him.

"Harold had a raincoat on and it was flapping in the wind and that got Native Dancer going," Claude Appley recalled. "He took a big jump and Bernie was dumped, and he was gone. There were people putting in flowers in the paddock and they were hollering like crazy in Spanish. It scared the hell out of everyone."

Vanderbilt's stable struggled through the meeting, seemingly operating under a dark cloud in the wake of the surprising news that Bed o' Roses had died at Sagamore Farm on January 5, an organic disorder cutting short her life just months after she had been retired from racing. Kercheval had planned to have her bred that spring to Count Fleet, the Triple Crown winner, but then she died and Vanderbilt horses made more than a dozen straight losing starts at Santa Anita.

The best three-year-olds of the meeting were Decorated, Correspondent, and Calumet Farm's Chanlea, winner of the Santa Anita Derby, California's biggest three-year-old race, in which Social Outcast finished fourth. But the best three-year-old on the grounds never raced. The Dancer made only one appearance under Vanderbilt's silks, jogging around the racing strip before 47,500 fans after the first race on February 7. Track officials had asked Vanderbilt to show the famous Grey Ghost under colors to boost attendance—some of the proceeds were going to charity—and promoted the appearance in ads as a chance to see "the great horse of the year." Everson was on him instead of Guerin because the horse's romp through the paddock had occurred just days earlier, and Everson was heavier and stronger. Guerin watched from the apron.

The *Los Angeles Times* reported that the crowd "gave the Dancer a big hand" as he circled the track and that he seemed to "sense the admiration as he proudly bowed his head and jogged jauntily" with "precautionary bandages on his high-priced legs." Vanderbilt watched from his box with Jeanne and friends. Though ordinarily opposed to displaying his enviable assets, especially around the racetrack, he didn't mind letting his Hollywood friends get a glimpse of his undefeated champion.

For the slender Everson, it was a rare moment in the spotlight, riding a champion for a cheering crowd while wearing Vanderbilt's silks. Exercising horses was not the career he had expected when he left school in Maryland at sixteen to become a jockey, but he had failed to establish himself, then spent five years in the army during and after World War II, working overseas in the office of a medical division that served in Italy and Africa. He settled for a career as an exercise rider upon being discharged—he was married, had a son, and needed steady work—and was valued by Winfrey and Vanderbilt, who considered him their top morning jockey. He would never achieve the great glories he had dreamed about, but with the crowd cheering him at Santa Anita, he was, at least for the moment, a star.

Back in the obscurity of the morning, he was on the Dancer when the horse finally resumed training on February 18, some twelve weeks after his ankles had been fired. Everson worked him three furlongs in 39 seconds, then breezed him the same distance three days later, this time in 37⅕ seconds. Soon the Dancer was back to his usual morning workout schedule. Horsemen flocked to the rail at Santa Anita to watch, as Winfrey oversaw the exercise from the back of a stable pony and Vanderbilt stood nearby. On March 13, the horse worked seven furlongs in a pedestrian 1:28—he wasn't ready to race yet—and boarded a train bound for Belmont the next day. His Hollywood star turn was over. The Derby was seven weeks away. It was time to go to work.

On the long train ride back east, the Dancer again rode in a car with Murray, Social Outcast, and Mom, his favorite cat. The horse, as always, drew great pleasure from playing with the cat, nudging her with his nose and nuzzling her while she slept. Mom, as always, didn't flinch at the touch of the massive animal looming over her.

Mom had been around Vanderbilt's farm for years, delivering an occasional litter of black kittens who either remained in the barn or found a home elsewhere along the backstretch. There were so many black felines in Vanderbilt's barn that Vanderbilt sometimes joked that he was "going to see the cats" when he left in the morning to see his horses work out. The Dancer had picked Mom out as his favorite, seemingly bemused by her imperturbable nature.

Not long after the horses disembarked from their California trip and were back in Barn 20 at Belmont in March 1953, Mom disappeared into a crevice in a wall, set to deliver a new batch of kittens. Such moments were heralded with joy and laughter on the premises, but this delivery stunned the grooms, exercise riders, and hotwalkers into silence. Out came five kittens, tiny, mewing, and grey.

"That old cat ain't never had nothing but black cats until now," Lester Murray told John McNulty, "and now she have five just as grey as that Dancer. Just as grey as him!"

The old groom just shook his head. His faith in the inexplicable had been justified.

"That Dancer," Murray said, "he's one powerful horse."

# EIGHT

he last Kentucky Derby Joe Palmer covered was the first to be televised live across America from coast to coast. That was just a coincidence, but viewed through hindsight's clear-eyed lens more than a half century later, the fleeting overlapping of eras was flushed with symbolism that all but shouted a message. The country's habits were changing, and if few knew yet how profound those changes were, Native Dancer, being readied for his three-year-old season, would soon help illustrate it.

Palmer, at forty-eight, symbolized the country's familiar syncopation of mainstream media, and in a broader sense, life as it had always been. He was racing's press box bard, a Kentucky native with a master's degree who had taught college English before switching to journalism. He brought wit and literacy to all of his endeavors—books on breeding and racing, columns in the *Blood-Horse,* and his beat work and "Views of the Turf" column in the *New York Herald Tribune.* He was also heard by millions on CBS radio's national broadcasts of major races.

"Joe was one of the great writers of our era, a tremendous composer of English," said John Derr, who worked as an announcer, producer, and executive for CBS radio and TV for more than a quarter century beginning shortly after World War II. "Clem McCarthy had been our race-caller and Joe came in and did a wonderful job. He did the radio broadcast of a number of Native Dancer's races [as a two-year-old in 1952], and people fell in love with the horse, with the way Joe described him in such endearing terms."

Newspapers and radio were long established as the country's fundamental conduits of images, information, and opinion, the channels through which racing—or any popular endeavor—was presented to most of the public. Palmer was at the forefront, a respected pro who was brilliant on deadline and generous in spirit. He worked with binoculars and a flask of bourbon in front of him and rows of admiring colleagues behind him, and no one was better at bringing to life the horses and horse people the public couldn't see.

Then he went to the Kentucky Derby in 1952, and suddenly, his kingdom was being threatened. The usual 100,000 spectators filled Churchill Downs and watched Eddie Arcaro's winning ride on Hill Gail, but a TV audience estimated at 10 million also watched on CBS. Palmer worked the radio broadcast and wrote a story in the *Herald Tribune,* but for the first time, his words and images merely supported what many in the public had seen for themselves.

He was dead before the year was over, just as racing, encouraged by the popular Derby telecast, stood at the threshold of a new era. It was about to be seen consistently for the first time by the vast audiences rushing to TV, which had emerged from radio's shadow since World War II and become a powerful force, expanding in size and influence as rapidly as any instrument in history. The Dancer, championed as a two-year-old in the trusted organs of Palmer's heyday—newspapers, radio, newsreels, and weekly magazines—would now be followed unlike any great horse before him: with a TV signal beaming a live view of his brilliance into millions of homes.

Such staggering fame had seemed unthinkable in 1939 when the National Broadcasting Company sent out its inaugural TV signal to four hundred "receiving sets" in New York, the nation's TV audience. Early programmers were drawn to sports because most of the sets were in bars; within five months in 1939, NBC broadcast the first televised sports event, a Princeton-Columbia baseball game, and the first televised boxing match, tennis match, pro football game, and major league baseball game. The NFL game featured a kicker for the Brooklyn Dodgers named Ralph Kercheval. With millions of radio listeners still entranced by programs such as *Amos 'n' Andy* and *Fibber McGee and Molly,* and early TV pictures ranging anywhere from murky to indecipherable, it was hard to imagine TV making a dent in radio's grip on the broadcast market.

"We watched TV in bars," recalled Clem Florio, a New York–area boxer and horseplayer in the 1940s, "and also, the stores that sold appliances always had TV going. The wrestling matches. They would drone on and on, and people would be out on the street, packed around the store window, looking in. That was TV. You'd go, 'This is coming from Madison Square Garden and we're in Ozone Park. How'd they do that?' We'd watch it and then read about it the next day. It was a miracle. We'd first heard about it at the World's Fair in 1939. They had an exhibit. Then they started showing the wrestling matches. They'd hold on to each other for hours, the most boring stuff in the world. They finally got smart and livened it up with guys gouging each other and fighting with the referee and stuff. They were trying to sell the product—the TV sets, not the wrestling."

Production of sets was halted during World War II, and only seven thousand were in use in 1946. But then mass-produced sets with long-lasting cathode-ray tubes began selling more briskly after the war. "It all started to pick up after the war," Florio recalled. "That was the first time we saw the [boxing] fights. I did some exhibition boxing for TV, got paid two hundred a fight to box two rounds with a guy in my stable. I was white and dark-haired, and the other guy had to be blond, or black. They had to have contrast. It was going out as an exhibit. They were trying to figure out how to broadcast it, going through a learning process. They would ask you to stay on one side of the ring, or close to this or that spot. They were trying to figure out the angles."

In 1948, NBC hired Milton Berle to host the TV version of a popular radio show, *The Texaco Star Theater.* A rubber-faced comedian weaned on vaudeville shtick, Berle was an instant hit with TV audiences able to see his slapstick, sight gags, and mild vulgarities. He made the cover of *Time* and *Newsweek* in 1949, and as his popularity soared, so, almost directly, did that of the nascent medium. Friends met in homes with TV to watch Berle's show, then went out and bought their own sets. An industry formed around the CBS, NBC, ABC, and DuMont networks, which organized schedules and developed programming.

Radio had controlled 81 percent of the broadcast audience when Berle first appeared, but it lost half of its listeners within two years. Movie attendance dropped 70 percent. Television was taking over. Ten million American homes had sets by 1951. The total had surpassed 17 million when Arcaro crossed the finish line on Hill Gail on the first Saturday of May 1952.

It was mostly an urban phenomenon at first: almost half of the 1.1 million TV sets in use in 1949 were in New York City, with most of the rest in other major cities. Small towns and rural communities were left out, unable to pick up signals from urban transmitting stations. But with movie theaters and minor-league baseball circuits closing in droves as city dwellers opted to be entertained in their living rooms, all barriers limiting TV's growth were bound to fall. The last obstacle was cleared with the laying of a signal-carrying coaxial cable stretching from coast to coast, completed in 1951. Now small towns and rural communities could have TV, too.

The first coast-to-coast national TV broadcast was on September 14, 1951, when millions watched President Harry Truman address the Japanese Peace Treaty Conference in San Francisco. A month later, *I Love Lucy* premiered on CBS, starring Lucille Ball and Desi Arnaz as a young couple in New York. Critics were dubious at first, but the half-hour comedy soon had a weekly audience of more than 7 million viewers. On April 7, 1952, an episode of *Lucy* became the first American show seen in more than 10 million homes.

Television was rapidly replacing radio as the modern version of the village storyteller. For a majority of the public, there simply was no comparison between listening to a program or major event and actually seeing it. "Television brought the outside world into the home in a way that had never existed before," recalled Leonard Koppett, a *Herald Tribune* sportswriter in the early 1950s. "People in the twenties had been completely knocked out by the phenomenon of radio, and that was just a voice box. They still got most of their information from newspapers, and few of them actually saw anything they read about. Everyone knew about Man O' War, but who had seen him run? Then along came TV, and no matter how scratchy the picture was, the connection experience was astounding. People went, 'Hey, this event is happening right now, it's important, and I'm looking at it. I don't know how this is happening, but it's fantastic.'"

Observing the public's fascination with the visual medium, *Herald Tribune* critic John Crosby presciently wrote that "the revolution in the entertainment world is only dimly understood [now]." For that matter, the revolution in basic human perceptions was only dimly understood. "Before TV, the printed word was the way you learned something," Koppett said. "When TV came along, it became the printed word in combination with a visual image. It was a wholly different internalizing process."

Berle's popularity was the first example of TV's ability to bond on-air personalities with individuals in a sweeping audience. The awesome power of that connection was soon demonstrated in other ways. After Senator Kefauver and his anticrime panel grilled mobsters on live TV in 1951, the obscure Kefauver became a presidential candidate in 1952. Coverage of that year's political conventions drew vast audiences and turned news anchors such as CBS's Walter Cronkite into household names. In September 1952, when it was reported that wealthy California businessmen were giving money to Republican vice presidential candidate Richard Nixon to help cover his personal expenses, Nixon went on national TV—on a Tuesday night, after Berle's show—and tried to clear his name in front of millions of viewers.

Sports also boomed in the early TV days. Boxing was a perfect fit, with dramatic, action-packed bouts taking place in tight, camera-friendly confines. *The Gillette Cavalcade of Sports,* a weekly series of Friday night bouts, drew large audiences after debuting in 1948 on NBC, and soon as many as six boxing programs were on every week, featuring Rocky Marciano, Sugar Ray Robinson, Archie Moore, and numerous lesser lights who became well known strictly because of TV. Boxing had a brief fling as the nation's sports obsession. Harness racing soared in 1949 and 1950 when NBC aired a show from New York's Roosevelt Raceway several nights a week. Bowling shows were also popular, leading to the opening of hundreds of new bowling alleys across the country. "The ability of TV to determine the popularity of sports was instantly evident," Koppett said.

Major league baseball and college and pro football were also programming mainstays, but they experienced notable drops in attendance at televised games. Sales of tickets for televised boxing cards also fell sharply. Suddenly, sports decision-makers were dubious about the marriage of TV and sports. Was the exposure gained from televising an event worth the apparent damage inflicted on ticket sales?

Opinion was divided. Tim Mara, owner of pro football's New York Giants, said, "There isn't the slightest doubt that TV murders you." Branch Rickey, baseball's famed builder of pennant-winners, wrote an essay titled "TV Can Kill Baseball." Grantland Rice labeled TV "a raging storm spear-headed by a wrecking cyclone." On the other side, more farsighted leaders such as Ned Irish, vice president of New York's Madison Square Garden, correctly sensed that exposing a sport to TV's vast audience was worth any short-term loss in revenue.

Alfred Vanderbilt agreed with Irish, becoming an immediate and outspoken advocate of the new medium. "He embraced TV," Clyde Roche recalled. "He thought the best thing to happen for racing was to build a big public audience for the sport at the highest level. He liked traditional things, but he also was very open to new ideas. It was a conflict in his personality."

His daughter Heidi recalled, "Dad was a proponent of TV. We watched it all the time. It was really important to the way he was with us. There was a set in the living room and another upstairs in the bedroom. We watched the cowboy shows and *Howdy Doody* with Dad. I'd sit on his lap when he watched the news in the morning. We watched *Omnibus* and *Kukla, Fran and Ollie.* And we always watched the races, of course."

Vanderbilt advanced the marriage of racing and TV in several ways. When his friend CBS president Bill Paley was looking for an announcer for a broadcast of the 1947 Belmont, Vanderbilt volunteered. He coolly handled forty minutes of interviews and chitchat before explaining to viewers that he had to go "because I have a horse in the next race." John Crosby reviewed him favorably. "When you were on TV," Alfred Vanderbilt III said, "all of your friends saw you and they'd call you up and say, 'Hey, Alfred, I saw you on TV.' What a great novelty. He was still young enough to enjoy it."

Sam Renick, a jockey who had ridden for Vanderbilt, became racing's first identifiable TV analyst after Vanderbilt suggested that, with his talkative nature, he was suited to broadcasting. When Pimlico needed a sponsor to get on the air in the late forties, Vanderbilt reeled in help from his late father-in-law's company, Bromo-Seltzer. "He understood very quickly what TV was about, how powerful it was, and that it was a way to show people how exciting racing was," Alfred Vanderbilt III said.

Despite Vanderbilt's position, racing proceeded cautiously in TV's early years, tiptoeing through the tracks of the learning curve set by other sports. Most track operators remained skeptical, refusing to show their feature races to afternoon audiences. "You can't sell a product and give it away at the same time," insisted Bill Corum, a former New York sportswriter who became president of Churchill Downs.

"The track owners and operators believed if we put the races on, people would stay home. We couldn't convince them otherwise," said Tommy Roberts, a longtime TV racing broadcaster and executive. "The only ones who saw the possibilities at the time were Vanderbilt and old Sunny Jim Fitzsimmons. Fitz said, 'This is the greatest thing, what a window into our world. People can see the fine clothes and celebrities and horses and color.' He was right. But the rest of the racing fraternity couldn't see it."

There were other problems as well. Even though racing's popularity was soaring, the Kefauver investigation into organized crime was a fresh memory, and many sponsors were reluctant to have their names and products associated with any endeavor involving gambling. "We couldn't give racing away, to be honest," CBS's John Derr said. "Couldn't give away golf or tennis, either. Wrestling was no problem. Boxing was no problem. But we couldn't find anyone to sponsor racing even when Bing Crosby was involved."

Racing's TV exposure was limited to occasional local broadcasts through the early fifties. The first TV show ever aired in Baltimore was the opening of Pimlico's fall meeting in 1947, with newspapermen calling the races and models putting on a fashion show on the clubhouse roof to keep viewers tuned in between races. Two races a day were broadcast through the meeting, but the impact was minimal with the city's TV audience limited to four hundred or five hundred sets in bars. In 1948, CBS televised the Belmont and Preakness live in New York, Philadelphia, and Baltimore, and NBC broadcast races from local tracks several times a week in New York, with Clem McCarthy and Fred Caposella calling them.

"Citation ran at Garden State Park one time, and CBS sent Ted Husing down to do the race on TV," Tommy Roberts recalled. "Ted was a legendary radio announcer, but he had never called a horse race. The producer said, 'Look, Citation will go to the front and all you have to do is look for those silks and say, "He's in front, Citation is in front . . . he's still in front."' That race was shown only on local TV in Philadelphia."

When racing's attendance continued to soar in these early years, unlike the attendance for sports seen more often on TV, Corum and other racing officials were hailed for their prudent handling of the TV "raging storm." Racing was booming, with Joe Palmer and his colleagues—newspaper columnists such as Red Smith and Rice, and radio race-callers such as Bryan Field and McCarthy—telling the stories, painting the images, and creating the legends. As had been the case for decades, the general public's only chance to eyeball top horses came in the brief newsreels shown in movie theaters before the feature.

"Movietone newsreels were where you got images of events," recalled Tim Capps, the racing executive and author. "They showed the races a lot. The newsreels were how my father learned what Whirlaway and Count Fleet looked like. That was the only way people saw racing. If you didn't grow up in an area with a track, you didn't see a horse race unless you saw the Movietone newsreels. Then TV came along and transformed the world of people who watched sports."

Indeed, TV was growing so quickly and becoming so prevalent

that it was impossible to resist. Many racetrack operators were less worried than they admitted in public, believing they could handle more TV exposure without experiencing a precipitous drop in attendance because, as Red Smith wrote, "until someone builds a set with a built-in mutuel window, every new fan created by TV will eventually show up at the track."

After refraining from allowing any broadcast of the Kentucky Derby through 1948, fearful of harming attendance, Churchill Downs allowed a delayed local broadcast in 1949. The next year, Field called the race into a CBS microphone, took a film of the race to the airport, and boarded a private plane for Dayton, Ohio, the city nearest Louisville with coaxial cable. (Louisville didn't get it until 1951.) The plane was equipped with a special device for developing film, and that night, four hours after the race, CBS viewers saw a tape of Middleground's victory. DuMont used the same complicated process to show racing from Hialeah that year; the first six races at the South Florida track were filmed in the afternoon, and the films were flown to New York and broadcast that night.

The first live national telecast of a race came on November 16, 1951, months after the job of laying the coaxial cable from coast to coast had been completed. CBS televised the Pimlico Special from Baltimore, with Dave Woods, Vanderbilt's longtime racing publicist, calling the race and urging viewers to participate in a Red Cross blood drive for U.S. soldiers fighting in Korea. The size of the viewing audience for the twenty-five-minute sponsor-free broadcast wasn't estimated, but the obscure $15,000 race, won by a colt named Bryan G., was surely seen by more eyes than any previous race in American history.

Months later, Churchill Downs reluctantly consented to the live national broadcast of the 1952 Derby. Corum predicted the show would command the "largest TV audience ever to view an on-the-spot event," but, ever dubious, he was careful to mute his enthusiasm in announcing the one-year deal he described as "experimental." Said Corum, "We're going to study the effect on the size of the crowd, betting and such before committing ourselves to any future contracts."

CBS went all out. Judson Bailey, the executive director of CBS-

TV sports, flew to Louisville to oversee a forty-man broadcast team. A pipe-smoking former baseball writer for the Associated Press, Bailey told reporters the broadcast would cost "well into six figures," making it the "most expensive half hour in TV's brief history." Four cameras would be used—one in the paddock, one in the infield, and two on top of the grandstand—and Field would call the race from a new press box above the finish line. An original "feed" of words and pictures would travel over the coaxial cable to WCBS in New York, where edits would be made, commercials would be inserted, and a finished product would be sent out. Viewers would see events one-hundredth of a second after they occurred.

The announcer, Bryan Field, like Palmer, was familiar to racing fans, trusted to bring order and context to unseen events. He had started out as a general sportswriter for the *New York Times,* then became a racing expert in the late 1920s, not only writing adeptly but also developing a flair for calling races in a faux British accent. By the late 1930s, he was writing for the *Times* and calling races as a radio broadcaster and track announcer in New York, and as if that weren't enough, he took on the job of director of public relations at Delaware Park, a track in Stanton, Delaware, in 1939. Soon he was running the track as its vice president and general manager, commuting back and forth every day from New York. He eventually had to quit his newspaper job as Delaware Park flourished and his prominence as a race caller increased with TV's rise.

Hours before Field took the microphone to call the 1952 Derby, President Truman gave the nation a televised White House tour before millions of viewers watching on three networks. A trio of newsmen followed him from room to room and asked questions as he chatted about paintings, china, and the history of the famous house. The president was so relaxed he sat at a piano and played a portion of Mozart's Ninth Sonata, leading Jack Gould, a *New York Times* critic, to label him "a born TV star."

Minutes after Truman went off the air, it was time for the Derby. The first fifteen minutes of the forty-five-minute show were broadcast on a "sustaining" basis—without a sponsor—and Gillette, the razor company, sponsored the race and its aftermath. Sam Renick handled the scene-setting, advertising pitches, and prerace interviews. Pete French, a Louisville broadcaster, interviewed several celebrities. Field called Hill Gail's victory with one minor gaffe, initially claiming that a colt named Pintor had nosed out Master Fiddle for third when, in fact, Blue Man had run third.

It was another of the major TV moments Americans were learning to share in their living rooms, or wherever they could find a set. The Associated Press reported that taverns in Buffalo were crowded with fans watching the race; TV sets in storefronts in Huntington, West Virginia, drew large crowds from a nearby high school band tournament; sportswriters and school officials turned away from a USC-UCLA track meet in Los Angeles to watch; management at Pimlico installed twenty-six sets in the grandstand so fans attending the races there wouldn't miss the big event; and the "sporting gentry" in New York "flocked to bars for the teleview" and "jettisoned the Kentucky tradition of mint juleps in favor of cooling draughts of brew."

It was easily the most watched horse race in American history, and Jack Gould's *New York Times* review was generally favorable. "The camera coverage of the race was excellent and Field's commentary on the race itself was outstanding," Gould wrote, "but the other announcers, in doing the color, indulged in the usual synthetic hoopla and contrived excitement. When will these tiresome children of broadcasting learn to shut up and behave as human beings?"

Of course, the only review Corum cared about was the review of the attendance and betting figures, and there, too, the news was favorable. Even though the race was shown live in Louisville, the usual crowd had swarmed Churchill Downs and bet enough to establish a new record for Derby day wagering. With that news, racing officially entered its TV age, however belatedly. Now that the Derby was on TV, other tracks were bound to follow with their major races, bringing the sport into focus as a TV entity along with boxing, baseball, and football. A vast audience lay untapped in America's hills and valleys, and the chance to introduce it to the sport was impossible to resist.

In the coming months, CBS signed a three-year deal to broadcast the Triple Crown, and NBC agreed to televise ten major East

Coast races from April through June 1953, with Gillette sponsoring the program as part of its popular *Cavalcade of Sports* anthology. Still unsure if racing would attract viewers, Gillette arranged to have a pony auctioned off during each of the hour-long broadcasts, with the proceeds going to the Damon Runyon Cancer Fund, a charity started by the late sportswriter. The races on the schedule included the Gotham Stakes, Wood Memorial, Dwyer Stakes, and Travers Stakes, all on the projected schedule for the Dancer that Winfrey and Vanderbilt had drawn up.

On October 31, 1952, five months after the Derby telecast and nine days after the Dancer's victory in the East View Stakes, Joe Palmer spent the day covering the races at Jamaica for the *Herald Tribune*. The early autumn weather was crisp, but no crisper than the prose Palmer batted out in the press box after the last race was over and the 15,687 fans had departed. "The weather was better than the racing," he wrote, chiding track management for the quality of "what it probably believed to be a feature" race, the Sanford Purse. By the time his story hit the streets, Palmer had suffered a heart attack and died in a hospital, leaving behind a wife, two sons, and millions of fans. "It can be stated only as one man's opinion, yet unquestionably it is shared by thousands, that he wrote better than anyone else in the world whose stuff appeared in newspapers," wrote Red Smith, Palmer's close friend and *Herald Tribune* colleague, in a tribute column.

Sadly, racing's best writer was dead, far too soon, and with him, fatefully, went an era. The information machinery of his lifetime would continue to publish and preach, wielding influence and telling the public what it should believe. But Americans were becoming addicted to the power of their own vision: the thrilling independence of seeing events for themselves and making their own judgments, instead of having events seen for them and translated.

Native Dancer, as if on cue, stepped into this confluence of technology and societal evolution in the spring of 1953. Adult Americans, raised in the Depression, were accustomed to horses, yet many had never seen a great one coming down the stretch. Racing, a sport riding a crest of popularity, yet still a newcomer to national TV, was set to offer them the chance. And the public's initial fascination with the new medium still hadn't worn off. The Dancer, with timing as momentous as his talent, would be the one to test the new era's limits of celebrity, like Milton Berle before him.

# NINE

W hen Native Dancer raced for the first time as a three-year-old in the Gotham Stakes at Jamaica on April 18, 1953, the rest of the sports world stopped to watch. The undefeated Grey Ghost hadn't raced in almost six months, and the public's curiosity was boiling over with the Kentucky Derby now just weeks away. Fifty thousand fans were expected, and 38,000 still came in a chilling rain. Millions more watched and listened on TV and radio; the race was televised nationally on NBC, marking the Dancer's first coast-to-coast exposure, and also broadcast nationally over ABC's radio network.

American horse racing had experienced swells of popularity before: the 1920s were a high time in the wake of Man O' War's career, and four horses—Whirlaway, Count Fleet, Assault, and Citation—had won Triple Crowns in the 1940s, drawing millions of new fans to tracks, particularly after World War II. But the sport had never been as popular as it was in the early 1950s. "Racing Now Virtual King of Sports, Topping Baseball in Gate Appeal," read an April 1953 headline on the front page of the *New York Times*. That was hard to believe, given baseball's long reign as the "national pastime," but the *Times* supported its claim with strong evidence: Thoroughbred and harness tracks had collected more than 45 million paid admissions in 1952, surpassing by 5 million the total at major league and minor league parks. Moreover, racing's attendance was rising, and baseball's was falling. The sport had struggled at times against persistent tides of skepticism and societal conservatism in the first half of the twentieth century, but it was booming now.

"What used to be called the sport of kings is now threatening to become the king of sports," the *Times* wrote, adding that fans were flocking to tracks because racing was "faster and more colorful" than baseball games, which "tend to drag," and football games, which amount to "a confusing pile-up of players or a tricky sleight-of-hand game more easily watched on TV."

The increase in popularity was attributable to numerous factors. The nation's sports calendar wasn't nearly as crowded as it would become. Baseball, college football, and boxing were popular, but pro football and pro basketball were just beginning to attract larger followings, and college basketball was reeling from a point-shaving scandal. Television would turn the latter three into major attractions and America into a country of sports-mad couch potatoes within years, with pro football surpassing baseball as the nation's primary sports obsession, but the public wasn't yet dizzy with choices in the early 1950s and the old-guard sports still ruled. Racing was at the forefront of the old guard, with a history dating to before the turn of the century and more tradition than any sport other than baseball.

Racing also still had the gambling market all to itself. Las Vegas was in its infancy, state-run lotteries didn't exist, and backroom bookmakers were hurriedly closing up shop in the wake of the Kefauver hearings. With the judiciousness of off-track betting still being debated, a racetrack was the only place where a person could legally gamble, and millions of Americans were exercising their right to do so. "It seems clear," the *Times* wrote, "that gambling blood runs strong in the veins of Americans."

That had not always been the case. Powerful voices had shouted down racing on moral grounds for decades, stunting its growth and occasionally even shutting it down. "There was always that Goody Two-Shoes stuff about it being a vice; it was equated with sin because of the gambling," Clem Florio recalled. "Millions of people loved it, treated it in a healthy manner. But the church people really held it back. There was a time when you said you were a horseplayer, that was a stigma. It was like, 'Uh-oh, we don't trust this guy, he's probably a killer and at least a degenerate.'"

Such notions were outdated by the early 1950s. The voices shouting down racing had lost the war. Racing's leaders had finally succeeded in refuting the long-held perception that their sport was a haven for cheats and shady characters. That perception had been warranted at times and still was in some cases, but the overall picture was far less murky. The Thoroughbred Racing Protective Bureau, organized by a coalition of major tracks in 1946, had created a powerful watchdog agency stocked with former FBI agents. The "film patrol"—teams of cameramen who filmed races from multiple angles to help stewards identify fouls—had spread across the industry in the 1940s and virtually eliminated jockey shenanigans. Pari-mutuel wagering, in which fans bet against each other, with the tracks holding the money, had become customary, putting bookmakers out of business and giving bettors the faith that their money was traveling through legitimate corridors. Racing would always have its share of dark corners, but in the early 1950s it was as well scrubbed and unpolluted as it had ever been.

At Belmont, there was talk of increasing the seating capacity to 32,000 and ultimately 50,000. The Jamaica Racetrack, built in 1903 with seats for 12,000 fans, now strained to handle four times as many on weekends. Hialeah had opened a new clubhouse. Santa Anita drew as many as 75,000 fans for handicap races at the peak of the winter racing season. Although some customers were unhappy about being squeezed into outdated facilities, most came back for more. The combined wagering at America's 127 tracks had totaled almost $2 billion in 1952, setting a record for one year and marking a 20 percent rise from the year before. The combined attendance of almost 29 million had set another record.

Racing was especially popular in Florida and California over the winter, Kentucky in the spring, Chicago in the summer—and New York for much of the year. From April through November, the big city paused and paid attention every time the starting gate opened at Jamaica, Belmont, or Aqueduct, which rotated meetings. Much as the scores of afternoon baseball games in progress were whispered through offices and communicated among strangers on the streets, the results from the track were heralded through the teeming city of big yellow cabs, brassy chatter, and smoky bars. It was appropriate that the city's nickname had racetrack roots—the *Morning Telegraph*'s John J. FitzGerald had started using the phrase "the Big Apple" in print in 1921 after hearing two black stable hands in New Orleans use it to describe the New York racing circuit—for the city and the sport were as intertwined as siblings.

"They'd open up at Jamaica in April and get 50,000 people and handle $5 million [in bets that day]," said Tommy Trotter, an assistant racing secretary in New York in the early 1950s. "It seemed like racing was in the best years I can recall. Racing had been shut down during the war [for five months in 1945], and when it came back, everything was going right. We had big crowds, lots of interest, great newspaper coverage. We had a lot of papers in New York and they all gave racing a lot of coverage with articles and pictures."

Costy Caras was working for the *Daily Racing Form* in New York in the early 1950s, helping Don Fair, the racing paper's legendary chart caller. Caras lived in Jamaica, where his father owned a restaurant located near the Jamaica track and popular with the racing crowd. "Jamaica was just a fantastic hotbed for racing," recalled Caras, who was later the longtime track announcer at Charles Town in West Virginia. "People took a bus or the elevated line to get to the track; it was very easy to get to, easier than Belmont, which was a little farther out from the city. They might have 65,000 people on a Saturday at Jamaica."

Caras's father's restaurant, the Louis Restaurant, was located at Merrick Boulevard and Jamaica Avenue. "We had pictures of jockeys and horses on the walls. A lot of the big-name people came in," Caras recalled. "We were near the Whitman Hotel, which was where the racing people who shipped in stayed. There was a lot of racing talk. I would bring in a tape of Fred Caposella's calls of that day's races, and we'd play it in the restaurant to warm up the supper crowd."

New York's racing fever originated in Jamaica and spread throughout the five boroughs. Anyone who might have doubted the

*Times*'s surprising claim about racing surpassing baseball needed only check the crowds at New York's tracks and ballparks in April 1953. The first day of the Jamaica meeting drew 40,364 fans in chilly, overcast weather. The Brooklyn Dodgers and Pittsburgh Pirates drew 12,433 fans on opening day at Brooklyn's Ebbets Field; Jamaica drew 20,767 the same afternoon. Several days later, a pair of afternoon ball games drew fewer than 12,000 fans combined (the Dodgers and Pirates drew 3,149, and the Yankees, on a streak of four straight World Series championships, drew 8,196 to Yankee Stadium for a game against the Philadelphia Athletics), and that night more than 30,000 crowded into a harness racing track in Queens.

Although the tracks were outdated and dilapidated and fans were grumbling—the New York Racing Association would be formed in 1955 to address the condition of the tracks and unify them—the thirst for horses and racing was almost insatiable, it seemed. Native Dancer loomed over this unprecedented fervor, the horse of all horses, casting a giant shadow as the Jamaica meeting began. The other three-year-old Triple Crown contenders were sorting themselves out in prep races in Florida, Louisiana, Kentucky, and California, but the Grey Ghost's superiority was so presumed that his odds were 7–5 in a popular Derby future book in Caliente, Mexico. Long-range bettors were already betting on him to win the Kentucky Derby at those marginal odds even though he hadn't raced since October.

His arrival at Jamaica's paddock minutes before the Gotham was presidential, lacking only blaring trumpets. Hundreds of fans swarmed the enclosure for a closer look at the unbeaten colt. They were stunned by what they saw. As a two-year-old, the Dancer had seemed coltish, immature, still lacking definition despite his size. That was no longer so. He stood 16.2 hands tall and weighed 1,200 pounds, with a powerful hind end to match his massive forelegs, which had seemed out of proportion when he was two. Other than the usual bulge in his right ankle, which Winfrey dismissed as insignificant, he was spectacular.

Eastern horsemen had noticed the differences when he returned from California with the rest of Vanderbilt's stable in March.

Rumors about his condition had circulated for months after his ankles had been fired and he was taken out of training for twelve
weeks, but it was clear, once he was back East, that he had benefited
from the time off. He covered five furlongs in 1:02⅖ on a muddy
track at Belmont on March 21, and his conditioning improved
rapidly from there.

The goal, of course, was to have him at his best for the Derby.
Winfrey plotted a short, intense course of prep races, all at Jamaica:
the Assault Purse, at six furlongs, on April 13; the Gotham, at a mile
and a sixteenth, five days later; and the Wood Memorial, at a mile and
an eighth, on April 25. That meant four races in nineteen days, count-
ing the Derby on May 2. It was a vigorous reentry to racing after such
a long layoff, but Winfrey had little choice. The Dancer's training had
been pushed back when his ankles were fired, and he was just getting
into shape.

Predictably, there was criticism. Some horsemen felt mid-April
was too late to start giving a Derby horse a diet of prep races; it was
already clear, they said, that the Grey Ghost wouldn't be in peak condition in Louisville. Others felt Winfrey surely knew what was needed
to have his horse ready, and the Dancer's training seemed to validate
their assumption. The colt worked a mile for the first time as a three-
year-old on April 4, covering it in 1:41⅖ on a fast track, then worked
the same distance in 1:39 on a muddy track four days later. The latter
was an impressive work seen by hundreds of horsemen at Belmont,
and "the workout combined with his unbeaten record, seems to have
terrified rival trainers," *Morning Telegraph* columnist Charles Hatton
wrote.

Just as the Dancer was preparing to make his debut in the Assault Purse, there was a distracting snag involving Winfrey. Kitchen
Maid, a Vanderbilt filly with a kidney ailment, ran second in a race
at Jamaica on April 10, and her urine test came back positive for caffeine, a banned stimulant. New York's racing commissioners inves-
tigated, and there was tension for a day with Winfrey facing a
possible suspension and Vanderbilt insisting the Dancer wouldn't
run in the Triple Crown without his trainer. But the commissioners
quickly exonerated Winfrey, determining that he had treated

Kitchen Maid with medicine from a bottle that didn't list caffeine among the ingredients.

Then there was another snag. Supporting Hatton's opinion that the Dancer had "terrified" rival trainers, only two other horses were entered in the Assault Purse on April 13. Jamaica officials initially said they would still hold the race, then changed their minds and canceled the Grey Ghost's three-year-old debut. The track caterers received a record number of cancellations for lunch, but more than 24,000 fans still came to the track on a rainy Monday, thinking the Dancer might still appear as originally scheduled. They went home disappointed. The Dancer worked three furlongs in 35 seconds that morning at Belmont and spent the afternoon in Barn 20.

The colt had been training at distances beyond the Assault's six furlongs, so he probably wouldn't have benefited much from the race. But he needed the work, and with race-goers desperate to see him, Vanderbilt proposed running him in a public trial with two other Vanderbilt horses in between races at Jamaica the next day. Jamaica officials consented. Winfrey drove over from Belmont the next morning and found the racing surface in good condition despite recent rains. The trial was on for that afternoon.

It so happened that John McNulty had chosen to spend that day at the barn researching his article on the Dancer for *The New Yorker.* McNulty observed Lester Murray standing on a bucket in stall 6 and meticulously braiding the colt's hair for a half-hour before the van arrived to take him to Jamaica. "I'm going to fix you up pretty, you big bum, before all those people look at you," said Murray, who continually moistened his fingers as he worked the braid until he got it just as he wanted. The van arrived then, and Murray gave the horse a hard slap on the rear as the Dancer was led outside.

The Dancer rode over in the van with his trial "opponents": First Glance, a six-year-old who had won the Excelsior Handicap in his last start, and Beachcomber, an unraced three-year-old gelding. The Dancer made his first public appearance of 1953 at 3:41 P.M. on Tuesday, April 14, at Jamaica, ridden by Eric Guerin in a yellow sweater and blue cap. Caposella introduced him, and a chilled crowd gave him an ovation. "Hundreds of horse players ran to the trackside from near the mutuel windows, where they had been engaged in the engrossing business of betting on the sixth race. Running out to see the Dancer close, they looked like hundreds of water bugs skating on the surface of a brook," McNulty wrote.

Winfrey wanted Beachcomber to challenge the Dancer early in the six-furlong trial, then have First Glance pressure him late, thereby giving the Dancer the exercise he needed. But it didn't work out as planned. Beachcomber broke slowly and lagged behind. The Dancer and First Glance were raced under heavy restraint. "The grey went past the stands with his head almost pulled around to face the crowd," the *Morning Telegraph* reported. The Grey Ghost covered the six furlongs in a slow 1:14. It was unclear if he had benefited. Still, Winfrey proclaimed him ready for the Gotham in four days.

After the Dancer was safely back at Barn 20, McNulty watched Winfrey, Murray, Harold Walker, and J.C. Mergler rub their hands up and down the colt's legs, checking for signs of distress—a routine safeguard. The Dancer was fine. Soon, McNulty was alone with Murray in front of the stall, eyeing the colt.

"He keyed up," Murray told McNulty. "He a little mixed up in his mind, but he all right. He don't know was that a race he was in or wasn't it. They had the gate, they had the other two horses, they had the crowd yelling. But you know what I think got him mixed up in his mind? It looked like a race to him except one thing. They never brought him back to no winner's circle. This horse never been in no place else but that winner's circle. Every single, solitary time he run a race. He don't know what to make out of it, no winner's circle this time. It's got him mixed up."

The public's fascination with the Dancer was evident in the response to the trial. Every aspect of the workout was analyzed and debated among horsemen and newspaper columnists, as if great truths were obtainable. How did he look as he came down the track? When he was eased up? Was this sufficient preparation for the Gotham? Was Winfrey still behind schedule? What about those ankles? *Morning Telegraph* columnist Evan Shipman wrote that he "couldn't see how the horse could have accomplished what he did with more authority," and wisely added that it was a mistake to make too much of the event.

"There is a brain there," Shipman wrote of the Dancer, "and nothing sluggish or idle about it. The horse is well aware that a work is not a race."

Shipman, an influential veteran columnist, was a great believer in the horse. "Native Dancer is well on his way to becoming a great popular champion in the world of sport, his appeal reaching far beyond the ordinary limits of racing," he wrote. "Sports writers naturally welcome such champions and do their part toward creating them, but there has been nothing artificial about the growth of this particular legend. Several unbeaten two-year-olds have failed to inspire anything like the same adulation, and some truly great thoroughbreds have failed to kindle the imagination of the larger public. But there is no denying that Native Dancer possesses the intangible quality we call 'color,' without which any champion is just another name in the record books. It is not forcing a simile to compare this rugged youngster with the great one-punch fighters. He appears to have the same instinct for competition, the same ability to force an issue to a conclusion at the crucial moment."

His popularity was undeniable. But the Kentucky Derby was less than three weeks away, and the horse still hadn't raced as a three-year-old. Critics continued to voice concern that Winfrey had brought him along too slowly, and Winfrey confessed years later that even he was concerned after the canceled race and botched trial. But "the only thing I could do was run him in the Gotham," he told the *Blood-Horse* in 1985.

The pressure was building. "Huge Audience to See Gotham on TV Saturday," blared a *Morning Telegraph* headline several days before the race. Caposella would call the race on the national telecast, with Sammy Renick handling the commentary and interviews. It was the Dancer's first appearance on TV, local or national, and "his presence in the starting field assures the largest TV and radio audience in the history of turf broadcasting," the *Morning Telegraph* wrote. Even larger, in other words, than the Kentucky Derby the year before.

Eighteen horses were entered in the Gotham, forcing Jamaica to split the field into two divisions. The Dancer landed in the weaker division, with no rival even close to his class other than a colt named Isasmoothie who had won the Pimlico Futurity six months earlier, and another colt named Magic Lamp who had occasionally shown promise. But although the other division featured Derby contenders Laffango and Invigorator and figured to be far more competitive, NBC wasn't televising it. The public didn't really care about Laffango and Invigorator. This was the Grey Ghost's show. Vanderbilt's friend Jock Whitney came to the paddock before the race to show support. Bettors sent the horse to the post at 1–6 odds. He had worked a speedy half mile in 46⅗ seconds at Belmont the day before.

The crowd cheered when the Dancer broke sharply from the starting gate, but Guerin, as he had in every race the year before, settled the horse off the lead. The Dancer raced along in fourth, to the outside of the front-runners, Magic Lamp and a sprinter named Virtuous, as the pack moved at a slow pace around the first turn, up the backside, and into the second turn. Then Guerin lowered himself and began scrubbing the horse's neck, asking for a run. The Dancer charged up to second, now trailing only Magic Lamp, then stalled, sending a shiver through the crowd as he turned for home.

But any concern quickly dissipated. Guerin drew his stick and waved it in front of the Grey Ghost's eyes as they headed for home, and the horse burst past Magic Lamp and opened up a lead. The outcome was never in doubt through the stretch, although the Dancer failed to continue to draw away from Magic Lamp as Guerin waved the stick at him. The winning margin was two lengths.

In the other division, Invigorator and Laffango pressed each other all the way up the backside, through the turn, and down the stretch. Laffango won in the end, and many observers felt that both horses looked sharper than the Dancer, not that that was a surprise with the Dancer coming off such a long layoff. "He got very, very tired in that race," Winfrey told the *Blood-Horse* in 1985, adding that it was the horse's "only race" in which he wasn't fit.

Yet Laffango's time of 1:44⅕ was only a fifth of a second faster than the Dancer's, and given the slow pace in the Dancer's heat, it was obvious the Dancer could have gone faster. As much as his time and his inability to put away Magic Lamp provided new fodder for the doubters, he was just warming up. His winning run in Gotham, wrote columnist Arthur Daley in the *New York Times,* was "not unlike Babe Ruth hitting one out of the park against batting practice pitching." The real show, in other words, had yet to begin.

# TEN

Five days after the Gotham, an unequivocal challenge was issued to the popular assumption that Native Dancer was so superior to the rest of his three-year-old class that he couldn't
lose the Kentucky Derby. A California-based colt named Correspondent blazed to a five-length victory in the Blue Grass Stakes, a major
pre-Derby test at Keeneland, in Lexington, Kentucky, outclassing two
horses that had excelled during the winter racing season in Florida:
Straight Face, winner of the Flamingo Stakes, and Money Broker,
winner of the Florida Derby.

With Eddie Arcaro directing him, Correspondent set a track
record on a sunny Thursday afternoon, covering a mile and an eighth
in 1:49, one-fifth of a second faster than Coaltown's winning time in
the 1948 Blue Grass. Coaltown was the memorable Calumet speedster who had opened a six-furlong lead on Citation in the Kentucky
Derby before finishing second to his stablemate and eventual Triple
Crown winner, so even though the Blue Grass was Correspondent's
first stakes victory and just his sixth win in fourteen career starts, he
was running in fast company now.

Owned by Gordon Guiberson, a Texas businessman now living
in California, and trained by Wally Dunn, a Canadian-born horseman
now based at Santa Anita, Correspondent instantly dropped to 2–1 in
the Kentucky Derby future book in Caliente, Mexico, as the clear sec-

ond choice behind Native Dancer. The nation's three-year-olds had been competing against each other through the winter in California and Florida and the early spring in New York, Maryland, and Kentucky, and the picture was finally beginning to crystallize as the Derby neared.

Tahitian King, the colt who had nearly upset the Dancer in the Futurity, had failed to fill out while wintering in New Orleans and was running well below his prior form; he was now deemed a long shot even to run in the Derby. Laffango, winner of the other division of the Gotham, was out after experiencing swelling in his left front ankle following his impressive victory. So much for the two horses weighted closest to the Dancer on the Experimental Free Handicap ranking of 1952 two-year-olds.

With those two out and Calumet Farm failing to produce a dangerous springtime three-year-old for only the second time since the end of the war, the horses emerging as the top threats to the Grey Ghost were Royal Bay Gem, Straight Face, and now Correspondent.

Royal Bay Gem was a late-blooming overachiever, an undersized black colt who had sold for just $7,500 as a yearling, and at first glance, appeared incapable of racing even a mile without faltering. He had made twenty-two starts, mostly in allowance races, as a two-year-old, winning only three with a late-running style. But his owner, a white-haired Texan named Eugene Constantin, and his bow-tied trainer, Clyde Troutt, kept believing in him and running him in Florida early in 1953, and their faith finally paid off. The Gem beat eighteen other horses, including Straight Face, to win a wild Everglade Stakes; his jockey, Jimmy Combest, rallied him from fifteenth on the first turn to a two-length victory. He then came from far back in the Flamingo Stakes and Fountain of Youth Handicap to finish second in both. In his most recent start, the Chesapeake Stakes, at Bowie, Maryland, he was last in a fifteen-horse field in the early going, then charged through the pack to win by two lengths. With his gaunt frame and lack of stature, he didn't look the part of a Kentucky Derby horse, but his formidable late move was a good fit for the race, which always had a big field.

Straight Face was a more typical Derby horse, a long-legged bay sired by Count Fleet and bred and owned by Jock Whitney's Greentree. He was so contrary as a yearling that he had been gelded and held out of competition until August 1952 while Tiger Skin raced as the stable's top two-year-old, but Tiger Skin was put to death after fracturing a leg in October and Straight Face emerged, winning two stakes races in Kentucky late in 1952 and then the Flamingo. He had come out of Florida with a sore knee, and Correspondent had put him in his place in the Blue Grass, but with his breeding and long stride, he was still regarded as a rising threat.

Other horses in the mix included Invigorator, who had finished in the money in nineteen of twenty-five starts and would have Bill Shoemaker, the nation's hottest young jockey, on him in the Derby; Ram o' War, a long shot who had won a division of the Fountain of Youth; and Money Broker, who had run in midwestern claiming and allowance races as a two-year-old but leaped forward at three, finishing second in the Louisiana Derby, first in the Florida Derby, and third in the Blue Grass. Winfrey and Vanderbilt were also considering running Social Outcast, who had finished fourth in the Chesapeake Stakes.

Correspondent was ahead of them all after having won the Blue Grass so impressively. Sired by Khaled—soon to gain fame as the sire of Swaps, the 1955 Kentucky Derby winner and later a popular handicap champion—Correspondent didn't have a typical Derby résumé. He had gone winless as a two-year-old, finally breaking his maiden in his seventh career start, a seven-furlong allowance at Santa Anita in late January 1953. A third-place finish in the Santa Anita Derby on February 21 had hinted at what was to come, but no one could have foreseen how brilliantly he would bloom upon arriving in Kentucky in early April as a fringe Derby horse.

With Arcaro on him—others had ridden him as he competed against Decorated and Calumet's Chanlea through the winter at Santa Anita—Correspondent easily outran Money Broker in a six-furlong allowance at Keeneland on April 10, then just missed setting the track record for seven furlongs in another allowance a week later. That day, Arcaro went to the whip when a long shot named Dark Star posed a challenge in the stretch, and Correspondent pulled away easily.

Straight Face was still the betting favorite in the Blue Grass six days later, the public choosing to put its faith in a Greentree colt with more than $150,000 in career earnings and a better record than Correspondent in stakes races. But as 10,824 fans watched at Lexington's intimate track, the second choice proved far superior to the favorite. Arcaro took him to the front and set a scorching pace—22⅖ seconds for the first quarter mile, 46⅖ for the half—and when Straight Face and Money Broker began to close on the far turn, Arcaro let out the reins and shook his stick, and Correspondent took off. The colt was in front by three lengths as he entered the stretch and never stopped pulling away.

"I don't know that there's a three-year-old in the country that could have beaten that colt today," said Greentree's trainer, John Gaver, who had traveled from New York to saddle Straight Face. Teddy Atkinson, Straight Face's jockey, refused to indulge reporters wanting him to compare Arcaro's horse to Native Dancer. "There's no common ground to make a comparison yet," Atkinson said.

Arcaro dressed quickly after the race. A private plane was waiting to take him to New York, where in forty-eight hours he would race against Native Dancer in the Wood Memorial, the final Derby prep race on the East Coast. Arcaro was booked on Social Outcast, Vanderbilt's second-string three-year-old. The jockey's choice for a Kentucky Derby mount was down to two, Correspondent or Social Outcast, and while the choice seemed obvious now, Arcaro refused to admit it.

"I told Mr. Vanderbilt that I'm coming to New York with an open mind, so you won't get any answers out of me!" Arcaro shouted good-naturedly to reporters.

"I'll bet you've got a lot in the back of your mind, though, Eddie," one reporter said.

"I guess I have," Arcaro said, "but I'm not going to tell you newspaper guys."

Arcaro, at thirty-seven, was racing's biggest star, its Rocky Marciano, its Joe DiMaggio, the athlete-cum-celebrity whose name resonated well beyond his sport's boundaries. Winner of five Kentucky Derbys and a pair of Triple Crowns—on Whirlaway in 1941 and Citation in 1948—he was a character Damon Runyon might have invented, brash and big-nosed (hence his nickname, Banana Nose), small and strong-armed, gifted and glamorous. Champion horses came and went, but Arcaro was always present, the familiar, flamboyant jockey who loved to tell stories and dance at nightclubs, yet still dominated his peers with a matchless blend of coordination, unerring judgment, and strength.

Born in Cincinnati in 1916, he had left school at fourteen, become a jockey at fifteen, and started riding for Calumet at eighteen. He won his first Derby in 1938 and led the nation in earnings for the first time in 1940, then again in 1942, 1949, 1950, and 1952 as long associations with Calumet and Greentree served him well. He was still in his prime, having won four Triple Crown races on four different horses since 1950, including the Derby the year before on Hill Gail. Gregarious and glib, he was beloved by reporters and was the darling of the manly racing crowd that admired his talent and winked at his lifestyle.

"He was the Babe Ruth of our game," recalled longtime *Daily Racing Form* columnist Joe Hirsch, a close friend. "There were always people around him. I said when he died [in 1996] that it was the first time he'd ever been alone. He was just a great people person."

"I conducted a poll in 1955 at Garden State Park: I asked fans if they could name the horse that had won the Triple Crown in 1948," TV executive Tommy Roberts recalled. "Only about 20 percent knew it was Citation. This was just seven years later. They didn't know Citation. But they all knew Eddie Arcaro."

Even his dark moments were imbued with a certain allure. In 1942, before the film patrol was popular, he had intentionally smashed his horse into one ridden by a rival whose horse had hit his in a prior race. The rival flew into the infield and Arcaro was suspended indefinitely after admitting to stewards he was "trying to kill the s.o.b." It was an embarrassing blemish on his record, but to many fans, merely indicative of the passion that made him such a great jockey.

He had ridden only occasionally for Vanderbilt over the years, seldom on the stable's top horses. Vanderbilt would surely have used him more, but poor timing had interfered: Vanderbilt's stable hadn't been strong enough during and right after the war for Arcaro to commit to it under a contract arrangement, and Arcaro was heavily booked when Vanderbilt's stable made its comeback starting in the late 1940s. Vanderbilt had ended up putting Guerin under contract after the young Cajun, whom Arcaro had mentored, rode Bed o' Roses and Next Move to so many big wins. Thus, although Arcaro, America's jockey, was a perfect fit for the Dancer, Guerin had the mount.

Did Arcaro want the mount on the Dancer? "I'm sure; and I'm also sure Eddie tried to submarine Guerin a few times," Joe Hirsch said. But as the Derby neared, Arcaro was mostly upset that fans and experts were already comparing the Grey Ghost to racing's greatest champions, even though the Dancer had only made ten starts. Comparisons to Citation particularly annoyed Arcaro, who had ridden Citation to his greatest triumphs and believed the Calumet star was a horse without peer.

Out of loyalty to Citation, Arcaro had subtly started taking shots at the Dancer. It had started during the previous fall, after the Dancer had rallied to beat Arcaro and Tahitian King in the Anticipation Stakes, a tune-up for the Futurity. Guerin told reporters the Dancer was "just playing" when he trailed and a victory had always been assured. Irritated, Arcaro lashed out at Guerin after the Futurity, in which Tahitian King came close to pulling off the upset.

"You're not going to tell me your horse was 'just playing' this time, are you?" Arcaro snapped within earshot of reporters.

"Oh, no, that's a real good colt you were on, Eddie," replied Guerin, embarrassed at having to defend himself when he had just been trying to compliment the Dancer after the Anticipation.

Arcaro was no fool. He knew the Dancer was special. But he felt it was too soon to shower such praise on a colt who had never raced outside of New York and, in his opinion, had merely defeated the same inferior East Coast competition over and over, mostly in races lacking early pace. The Master had serious doubts about how the Grey Ghost would respond in the Derby when confronted for the first time with speedy front-runners such as Correspondent.

For now, though, he would wear Vanderbilt's silks in the Wood

Memorial, temporarily teamed with Guerin and the Dancer. His chances of success were slim. Social Outcast was a Maryland-bred chestnut who had romped with the Dancer as a youngster at Sagamore Farm and, like the Dancer, was a grandson of Discovery, but the comparisons stopped there. Social Outcast had earned just $29,100 as a two-year-old, winning only maiden and allowance races, and had yet to win in six starts as a three-year-old. But he had finished second in the Remsen Handicap as a two-year-old and recently run well behind Royal Bay Gem in the Chesapeake Stakes, losing a three-way photo finish for second. He was improving.

Conspiracy theorists believed that Winfrey and Vanderbilt were running Social Outcast in the Wood and bringing in Arcaro just to ensure a faster early pace and prep the Dancer for the Derby. In reality, Social Outcast wasn't comfortable as a front-runner, preferring to come from off the pace, like the Dancer. Winfrey and Vanderbilt were running him because they were still trying to gauge his Derby potential.

The Wood had been run at Jamaica since 1925, evolving into the East's top race for likely Derby contenders. Five horses other than the Dancer and Social Outcast were entered this year, with the race billed as the richest for three-year-olds ever run in New York, its purse totaling $123,750. It was certain to provide a better test for the Dancer than the Gotham, even though Laffango was out. Invigorator and Tahitian King were in, as was a long shot named Jamie K.

In the week between the Gotham and the Wood, run on successive Saturdays, the Dancer worked once, on Tuesday, covering a half mile on Belmont's training track and then a mile in 1:40⅘, with the last quarter in twenty-seven seconds, on the main track. It was an average work, and by Friday, according to Evan Shipman's column in the *Morning Telegraph,* many Belmont horsemen were expecting the Grey Ghost to lose for the first time the next day.

Shipman wrote, "The public has put its faith in Native Dancer. The aura of invincibility sheds a golden glow on him, and the crowd takes a warm and commendable delight in frank hero worship. [The] horsemen are reacting strongly to this uncritical admiration, insisting not only that the Dancer can be beaten, but that he will be beaten in the Wood. Their attempt to maintain a cool detachment in the face of the adulation inspired by the Dancer's record inclines these critics, we believe, to prejudice. We suspect that envy and a human tendency toward iconoclasm have played a part in their attitude."

Vanderbilt also scoffed at the critics, using his trademark wit to suggest that, indeed, they were just jealous. "The main trouble with Native Dancer is the same thing that used to be the matter with Citation—he goes back to the wrong barn," Vanderbilt said. Someone else's barn, in other words.

Saturday's weather was vastly improved from that of the week before. Sunshine and warm temperatures lured more than 40,000 fans to Jamaica. NBC was back for another national TV broadcast, with Caposella calling the race and Renick handling the interviews. The atmosphere in the paddock wasn't as electric as before the Gotham, but with the Derby now just a week away, the anticipation was still palpable. Six Wood winners, including Gallant Fox and Count Fleet, had gone on to win at Churchill Downs. Here, perhaps, was the best of them all.

The entry of the Dancer and Social Outcast went to the post as a 1–10 favorite, the teaming of an unbeaten colt and Arcaro proving irresistible to bettors. Of the $448,689 wagered on the race, $362,620 was bet on the entry. Invigorator was the second choice at 6–1, followed by Tahitian King at 15–1 and Jamie K. at 16–1. Arcaro had given up the mount on Tahitian King even though the colt was out of a mare named after Arcaro's daughter. Despite the sentimental attachment, the Master had become frustrated with Tahitian King's lack of progress. Hedley Woodhouse would ride Tahitian King in the Wood, and he was expected to set the early pace.

Sure enough, Woodhouse took the lead once the starting gate opened and held it through the first turn and up the backstretch, setting the dawdling pace the Dancer was accustomed to: a quarter mile in 24⅘ seconds, a half in 50. Guerin, forced to place the eager Dancer closer to the front than usual, was running second, ahead of Invigorator. Social Outcast was near the rear.

Heading into the second turn, Invigorator, Native Dancer, and Tahitian King were virtually even. They all began to run. Guerin took out his whip and struck the Dancer once—it was just the third time in the Dancer's eleven races that Guerin had used the whip—and the Dancer surged into the lead, opening up three lengths on Tahitian King as they turned for home.

He was a fearsome sight coming through the stretch, his powerful body pushed to its limit. After meandering to the finish line in the Gotham, he almost resembled a greyhound at full speed now, kicking so hard that you could draw a horizontal straight line from his airborne back feet to the tips of his forelegs. With the crowd roaring its appreciation, he reached the finish line four and a half lengths ahead of Tahitian King. Invigorator was far back in third, Social Outcast a distant fourth. "Even those customers who had bet against him were viewing the grey colt with admiration," James Roach wrote in the *New York Times*.

Not even his persistent skeptics could find fault in this performance. After the slow start, the Grey Ghost had covered the final half mile in 47⅕ seconds, a rousing finish that drew him within a second of the track record for nine furlongs, held by an older horse who had carried nine fewer pounds. If the Gotham had raised doubts about the Dancer, the Wood had quelled them.

"I don't know if any horse is going to beat Native Dancer [in the Derby], but the ones around here don't have a chance," said Arcaro, confirming that he would ride Correspondent in Louisville.

Swept up in the moment, Guerin repeated the comment that had irked Arcaro months earlier. "He was just playing out there," the jockey said of the Dancer. "I could have gone to the lead earlier, but I decided to wait." Why, then, did he use the whip? "I hit him just once to see what he would do, and he responded," Guerin said.

Standing in the winner's enclosure, in the shadow of the grandstand, the Dancer was a portrait of power and glory. He had won eleven races without a defeat and earned $341,995, each a record for a horse heading into the Kentucky Derby. A TV audience numbering in the millions had just watched him win the Wood with ease. His moment to make history was at hand.

There were horses waiting in Kentucky to take him on. Royal Bay Gem, the little black colt, was all heart. Straight Face, the Greentree gelding, had a champion's pedigree. The speedy Correspondent, with Arcaro directing him, would pose a sterner challenge than the Dancer had ever faced. But the Dancer was on another plane, seemingly invincible, his forceful finishing kick yet to encounter a wall it couldn't knock down. Alben Barkley, the Kentucky lawyer who had served as Harry Truman's vice president, had once said that "one of the joys of man is to see a real thoroughbred horse perform," and after this performance, seen by millions on TV, there was little doubt that the Dancer had a firm hold on the country's hearts. Later that week in Queens, not far from Jamaica, a construction worker would remove $13,000 from his widowed mother's safe-deposit box without her knowledge, buy a car, drive to Churchill Downs, and bet everything on the Dancer to win the Derby, vividly illustrating the difference between the Dancer and his likely Derby rivals. The others were capable, talented, even dangerous in some cases. But the Grey Ghost was a horse who could make you lose your mind.

▲ Lester Murray walks the Dancer at Saratoga in August 1952. On some level, they were in love. *Courtesy Alfred Vanderbilt III*

▲ Eric Guerin and the Dancer. *Courtesy Olive Cooney*

The Dancer breaking his maiden at Jamaica in April 1952. "Jumped a mud puddle at the sixteenth pole and still won easy," Bill Shoemaker said. *Keeneland-Morgan* ▼

▲ Eddie Arcaro prepares to exercise the Dancer two days before the 1953 American Derby in Chicago. "If I get beat on this horse, I'm the biggest bum alive," Arcaro said. *Courtesy Carey Winfrey*

▲ Fred Astaire, Bill Winfrey, Jeanne Vanderbilt, and Alfred Vanderbilt, in Vanderbilt's box at Santa Anita. *Courtesy Carey Winfrey*

▲ Dining al fresco at Broadhollow, a "modern Shangri-la." Louis Cheri, Alfred Vanderbilt's valet and confidant, serves oatmeal to young Alfred out of a silver bowl. *Courtesy Alfred Vanderbilt III*

The Dancer (4) runs fourth early in the Preakness behind the leader, Dark Star (3). They changed places at the head of the stretch. *Baltimore Sun* ▼

▲ Dark Star holds on at the end of the 1953 Kentucky Derby. "The best horse got beat." *Kinetic Corp.*

▲ The Dancer narrowly defeats Jamie K. in the 1953 Belmont Stakes.
*Getty Images*

Jock Whitney and
Alfred Vanderbilt.
The public yearned to
see their champion
horses, Tom Fool and
Native Dancer, meet
on the track. *Courtesy
Alfred Vanderbilt III*

▶

▲ The Dancer winning the Travers Stakes at Saratoga in August 1953.
*Keeneland-Morgan*

Guerin and the
Dancer surounded
by their public
after the 1953
Preakness. "It was
like the scenes
with the Beatles a
decade later."
*Baltimore Sun*
▶

▲ The Dancer in retirement at Sagamore Farm in 1966. *Winants*

# ELEVEN

As stable hands on Churchill Downs's backside watched NBC's telecast of Native Dancer's victory in the Wood Memorial, an obscure brown colt rested in his stall in Barn 12. If the famous undefeated Dancer was at one end of the Derby spectrum one week before the race, the colt, named Dark Star, was at the other end: largely unknown, perhaps not even worthy of running in the Derby. The $87,000 the Dancer had earned in 110 seconds in winning the Wood was almost three times as much as Dark Star had earned in his entire career.

The owners and trainers of horses in the Derby mix still had four days to decide whether to enter, and Dark Star's trainer, Eddie Hayward, and his owner, Harry Guggenheim, were still trying to make up their minds. Dark Star had shown flashes of ability at times in his nine-race career but had finished last in a thirteen-horse field in the Champagne Stakes the previous autumn and out of the money in the Florida Derby in March, raising doubts about his capacity for handling top competition.

Hayward, a fiftyish Canadian-born trainer who had never run a horse in the Derby, had decided to give Dark Star one last chance to prove himself—in the Derby Trial, the one-mile event run at Churchill Downs on the Tuesday before the Derby. If Dark Star ran well in the Trial, he would be entered in the Derby; the year before,

Hill Gail had won the Trial and come back later in the week to win the Derby, so it was a reasonable plan. On the other hand, if Dark Star ran poorly in the Trial, as Cousin had the year before, he wouldn't go in the Derby.

Dark Star's sire, Royal Gem II, was an Australian horse who had competed Down Under from 1944 to 1949, winning twenty-two races at every distance from five furlongs to a mile and a half. His reputation spread to America, and Warner Jones, the eminent Kentucky breeder, put together a syndicate that bought the horse for a sum estimated at $150,000. Royal Gem II sailed for America on a Swedish vessel, accompanied by his trainer. Twenty-five days later, Warner Jones met them in port in San Francisco and transported them to Jones's Hermitage Farm in Skylight, Kentucky, where Royal Gem II started his stud career.

One of the first mares he was bred to was Isolde, a nine-year-old who had won some allowance races and competed until age six, and had yet to produce a stakes winner. She gave birth to a foal on Jones's farm on April 4, 1950, a week after Native Dancer was foaled some sixty miles away at Dan W. Scott's farm. Jones raised the baby along with some others from Royal Gem II's first crop, then put them up for sale as yearlings. Guggenheim, a prominent philanthropist from one of America's wealthiest families, bought Isolde's son for $6,500, picking out the horse himself. Royal Bay Gem, now one of the most prominent three-year-olds in the Derby picture, was also sold out of the crop.

Harriet Jones, Warner's wife, later told *Cincinnati Times-Star* columnist Douglas Allen that there were two brown yearlings to choose from in the sale, and Guggenheim had "picked out one" and "picked up the other," ending up with the wrong horse. "When we discovered [the mistake]," she told Allen, "we offered to let him switch, but he said, 'Never mind, I've got this one now and I kind of like him.'" Guggenheim later denied the story.

Like Alfred Vanderbilt, Guggenheim was descended from the cream of America's Gilded Age. His grandfather Meyer Guggenheim was a Jewish industrialist who immigrated from Switzerland to Philadelphia to escape anti-Semitism in 1848, and with the help of his sons, developed a worldwide empire of mining and smelting interests that was generating immense wealth by the turn of the century. Harry, born in 1890, fought as a naval aviator in World War I and fell in love with air travel. By 1950, he had served as the American ambassador to Cuba, bankrolled rocketry pioneer Robert Goddard's early experiments, founded *Newsday*, a Long Island newspaper, with his wife, and established a foundation that funded aviation research and helped the American airline industry get off the ground.

At age sixty-two in 1953, Guggenheim was friendly with Vanderbilt, traveled in the same social circle, and shared interests, but he was closer to Vanderbilt's mother, Margaret Emerson, his Long Island neighbor. Every year, he visited Margaret at Sagamore Lodge in the Adirondack Mountains, where she brought together figures from politics, business, and the arts. Signing the camp's guest register on August 6, 1950, Guggenheim wrote, "Even these grim times look better with Margaret at Sagamore."

Guggenheim had owned, bred, and raced horses since 1934. He started with six yearlings, calling his outfit the Falaise Stable, then changed the name to Cain Hoy Stable after his 27,000-acre Cain Hoy Plantation in North Carolina. Over the years, he had invested neither as much time nor as much money in racing as Vanderbilt; he didn't own a horse farm, preferring just to board his mares at Claiborne Farm in Kentucky. Now, though, with his business demands ebbing in the 1950s, he was becoming more involved in racing. The Jockey Club had made him a member and assigned him to a task force charged with improving the conditions at New York's overcrowded tracks. And his stable was becoming more prominent. Cain Hoy had produced the Kentucky Derby favorite in 1951, a colt named Battle Morn who ran sixth, disappointing Guggenheim but whetting his appetite.

Moody Jolley, a hard-edged, taciturn Tennessean, had trained Battle Morn and was still working for Cain Hoy when Dark Star turned two and began racing in 1952. The colt broke his maiden in February and then won the Hialeah Juvenile Stakes, a three-furlong race with nineteen entrants, finishing two lengths in front of the pack and earning almost double his purchase price. Guggenheim was pleased at the success of a horse he had selected himself.

After finishing third in Belmont's Juvenile Stakes in his next start, Dark Star developed osselets and had his ankles fired, like the Dancer, and was sidelined for four months. Returning in September, he won an allowance race on the Widener Straight Course, then finished a distant third to Native Dancer in the Futurity. A week later, he all but quit in the Champagne in a miserable performance. At the end of the year, twenty-two two-year-olds were ranked ahead of him on the Experimental Free Handicap.

Guggenheim, who had been known to change trainers, parted ways with Jolley in November. Cain Hoy's new trainer was Hayward, a former jockey who had conditioned horses since the late 1920s. Guggenheim's expectations were high, perhaps unreasonably, when he turned Dark Star over to Hayward with a record of three wins in six starts and earnings of $24,087. "Now train the horse and win the Derby," Guggenheim reportedly said.

Hayward had moved slowly. Dark Star began his three-year-old season with a victory in a seven-furlong allowance race at Hialeah in February, then finished out of the money in the Florida Derby and second behind Correspondent in an allowance race at Keeneland. That was his most recent start. With the Derby looming, Dark Star had never won any race longer than seven furlongs and had never won a stakes race longer than three furlongs. That was hardly a Derby résumé.

Hayward had not given up, though. The colt had run well in finishing second to Correspondent at Keeneland, and Hayward was hopeful of seeing the performance repeated or bettered in the Trial. The Keeneland race had been Dark Star's first with Henry Moreno, a twenty-four-year-old California-based jockey whose contract Cain Hoy had just purchased. Maybe the horse and jockey were a good mix.

Moreno had been introduced to racing a decade earlier while sweeping the floor at his father's barbershop in Chicago; there was a lot of racing talk in the shop, and one customer was a horseman who brought Moreno to the track and tutored him as a rider. Moreno wound up in Northern California, rode his first winner at the Alameda

County Fair, and started working his way up the ladder. He had soft hands and steady nerves and had experienced his share of success, but he was still unknown in the East and hardly at the top of the game. Before signing with Cain Hoy and coming to Kentucky in early April, he had been struggling for mounts at Tanforan, a smaller track in San Bruno, California. In Kentucky, he and his wife and young son were staying at a tourist camp, a crude cabin hostelry outside Louisville.

Hayward hadn't purchased his contract without reason, though: Calumet trainer Jimmy Jones had seen enough in Moreno to give him the first call on Calumet's horses at Hollywood Park the previous summer. Moreno rode Two Lea to victory in the Hollywood Park Gold Cup, a $100,000 race, and delivered a handful of other stakes wins. He eventually lost Calumet's first call in California when Eddie Arcaro chose to ride at Santa Anita over the winter of 1953, but Hayward had seen enough to offer him a contract.

Even if they fared well in the Derby Trial, however, Moreno and Dark Star were destined to be the longest of Derby shots along with Spy Defense, winner of four allowance races in fourteen starts; Curragh King, a former claimer who had won the Arkansas Derby in a major surprise; and Ace Destroyer, a colt who had finished out of the money in six straight starts. Dark Star belonged in that company, a fringe contender blotted out by the Dancer's luminous presence. Most horsemen agreed that if the sire Royal Gem II was going to leave a mark on the Derby with his first crop of horses eligible for the race, it would be with the stretch-running Royal Bay Gem. Dark Star? Even with Guggenheim's name working for him, the lightly raced colt with an unknown jockey and less than $30,000 in career earnings was as invisible as a springtime breeze.

# TWELVE

acing fans in New York who stayed home and watched
NBC's national telecast of the Wood Memorial knew what
was coming when broadcaster Win Elliott pulled Eric
Guerin aside for an interview after the race. "First of all," Guerin said
to Elliott, "I've got to say hi to my son at home." The jockey then
turned, looked at the camera, waved, and shouted, "Hi, Ronnie!"

He had begun his TV interviews with greetings to his son since
local coverage of racing had started in New York in the late 1940s. "It
was the early days of TV and [the greetings] had quite an impact on
people," Carey Winfrey, Bill's son, recalled. "Eric became well known
for it. I used to nag my father about it. I'd say, 'Eric says hello to his
son; what can't you say hi to me?'"

Now, on successive Saturdays, during NBC's coverage of the
Wood and Gotham, Guerin, twenty-nine, had introduced the custom
to millions of viewers across the country. His rise from a meager upbringing in a sparse Cajun backwater had moved slowly, if steadily, for
years, but it was accelerating dizzily now. Improbably, a blacksmith's
son with a ninth-grade education was linked with a Vanderbilt and
America's most popular horse, at the forefront of the public's sports
awareness.

Guerin was already living far beyond the most fortunate circumstances he could have imagined as a boy growing up in the 1930s in

Maringouin, Louisiana, sixty miles northwest of New Orleans. He, his wife, Gloria, a dark-haired New Orleans native, and Ronnie, aged seven, lived in a large home near the Jamaica Racetrack, with their basement fashioned after the dance floor of their favorite nightspot, the Copacabana in Manhattan. Guerin shared tables with famous athletes and entertainers and had made enough money to maintain a high lifestyle and buy a home for his parents in New Orleans.

Now he had the keys to the mightiest of equine rides, an undefeated Kentucky Derby favorite, raising his circumstances even higher. If Eddie Arcaro was the face of racing in America, Guerin, for the moment, was a close second, his smiling face and Cajun twang burnished into the minds of millions of fans watching at home on TV. He was the jockey who rode Native Dancer and never forgot his son, not even in the winner's circle.

The scrutiny was intense, but Guerin had deftly handled such pressure since his first winning rides in the early forties. Like Teddy Atkinson, Conn McCreary, and the rest of the top jockeys other than Arcaro, he was cast in the Master's shadow and relegated to a second tier; but he was successful in his own right and possessed an assortment of winning qualities. With calm and consistency, Guerin excelled at breaking quickly from the starting gate, judging pace, and avoiding trouble. "He took a very mathematical approach, knew where he was going all the time and didn't take a lot of crazy chances," Arcaro said years later.

Then there was his greatest attribute, unseen by the public. "The guy just absolutely loved horses, lived and breathed them; and loved being around them," recalled Frank Curry, Guerin's nephew, years later. His affection for the animals enabled him to get more out of skittish fillies and two-year-olds than other jockeys. "He was maybe the best filly rider there ever was," trainer Allen Jerkens recalled. "He liked horses, fillies especially. Some jockeys would lose patience with them, but Eric never did. He was a levelheaded, natural jock with a great affinity for horses, and that served him well."

Relationships between jockeys, trainers, and owners could be fragile and rife with distrust, but Winfrey and Vanderbilt were comfortable with Guerin. Unlike some jockeys, he was dependable on and off the track, courteous and professional in his dealings, and never rash; he had many friends and few enemies. And although he was easygoing, there was no doubting his will: he had come back from several horrific accidents early in his career and had struggled constantly with his weight, yet here he was, at the top of the game. He had won numerous races on Bed o' Roses, Next Move, Loser Weeper, and others in recent years, and with those memories still fresh as the 1953 Kentucky Derby neared, Winfrey and Vanderbilt were brimming with confidence in their jockey.

He wasn't the first jockey to come out of Louisiana's bayou country; a generation of hard-driving boys named Hebert, Martin, Duhon, Dubois, and Leblanc had carved out the pipeline before him. They were descendants of the French Canadians who had migrated to Louisiana after the British exiled them from Acadia, near Nova Scotia, in the 1750s, and these Acadians—nicknamed Cajuns—developed unerring balance while navigating narrow bayous in pirogue canoes twelve inches wide and ten feet long. Decades later, that exceptional balance gave Cajun jockeys an advantage, or so the story went.

The prototypical Cajun rider started at the bawdy, unlicensed "bush tracks" around Lafayette, where there was weekend racing for raucous fans who wanted to drink, gamble, and see fearless boys ride to win at any cost, even tying rocks and cans to their quarter horses to "make weight" and shock the animals into running. Guerin never rode at such a track: Maringouin was forty miles from Lafayette, and his family had no car to get him there. "We were poor as hell," said Charles Ray Leblanc, who was Guerin's first cousin and, like Guerin, grew up in Maringouin and became a jockey.

Maringouin was little more than a main street and a few side streets, a church, an oil company office, and a few houses; only the wealthy had cars, and the rest depended on horses and wagons for transportation, even in the 1930s. "It was pretty unsophisticated; when the little plane carrying the mail flew over, we all ran outside to look," Leblanc said. The weather was stiflingly hot and humid in the summer, and people worked hard for small wages and hunted possum and squirrel on weekends. "Eric's father would come home with a catch and his mom would cook it up for dinner," said Frank Curry, who was the eldest son of Guerin's sister.

The Leblancs were sharecroppers; the family rented a small farm and gave a share of their crops and proceeds to a landlord. Guerin's father, Oliver, worked as a blacksmith at a farm machinery shop he owned with a partner, and moved his wife and three children from house to house while carving out a living. Oliver never shod horses, and his son Eric didn't ride much. "I would ride a horse to the store for my mother, but Eric didn't live on a farm and didn't do that kind of stuff," said Leblanc, who was three years younger than his cousin.

Leblanc's older brother, Norman, served as the family's instrument of change. He became a jockey at a track in nearby Plaquemine and went on to ride in New Orleans and elsewhere, his career peaking with a victory in a stakes race at Saratoga. His travels and tales from the racetrack sounded impossibly exciting to his brothers and cousins back in Maringouin, who knew of little beyond their rural environs. By 1935, Norman had retired and become a trainer, and, one by one, began bringing his kinfolk to the track as jockeys. His brother Hubert joined him in New Orleans, spent two years learning to ride, and went out on his own, later winning the Widener Handicap and other races. Another brother, Euclid, followed Hubert and developed into a highly successful rider, the best of the Leblanc brothers.

But the best in the extended family was Guerin, who dropped out of school at age fourteen, in 1938, and joined Norman in New Orleans, intent on immersing himself in racing and learning to ride. For two years, he mucked stalls, exercised horses, and kept his eyes and ears open. Norman then sold his contract to Fred Wyse, a mannerly Texas businessman who operated a stable and took the sixteen-year-old Guerin around the country for a year, giving him mounts and breaking him in as a rider. The older man's influence was invaluable; Guerin's respectful behavior was attractive to clients throughout his career. "Fred Wyse was like a father to me; I learned more from him in one year than most people learn in 10, and I don't mean just about horses," Guerin told the *Blood-Horse* in a 1975 interview.

He finished ninth in the first race of his career at Florida's Tropical Park on March 12, 1941, then made thirty more starts for Wyse before winning for the first time on a filly named Sweet Shop at Boston's Narragansett Park on August 29. Less than a month later, he fractured his skull and collarbone in a fall at Narragansett and was in the hospital for a month. He came back strong, winning a riding title back home at the Fair Grounds in New Orleans, with the help of the apprentice's bug (weight advantage). When Wyse decided to get out of racing, he sold Guerin's contract to Joe W. Brown, a wealthy New Orleans sportsman and bookmaker who operated a top stable.

Riding for Brown and trainer Johnny Theall at age seventeen, Guerin was flying high—but not for long. He was leading the nation in wins in the summer of 1942 when he took a hard fall at Chicago's Washington Park that left him unconscious for twelve hours and out of action for six weeks with a concussion. His year with the apprentice's bug [weight allowance] was up when he returned, and the slump that often befalls young jockeys at that point in their careers hit Guerin hard. He slumped miserably in 1943, ending the year with yet another fall that resulted in a broken shoulder, a concussion, and seven weeks in the hospital. Then he tried, without success, to establish himself in New York in 1944 and 1945, attracting attention only as one of the riders in a rare triple dead heat at Aqueduct.

"It was a tough time to be a jockey," Clem Florio recalled. "The money was bad. A couple of guys had contracts or understandings that they would get 10 percent, and everyone else had to fight for everything. There was no obligation. You might get forty bucks if you won, and if you didn't win, you got blamed. They were paying guys off in the dark. Jockeys were the most underpaid, undervalued guys in the business. That's when they had big fields, with guys all hungry, trying to get every hole. Sometimes guys would cook something up and split the money. It's surprising there wasn't more larceny."

Guerin had talent, but he was over his head competing at age nineteen against Arcaro, McCreary, George Woolf, and others. The older jockeys took his mounts and took advantage of him before the advent of the film patrol, elbowing him and cutting him off. "A lot of things happened that officials didn't see; the film patrol changed everything," said Charles Ray Leblanc, who followed Guerin's career path, breaking in with Norman in 1941 and ultimately riding for Joe W. Brown.

Still, Guerin's biggest problem came from within as he struggled to establish himself. Tall for a jockey at five foot four, he gained weight easily and had to go to extremes to get the extra pounds off. He jogged in the heat, spent hours in jockeys' room "hot boxes," read books in his car with the windows rolled up, and when all else failed, stuck his finger down his throat. "Eric did that a lot," Leblanc said. His normal weight was close to 130 pounds, but he raced at 115, and sometimes even less.

Such harsh reducing left him weak and unable to ride up to his potential. Fortunately, Theall, a fellow Cajun, continued believing in him, and he remained under contract to Brown. Theall's faith finally paid off in 1946. Guerin, at twenty-one, spent the summer dueling with Arcaro in New York and won his share of races. "It's funny that you fellows who write for the papers seldom give Eric Guerin the credit he deserves. He's a pretty slick rider," Arcaro told reporters one day. The secret was out by the end of 1946. Guerin's total of twenty-one wins in stakes and handicap races ranked among the nation's best.

He earned his first Kentucky Derby mount the following year on Jet Pilot, trained by Silent Tom Smith, the reclusive legend who had conditioned Seabiscuit. Jet Pilot had won five races and more than $87,000 as a two-year-old with Guerin on him, and he was the second choice in the Derby, behind Phalanx, ridden by Arcaro. Smith had brought Jet Pilot along slowly because of sore feet, but figuring the chestnut colt had one good race left, he hoisted Guerin up before the Derby with simple advice: "Take him to the front and don't look back."

Guerin broke to the lead and slowed the pace to a crawl—a half mile in 49 seconds—leaving Jet Pilot with enough energy to hold off Phalanx and Calumet's Faultless down the stretch. It was a brilliant ride. Guerin had won the Kentucky Derby at age twenty-two. "I was at Churchill Downs that day, riding for Joe W. Brown," Leblanc said. "Jet Pilot wasn't the best horse in the race, but Phalanx didn't run for Arcaro and Eric rode a nice race."

A rush of bad luck immediately ensued, as if the racing gods were punishing Guerin for winning the Derby before he had paid his dues. He made seventy-five straight starts without winning, and the streak was halted not by a victory, but by the fourth major fall of Guerin's career. This one resulted in a fractured vertebra that laid him up for three months, giving him time to ponder his many ups and downs. He made a fateful decision, realizing that his persistent weight problem and resulting lack of strength had contributed to this latest fall. It was time to start eating right.

For years, he had eaten one major meal a day and otherwise starved himself on a liquid diet. That had allowed him to ride, but he wasn't winning the war. Lying in the hospital with a broken back, he listened as Dr. Alexander Kays, the medical adviser to the Jockeys' Guild, prescribed a new eating regimen: a poached egg, toast, and coffee for breakfast; no lunch; a slice of lean meat and a vegetable for dinner; and minimal intake of liquids. It was a diet that could help Guerin control his weight with doses of vitamin supplements, weekly shots of vitamin $B_{12}$, and, of course, willpower. "It wasn't an easy way to live," Guerin told the *Blood-Horse* years later, "but the vitamins and diet enabled me to keep riding."

Leblanc said, "The one thing you could never take away from Eric was that he had a lot of willpower. He had a real weight problem and he had to reduce hard for a long time to keep riding, and he did."

By 1949, Guerin was healthy and stronger, and his career was on the upswing. Vanderbilt and Winfrey called, looking for a rider. The timing was perfect. Vanderbilt's stable was on the rise. Guerin won on Bed o' Roses, Loser Weeper, Next Move, Foreign Affair, and Cousin, and also rode stakes winners Crafty Admiral and Royal Governor for other stables, including the King Ranch, which gave him a mount in the 1950 Kentucky Derby. Vanderbilt and Winfrey loved his soothing way with fillies and his nose for the finish line: at one point in 1949 he won five stakes races within three weeks, all photo finishes. In January 1951, he signed a contract with Vanderbilt; he would earn $1,000 per month, plus 10 percent of the stakes earnings his horses accumulated.

"Eric was in a beautiful spot, getting to ride all those good horses, but he made the most of it; he really produced," recalled Costy Caras. "He was a big name around New York. He and Arcaro and Teddy Atkinson were the key guys, the guys that dominated. Eric would come into my father's restaurant. I got to know him very well. We became quite buddy-buddy. We both liked big-band music, and we liked to play softball. I went with him to New Orleans one time when he was suspended for a week, and as big as he was in New York, you would have thought God had walked into the room down there."

The media's typical depiction of him as a "quiet youngster" was good for business but not entirely accurate. He was young, success-ful, and making more money than he could believe, and "like a lot of the jockeys back then, he spent whatever he made," Allen Jerkens said. Recalled Frank Curry, "When he'd come to New Orleans, there would be a party lasting two or three days. They'd rent out a restau-rant and go to the jai alai at this place Joe Brown ran, and it was just lights-out. And Eric was picking up the tab."

Inevitably, with so many jockeys in the family, his success caused problems. "We were close growing up, but we drifted apart: he was famous and I wasn't," said Charles Ray Leblanc, who later be-came a racing official in Chicago and New Orleans. "My brother Eu-clid resented that the whole family kowtowed to Eric, and he moved out to California to get away from it, to get out of Eric's shadow and the whole family talking about him. It got to Euclid."

Family issues aside, Guerin was on a roll, as popular as he was successful, as famous as he was dependable, and then Native Dancer came along in 1952, fitting seamlessly into the positive tide. Guerin knew by the Dancer's second victory, in the Youthful Stakes, that this was a horse that could take him to a place few jockeys reached. Now, indeed, the possibilities lay in front of him as the Derby neared, a feast of temptations, unseen but indisputably available: another Derby victory, a Triple Crown, a place in history on a horse for the ages.

If Vanderbilt and Winfrey had compiled a list of potential down-falls that could bring about the unthinkable, a loss in the Derby, a problem with Guerin's ride wouldn't have made the list. The jockey had overcome injuries, failure, and weight problems to become one of

America's best, and now he was riding a magnificent horse with supreme confidence, never moving too soon, always unleashing the Dancer's powerful finishing drive at just the right time. There was pressure, sure, but what did that matter? Guerin and the Grey Ghost were, it seemed, an infallible team.

# THIRTEEN

Few sports events were more important than the Kentucky Derby in the early 1950s. Along with college football's Rose Bowl, auto racing's Indianapolis 500, and golf's Masters, the Run for the Roses was one of the few events affixed to a time and place. Just as the start of the World Series was a sign that autumn leaves would soon be falling, the running of the Derby on the first Saturday in May in Louisville had become an emblem of America's spring.

Inaugurated in 1875, the race had traveled an arduous road to prominence, surviving antigambling crusades, financial crises, political opposition, a depression, and two world wars. One man, Matt Winn, a Louisville businessman and handicapper at the turn of the century, had kept it going and built it into a landmark.

Other races such as Chicago's American Derby had been just as important in the late 1800s; Kentucky racing was struggling and the Derby was in jeopardy, with Churchill Downs on the brink of becoming the fourth Louisville track to fail. Winn put together a group including hotel owner Louis Seelbach and Louisville mayor Charles Grainger and saved the Downs in 1902, then sold his interest in a tailoring business a year later and became the track's general manager. He was taking a great personal risk—Winn had eight daughters to support—but it was a turning point for the Derby.

Over the years, Winn installed pari-mutuel machines and a public-address system, lured fans with bands and air shows, brought in celebrities and politicians, put the race on radio, and courted New York's finest sportswriters, enhancing the Derby with a sheen of glitter and distinction. Kentucky was already horse heaven, the heart of the nation's breeding industry, and the Derby evolved into the state's signature event. By the time Winn died in 1949, the race faithfully transformed the nation into a community of railbirds for a few days every spring. The first live national telecast in 1952 had widened the audience, and now, a year later, with the lure of the undefeated Dancer, and the nation reaching out for assurances at an uneasy time, enthusiasm for the Derby was at a crescendo.

A cadence of familiar customs marked the weeks before the race. The trainers of most Derby contenders arrived at the Downs in early April and drilled their horses on chilly mornings in the shadow of the twin spires atop the grandstand. The backside hosted a convocation of racing's best horsemen, including Sunny Jim Fitzsimmons, Calumet's Plain Ben Jones, Greentree's John Gaver, and Whitney's Syl Veitch. The Derby horses' owners and jockeys trickled in later with reporters from across the country, and a crush of humanity descended on Derby eve, the fans coming by plane, train, and car and getting little sleep in between their Friday night parties and Saturday trips to the Downs.

The event was an American Bacchanalia, the scent of big money and fast horses colliding with Kentucky bourbon and pretty women to create a weekend of Roman excess in a conservative Mississippi River town. Comedians and congressmen vied with starlets and sports stars for invitations to private clubs and all-night parties. Hotels and cabdrivers tripled their rates. High rollers came in private railcars, drank champagne for breakfast, and shoved fistfuls of bills through the betting windows at Churchill Downs. At least one new story of laughable extravagance made the rounds every year. In 1953, Dick Andrade, a flamboyant oilman and bon vivant, brought a horse up to his suite at the Brown Hotel to mingle with guests at his Derby eve party.

Native Dancer, the horse everyone was talking about, took a

train down from New York, his every step chronicled. Winfrey had wanted him to make the 757-mile trek from Belmont Park to Churchill in the White Ghost, the Vanderbilt stable's massive van, but Vanderbilt preferred the train, having transported his horses by rail since Discovery's days. The Dancer was booked on the Cincinnati Limited, departing New York on the Sunday afternoon after the Wood and arriving in Louisville a day later. Social Outcast was also on the trip, as was Invigorator, after having finished third in the Wood.

The trip became a media event. Several of New York's best sportswriters, including Frank Graham of the *Sun,* Joe Williams of the *World-Telegram,* Red Smith of the *Herald Tribune,* and James Roach of the *Times,* booked overnight berths and traveled with Winfrey and his wife. Lester Murray stayed with the Grey Ghost in a special car as the train chugged through Pennsylvania and Ohio during the night. Murray draped a blanket over the horse as temperatures dipped into the thirties.

"Don't want you catching no cold," the groom said in the railcar illuminated by a dim lantern bulb. "You can't be going and getting sick now."

In the middle of the night, outside Columbus, Ohio, the train stopped suddenly to avoid hitting a car, and the writers "were jolted almost out of their berths," with one hurting a rib, reported Jerry Mc-Nerney in the *Louisville Courier-Journal.* Winfrey dashed from his berth to the Dancer's car. "My horse!" he shouted worriedly. Murray said Invigorator had been lying down when the jolt occurred, so he was fine, but the Dancer and Social Outcast had been standing and the Dancer "got bumped plenty." Fortunately, the Grey Ghost was wearing a leather headgear—standard equipment for horses traveling in trains—and wasn't seriously injured.

The jolt received little play in the papers and was quickly forgotten, but it resurfaced thirty-six years later when Ralph Kercheval told *Los Angeles Times* turf writer Bill Christine that Native Dancer had injured his right front ankle in the incident and "wasn't in the best of shape" arriving in Louisville. The ankle was "this big around," Kercheval told Christine, forming a sphere the size of a grapefruit with his hands. If it was, McNerney didn't notice. "I've watched about

20 Derby winners arrive in Louisville, including Count Fleet, Citation and Whirlaway, and none gave the impression of such sheer power and bubbling-over energy as this big grey," McNerney wrote in the *Courier-Journal* the next day. There was no mention of a lump on his ankle.

The car carrying the Dancer, Social Outcast, and Invigorator arrived early in the afternoon at a small rail yard three blocks from the Downs. Tom Young, Churchill's longtime track manager, drove over to greet Winfrey and the horses and guide them through the sea of reporters, photographers, and cameramen there to record their arrival.

"Don't block the platform with those cars!" Young shouted as they waited for the train. "Leave him plenty of room to walk!"

Soon the engine and car chugged into the yard, eased up to the platform, and stopped. "Here he is!" someone shouted. The media horde gathered at the door of the car, and after a moment, the door slid open and Winfrey popped his head out.

"Who's he?" someone asked.

They had come to see the horse, not the trainer.

Winfrey jumped out and cleared a path for the Dancer to disembark. A wooden gangplank was set down between the car and the platform, with strands of straw littered on the plank and bales of hay banked on either side.

"Okay, bring him out!" Winfrey shouted.

The cameramen formed a semicircle around the door, and after a dramatic pause, out came the Dancer. As cameras whirred and clicked, the grey colt marched down the plank in his headgear, blanket, and leg wrappings, with Harold Walker in front of him, holding the shank, and Murray to the rear, holding his tail with both hands. Social Outcast and Invigorator followed. The caravan proceeded straight to a yellow truck, which the Dancer coolly boarded, as if he had reserved a seat. The truck drove Winfrey and the horses over to the Downs, through the stable gate, and down to Barn 16, where, like a diva at an opening-night gala, the Dancer made a second grand entrance, departing the truck to another round of camera clicks.

"Easy now, no mistakes here," Winfrey said.

The trainer had asked Young to make sure a heavier bed of straw was laid in one of the stalls: the Grey Ghost liked a thick mattress.

"We did what you asked," Young said. "There's extra straw in the second stall."

Calm and compliant, the Dancer moved into his stall and immediately dropped to the ground and rolled back and forth in the straw, gleefully kicking and stretching and shaking his mane. It was as if he knew the long trip was over and he could finally cut loose.

"You like that, Pop? Well, go to it," Winfrey said, smiling with relief now that the trip was over.

McNerney asked Young, who had worked at Churchill since 1911, if he had ever seen a Derby arrival that looked more the part of a champion. Only one, Young said: Twenty Grand, the strapping bay that had won the 1931 Derby in record time and held the record until Whirlaway broke it in 1941. McNerney was also obviously impressed with the Dancer. "He's a big, healthy athlete; just looking at him, you know he's good," McNerney wrote.

The Dancer made his first trip to the track the next morning at nine o'clock, with Bernie Everson on him, Winfrey leading him on a stable pony, and a clattering mob of cameramen and reporters trailing him. He walked through the backside and entered the track on the backstretch at the height of rush hour for morning workouts, with horses and trainers and grooms and exercise riders coming and going. All activity stopped as the Grey Ghost stretched his legs and walked up the backstretch toward the second turn. Horsemen who had never seen the famed horse from the East flocked to the rail to look. Jockeys riding past on other horses slowed and looked back over their shoulders.

The Dancer was on the slightly damp oval for fifteen minutes. He took a walk around the track, then jogged around a second time. "The most talked-about horse since Man O' War seemed to know he was the center of attention," the Associated Press reported. His reputation and physical appearance made an impression. McNerney wrote that "the big grey wins friends and influences people just by his looks." Eddie Hayward, trainer of Dark Star, laughed when asked if he was still considering entering another Cain Hoy Stable long shot, Bimini Bay, in the Derby. "Oh, no," Hayward said, "now that he's gotten a look at that grey colt, he won't eat for a week."

As the Dancer was leaving the track, he lashed out with his hind legs at a horse cantering close by. His aim was off, but the *Morning Telegraph* reported that the Dancer "corded up a bit" in his excitement and had to be massaged with oil to relax his tight muscles. The colt quickly cooled off and was back in his stall within minutes, seemingly unharmed, but in fact, the incident was the start of a major scare, according to famed Derby veterinarian Alex Harthill.

The Dancer "tied up badly," Dr. Harthill recalled years later. "It was a muscular spasm, like a charley horse. It was very painful and the horse broke out perspiring. Everyone was wanting to scratch him. I had just met Mr. Vanderbilt that winter at Santa Anita. He was keen to win the Derby, and he had a large entourage coming down from Maryland and New York as his guests for the race. He didn't want to hurt the horse obviously, but he wanted to run. We gave the horse a large dose of what amounted to Gatorade, four or five gallons of electrolytes passed through a stomach tube. We did that for several days with him, as a matter of fact. He recovered very nicely."

The news that the Grey Ghost was being treated with a stomach tube would have generated headlines from coast to coast, but it went unreported, and neither Vanderbilt nor Winfrey mentioned it over the years in any of the many interviews they gave about the Dancer. "I never tried to keep it quiet, but horse trainers have never been ones to advertise the little things that go wrong with their horses," Harthill recalled. "The boss [Vanderbilt] knew about it, I know that. I can't say if it affected the horse in the race or not. He was fully recovered by then. But it certainly didn't help him."

Vanderbilt was an old-school sportsman known for putting his horses' best interests ahead of all else, and it is unlikely he would have allowed the Dancer to run in the Derby if there had been any risk of injury, even knowing how much the public—and Vanderbilt himself most of all—would have been disappointed. In any case, there was relief, no doubt, when the colt quickly returned to health.

Winfrey set down stringent house rules for the rest of the week, probably reacting to the incident. The doors to the Dancer's stall would be closed at all times. He would leave the barn only to train. There would be no posing for pictures, no afternoon grazes. The horse was just too fit and full of himself, Winfrey felt, to expose him to many new and different circumstances.

Winfrey spoke to reporters outside Barn 16 after the Dancer's workout, as he would every morning leading up to the race.

"Is this a little different than last year?" he was asked, referring to the fiasco with Cousin.

"What a difference from last year," Winfrey said. "The press boys forgot all about me last year. I think they're going to be flocking around this year." He continued: "I guess I can stand one hectic week. This grey is the kind of horse you get only once in your life."

The Dancer's first appearance on the track dominated Tuesday's news dispatches from Louisville even though the Derby Trial was run later in the day before 23,000 fans. Fourteen horses were entered in the race, many being given a final chance to prove they belonged in the Derby, but they were "mostly second stringers," according to the Associated Press, and the race was assigned little importance.

The horse to watch in the Trial, many thought, was Royal Bay Gem, the undersized late-running colt that had come from fifteenth to win the Chesapeake Stakes. But after being sent to the post at 5–2 odds, he was blocked at the half-mile pole and was never a factor, with jockey Jimmy Combest strangely never asking for much effort. The Gem did close hard, however, coming from last to fourth with his customary finishing kick, and he would still have his backers in the Derby.

Dark Star won the Trial. The third betting choice at 9–2 odds, he sat in second behind a long shot for a half mile, then shot into the lead on the turn and pulled away to win by four lengths, with jockey Henry Moreno urging him to the finish line in 1:36, just three-fifths of a second off the track record for a mile. Money Broker, the Florida Derby winner, ridden by Al Popara, passed a quartet of horses in the stretch to finish second. Dark Star's shaky credentials as a Derby horse had been solidified. "I just wish we could have run the Derby today," trainer Eddie Hayward told reporters.

But even though Harry Guggenheim's little-known horse now had to be taken seriously, few really believed Dark Star would challenge the Dancer or Correspondent in the Derby. Correspondent, after all, had whipped Dark Star in an allowance race at Keeneland eleven days earlier, easily fending off a challenge in the stretch. After the Trial, Arcaro, who would ride Correspondent in the Derby, made sure reporters remembered that. "Dark Star just made Correspondent look even better," he said with a grin after finishing seventh in the Trial on a colt named Berseem.

Leaving the Downs after the race, Hayward was sitting in traffic when the car behind him suddenly accelerated, ramming the rear of his car and causing significant damage. "I'm going to need to win the Derby to get my car fixed," Hayward told the crowd at the annual Derby trainers' dinner later that night at the Brown Hotel. Despite Dark Star's victory in the Trial, it was hard not to see the horse and his trainer as star-crossed.

The Dancer was back on the track for a light workout the next morning, again stirring up a commotion. "This observer has been coming to the Derby since 1916, but never have I known a candidate for the Downs classic to excite quite such interest as Native Dancer," columnist Charles Hatton wrote in the *Morning Telegraph*. "When the strapping grey colt walks beneath the shed in Barn 16, the rail is lined with fully as many of the curious as most paddocks before a race. A score or more of newsmen, feature writers for slick magazines, newsreel, *Life* magazine, TV and daily press photographers follow him to and from the track during training hours, and each morning there is a parking problem in the vicinity of his barn. Not even Citation stirred such keen interest. Clearly, Native Dancer is 'the public's horse.' Thanks to TV, countless thousands of fans have become interested in him, as they used to be interested in outstanding ball players. Someone has well said that 'all the world loves a champion,' and Saturday, people will be rooting for the Dancer who will not wager a farthing on the outcome."

More reporters were arriving every day, with *New York Times* columnist Arthur Daley among Wednesday's newcomers. He began his morning at dawn, trying to coax responses from Plain Ben Jones outside Barn 15. Jones, who had trained three of the past five Derby winners and six overall, shooed Daley away. "You get on away from here, there ain't no Derby horses here," he said. "Just go on down the line and look at that grey. That's the horse to watch this year."

Winfrey was holding court again outside Barn 16. "One of the photographers asked me if I wouldn't take his bridle and lead him out in the sun for a picture—'not me,' I said, 'I wouldn't dare,'" Winfrey said. "I've got a 260-pound man leading him around now. If I could find a bigger man, I would."

Vanderbilt was at the barn for the first time, having flown into Louisville late Tuesday night after watching Indian Land, another of his horses, run in the feature race at Garden State Park. He smiled at Winfrey's caution. "That's right," Vanderbilt said. "He might decide to get playful and throw you over the roof."

Winfrey continued: "I wouldn't let him be photographed grazing on the grass, either. If some of those other horses with coughs grazed on the same grass, our horse could catch a cold and there goes the ballgame. No, sir, I'm taking no chances."

Joe Tannenbaum, a young racing writer for the *Miami Daily News,* was covering his first Kentucky Derby. The size and intensity of the hordes around the Dancer awed him. "Winfrey had big crowds of reporters around him every morning," Tannenbaum recalled years later. Tannenbaum was also fascinated with Vanderbilt: "A lot of people thought he was one of those aloof society people, but he was not around the barns; he was tense about his horses, like a horseman."

The writers were following their usual Derby week routine: morning interviews at the barns, afternoons in the press box, evenings at dinners or parties. Joe Palmer, sadly, was missing for the first time since the early 1930s, and CBS, again televising the race nationally, with Bryan Field handling the call, had several dozen technicians on the premises. The network was trying out a new blueprint for its forty-five-minute Saturday afternoon telecast. The first fifteen minutes would emanate from a New York studio, with Mike Wallace and Buff Cobb, the popular husband-and-wife interviewers, previewing the race. They would then throw it to Kentucky, where Mel Allen, the famed baseball announcer, would set the scene. After Field's call of the race, Allen and Louisville broadcaster Phil Sutterfield would cover the trophy presentation and interview the connections of the winner.

Many more people would see CBS's broadcast than any of the newsmen's stories, a reality beginning to sink in with the citizens of the press box. "Very quickly," Tannenbaum said, "many reporters rightfully changed their reportorial styles because they believed that most people had seen the race. It was a landmark change in how the job was done."

Tommy Roberts recalled, "There's no doubt the old-time newspaper guys saw their importance being eroded, and they didn't want to give that up. Before, when Red Smith or Grantland Rice walked into the track, everyone said, 'Hail Caesar!' But these new popular figures were emerging through TV, guys like Bryan Field and Fred Caposella. That worried the guys who ran the racetracks. They had grown up with the newspapermen and that world. That was one of the reasons racing was so reluctant to go with TV originally, because the newspaper guys had such sway with the track operators. No one really understood the power of the medium yet. But it was starting to change."

Winfrey had told the writers he planned to give the Dancer a final pre-Derby work Thursday morning, but the weather forecast was ominous, calling for thunderstorms. Winfrey considered his options. He didn't want to work the Dancer on a wet track, and he couldn't put off the work until Friday, just a day before the Derby. With Vanderbilt's help, he concocted a plan and proposed it to Churchill officials: the Dancer and Social Outcast could appear in a "trial" between races that afternoon, before the rains came overnight. Churchill agreed to the idea just in time to have the Dancer's appearance trumpeted in the last edition of the afternoon paper.

There were gasps and cheers when the two Vanderbilt horses appeared on the track hours later, after the third race. Bernie Everson was riding the Dancer, and Willie Nertney, a former jockey who now exercised horses for Vanderbilt, was aboard Social Outcast. Winfrey's plan was for the two to cover a mile, with Social Outcast breaking in front early to give the Dancer a target to shoot for down the stretch.

Unlike the botched trial before the Gotham, this went smoothly.

The horses broke to a start from under the finish line, and as planned, Nertney and Social Outcast jumped in front by five lengths. They increased the margin to eight lengths in the backstretch, with Everson keeping a tight hold on the Dancer. When Everson finally asked him to run as they turned for home, the Grey Ghost put on a show. Picking up steam, he closed to within five lengths of Social Outcast, then four, then two. He was within a head as they crossed the finish line, and although Social Outcast was in front, the Dancer's devastating finishing kick had the crowd buzzing. Clockers timed him over the final quarter mile in 23⅕ seconds—almost a second faster than any winning horse had ever run the final quarter mile of the Derby. That more than made up for the relatively slow overall clocking of 1:39⅗ for a mile.

As he watched the horses cool out back at the barn minutes later, Winfrey said he was pleased. "I would have preferred that he run a faster first half and a slower second half, but I'm not kicking," the trainer said. "He's ready to run Saturday."

The crowd watched five more races, but left talking about the Dancer's remarkable stretch run. It was instant Derby lore. More than 100,000 fans and a TV audience in the millions would see the horse's expected coronation in the Derby in a couple of days, but those who had seen him run down Social Outcast that afternoon had been given a private exhibition of his greatness. How lucky they felt.

The field was finalized Friday morning when the owners of a dozen horses paid the $250 to enter. The last horse entered was Dark Star, Eddie Hayward arriving with Guggenheim's money just twenty-one minutes before the entry period closed. Post positions were drawn in Churchill racing secretary Lincoln Plaut's office. Plaut placed twelve numbered pellets in a container and withdrew them one at a time. The Dancer drew the seventh post, in the middle of the starting gate. That pleased Winfrey and Vanderbilt.

The field was easily separated into three distinct groups. The Dancer and Correspondent were at one end, the favorites, and five long shots—Spy Defense, Social Outcast, Ace Destroyer, Ram o' War, and Curragh King—were at the other end, seemingly overmatched. In between were five horses with legitimate Derby credentials. Royal

Bay Gem figured to be the third betting choice, followed by Straight Face and Dark Star. Money Broker had finished in the money in all but one of his eight starts as a three-year-old. Invigorator was always competitive.

But the Grey Ghost loomed mightily over them all, his record, reputation, and physical presence convincing many on-the-scene observers that this Derby was a constellation with but one star. In a *Courier-Journal* poll printed on Friday, forty-one of sixty-seven journalists picked him to win. Support for the others was minimal, with ten backing Royal Bay Gem, nine taking Correspondent, three picking Straight Face, two taking Social Outcast, one taking Spy Defense, and one taking Dark Star.

The Dancer's hype and popularity were becoming too widespread for some horsemen, most notably Arcaro. Hours after the poll appeared in print, the Master gave scalding answers to several questions from Associated Press reporter Kyle Vance, complaining that Churchill's racing strip was "full of holes" and "the worst possible track" and that Native Dancer was overrated. "He had better be a hell of a horse," Arcaro told Vance in a story that moved on the national wires. "He hasn't proved he is yet. It isn't fair, the way they're building him up. It isn't fair to the horse and it isn't fair to the jockey."

There were other dissenters. Rip Newborn of the *Cleveland Press,* the one writer who had picked Dark Star in the *Courier-Journal* poll, explained in an accompanying article that he wasn't supporting the Dancer because "Polynesian has to show me he can beget a top stayer." In other words, because the Dancer's sire had raced most effectively at shorter distances, Newborn was unsure whether his grey son could race the mile-and-a-quarter Derby distance without tiring. It was a criticism that had dogged the Dancer, and now, on the eve of the Derby, it was one of several arguments his few critics were using to pick against him. A grey had never won the Derby. And only fifteen of the twenty-six odds-on Derby favorites had won.

As much as it seemed unlikely that the Dancer would lose, history suggested that, at the very least, the possibility existed. Thirteen years earlier, a magnificent colt named Bimelech had come to the Derby in circumstances similar to the Dancer's. Owned by E. R.

Bradley, already a winner of four Derbys, the colt was 11–0 and had been saluted by Bradley, one of Vanderbilt's racing mentors, as "my finest horse." Bet down to the shortest price in Derby history, forty cents on the dollar, Bimelech raced near the front, took the lead on the second turn, and held it driving for home, only to have a 35–1 shot named Gallahadion overtake him in the final furlong. Remembering the upset thirteen years later, *Courier-Journal* assistant sports editor Dean Eagle wrote a column headlined, "Don't Hock Your Car to Back Native Dancer! Remember Bimelech?"

On the other hand, two other favorites since Bimelech had run in the Derby at odds of forty cents on the dollar, and both—Count Fleet in 1943 and Citation in 1948—had won. The Dancer would draw similar support. Anyone who knew racing understood that any number of problems could arise in any race to keep the best horse from winning, but the Dancer, many believed, was so plainly superior that, like Count Fleet and Citation, he would sail past any obstacles on his way to the winner's circle.

During training hours on Friday, Vanderbilt was standing along the rail watching the Dancer jog by when Clyde Troutt, trainer of Royal Bay Gem, happened by on a pony. After waiting until the Dancer passed, Troutt leaned over and congratulated Vanderbilt.

"He's just a splendid horse, sir," the trainer said. "I've got a game one myself, but I can't beat you."

Vanderbilt smiled. The week had been a swirl for him from the moment he arrived, his many friends in racing wanting to help him celebrate the triumph of the Dancer's greatness. Louis Cheri, his valet, was with him—Louis had become a racing expert himself and wouldn't have missed the Derby—and Jeanne had joined them later in the week. Vanderbilt had a cold he jokingly attributed to "rose fever"—"If Native Dancer runs as fast as my nose, we're in," he said—but it didn't stop him from making his rounds. Every day he rose early and went to Churchill to watch the Dancer train and to soak up the scene, drinking coffee and giving interviews as the tension built. Other obligations occasionally distracted him—a society hostess gave a luncheon in his honor one afternoon—but he was increasingly fixated on the real reason for his trip, the momentous occasion for which he had waited so long: his chance to win the Derby.

He and Jeanne were staying at the home of Baylor Hickman, a wealthy Louisville horseman and businessman who had once served on the Kentucky Racing Commission. Hickman lived at Glenview, a magnificent acreage located up the river from downtown Louisville. "There were a lot of people around and they were having quite a time out there; lots of parties and lots of corks being popped," recalled Dr. Harthill, who was dating and later married Hickman's daughter, and attended many of the parties that week. "They were celebrating. Everyone thought the Dancer was going to win. It was like it was a foregone conclusion."

# FOURTEEN

The sun shone on the Dancer's Derby. The weather forecasters had called for storms and a sloppy track, but Saturday dawned clear and bright, with temperatures headed for the seventies, no ominous clouds in the distance, and a fast track assured. An existential handicapper might have suggested that the racing gods wanted the Grey Ghost illuminated in the ultimate spotlight on his most important day.

The colt had gobbled down four quarts of oats at 1 A.M. and slept in the straw until dawn, when Lester Murray brushed him and put fresh bandages on his legs. Bernie Everson took him to the track for a jog after Winfrey, Vanderbilt, and Kercheval arrived. Everson was wearing a cerise and white sweater over a cerise sports shirt with cerise diamonds on white sleeves—no doubt as to whom he worked for. The Dancer cantered up the backstretch and around the turn, accelerated for a quarter mile, then eased up at the finish line and jogged all the way around the track again. Just stretching his legs. Ever curious, he breezed with his head cocked at a detachment of National Guardsmen mustering in the infield.

Red Smith, the columnist for the *New York Herald Tribune*, was spending the morning at the barn, recording a minute-by-minute account of the Dancer's day, as if it were destined to become racing history. According to the column, which ran the next day, Everson was

on the shank as the horse cooled out, circling the barn with two blan-
kets over him at first, then one. "Don't let's walk all the speed out of
him," Winfrey said after twenty minutes. The horse was put back in
his stall, which was freshly laid with new straw. Murray tied his tail
up, removed his bandages, and rubbed him down, and he snoozed upright—"like Joe Louis sleeping in the dressing room before a fight,"
Smith wrote—before eating two more quarts of oats and snoozing
again.

Someone brought in a copy of Saturday's edition of the *Morning
Telegraph,* which included long profiles of Winfrey and Vanderbilt.
Winfrey glanced at the story, which noted that he had already been a
trainer for twenty-one years even though he was just turning thirty-
seven. "Why, I just started shaving," he told Smith. His father, George
Carey Winfrey, who had taught him so much, was back in New York,
putting his horses through their morning works at Jamaica. The elder
Winfrey had never run a horse in the Derby, so when a reporter
asked Bill Winfrey if the hullabaloo of the past week had aged him, he
knew better than to sound a jaded note. "Far from it; this is what I've
waited for for 37 years," Winfrey said.

Churchill Downs's gates had opened at 8 A.M., and a great crowd
was steadily building. The backside was overrun with grooms, fans,
horsemen, reporters, and children, and a steady stream of visitors
dropped by Barn 16 to offer best wishes. One, Smith wrote, was a
man who had served in the South Pacific with Winfrey during World
War II. Another was a newsreel photographer who shot film of the
owner and trainer laughing and smiling. "Do you want long faces, too,
in case we lose?" Vanderbilt asked. Vanderbilt and Kercheval left at
9:30, just before Johnny Adams, the veteran jockey who would ride
Social Outcast in the Derby, came by to discuss tactics with Winfrey.
The trainer left shortly after that.

Tension slowly built as the hours passed. According to Smith's
column, Everson's wife came by with her husband's lucky socks—
cerise with white diamonds, of course—which he had worn each time
the Dancer raced, and Murray and Harold Walker cleaned the barn
and ate lunch in a stall. The blare of the track announcer and occasional roars from the crowd interrupted the reverie. Winfrey re-

turned with his wife Elaine, who was pregnant, and showed her around the barn before taking her over to the grandstand to get her settled in Vanderbilt's box. A young boy leaning against a fence stopped them on their walk and offered Elaine a tip on the race. "Dark Star's gonna win," the boy said. The tip was ignored.

Word arrived that Spy Defense, one of the longest shots in the Derby field, had scratched, with trainer Jack Hodgins offering this explanation to reporters: "I've got a good reputation, and I'm not going up against the grey one. Native Dancer is a champion, and you don't see many champions, so why don't we just admit it?"

The nine-race card started at noon in weather so pleasant "many of the male customers put aside their coats and rolled up their shirtsleeves," wrote James Roach in the *New York Times,* and "those who were in the infield were able to get a full day of sun-tanning that was at least a reasonable facsimile of the Miami Beach type." It was a classic Derby crowd, a convivial blend of fashionable women and powerful men. They drank mint juleps, studied the *Racing Form*, bet, and bought souvenirs including fringed pillow covers, bugles, parasols, and julep glasses.

Churchill president Bill Corum had hoped Judy Garland and Bob Hope would lead the list of celebrities in attendance, but Garland had become ill after a concert the night before, and Hope had gone to Washington after attending the races on Friday. The list of faces-to-be-seen was still long and impressive, including U.S. senator Lyndon Johnson of Texas and a half dozen of his colleagues; four governors; FBI chief J. Edgar Hoover; former vice president Alben Barkley; actor Charles Coburn, singer Marilyn Maxwell, and Happy Chandler, the former baseball commissioner and governor of Kentucky. The Derby did bring out the heavyweights.

Mutuel clerks started selling tickets for the Derby at 9 A.M., with the resulting odds unannounced until after the sixth race, the race before the Derby. The Dancer, paired as a betting entity with Social Outcast, was 3–5 on the track-sponsored "morning line" printed in the program, but surprisingly, when the odds reflecting the daylong "blind betting" were posted after the sixth race, there was more money to win on Correspondent. The Dancer wasn't even the favorite! That changed quickly, of course. Even though Churchill bettors obviously loved Arcaro, who was riding Correspondent, they still preferred the Dancer. Within minutes, the Grey Ghost and Social Outcast were down to 6–5 and Correspondent was 2–1.

Winfrey left Vanderbilt in his box and returned to Barn 16 before the sixth race. Murray put the racing bandages on the Dancer's legs and brushed him yet again, his coat glistening in the sunlight filtering through his stall. A roar from the crowd signaled the end of the sixth race. A garbled voice on the scratchy backside public address system announced that it was time to take the Derby horses over to the paddock. The horses walked over on the track, traveling clockwise around the outer rail, right in front of the crowd. Harold Walker led the Dancer, with Murray bringing up the rear; it was the first time many fans had seen the favorite live, and they cheered and shouted their support.

The Dancer was calm in the crowded saddling paddock, where Vanderbilt and Jock Whitney, owner of Straight Face, chatted. Winfrey offered encouragement rather than instructions as he gave Guerin a leg up onto the colt's back; they were on the same page, knowing how the Dancer needed to run. As always, Guerin would fall off the early pace, stalk the leaders, and make a move turning for home. The jockey's only concern was that he didn't fall too far behind this time, with the Dancer racing farther than ever before against ten top opponents.

The horses stepped onto the track for the post parade, and a line of soldiers and sailors stepped forward in the infield holding the Kentucky and American flags. The University of Louisville band played "My Old Kentucky Home," and the Armored Center Band from nearby Fort Knox played the national anthem. The sun was casting longer shadows as the horses jogged clockwise through the stretch to the second turn, reversed direction, and approached the starting gate. The crowd loosed a roar of anticipation as Ace Destroyer went into the first stall, followed by Correspondent, Ram o' War, Invigorator, Curragh King, and Native Dancer, then Money Broker, Social Outcast, Straight Face, Dark Star, and Royal Bay Gem.

The eyes of the nation were on the race. Television industry analysts later estimated that almost 20 million viewers were watching CBS's live telecast in almost 8 million homes, the totals equal to those for the World Series and far exceeding those for any previously televised horse race. Seventy-two percent of the TV sets that were on from coast to coast were tuned to the Derby as Bryan Field gathered himself in front of the microphone and prepared to call the race. America was riveted. Man O' War had raced to immortality more than three decades earlier, before radio, with few of his fans seeing him run; and then Seabiscuit and Citation had come along as the champions heard 'round the country, the heroes of racing's radio days. Now the Grey Ghost was on the verge of joining them as the first great horse America had actually *seen*.

At the Louis Restaurant, the racing-mad eatery near the Jamaica Racetrack in New York, a packed house of customers was gathered around a TV set. There was no doubt where their allegiances lay. "We had a big picture of Eric Guerin on the wall; he had come in to eat and we were big fans of his," Costy Caras recalled. "Plus, Vanderbilt was a very popular man with the racing crowd. They knew he had put a lot into the sport. People wanted him to win."

Halfway across the country, in New Orleans, Tim Capps, destined to make racing his career as an author and industry official, was also watching TV. He was eight years old. "We didn't have a TV in our house, but our neighbor across the street did and we went over to watch the race there," Capps recalled. "We had just moved down from North Carolina and my father was in the seminary. I was just starting to read about horses and get interested. I was enthralled by Native Dancer. He was my first 'favorite' horse. I thought his name was great. I had read enough to know Alfred Vanderbilt was famous. And he was grey. He just jumped off the screen. We had gone over to our neighbor's house to watch some other things on their TV, college football bowl games, but the Derby really grabbed me. I wanted Native Dancer to win."

So did Judy Ohl, a seventh grader in Mauch Chunk, Pennsylvania, north of Allentown at the foot of the Pocono Mountains. "My father worked at Bethlehem Steel and brought the New York papers home in the evenings," she recalled years later. "There was always an article about Native Dancer, and I had become a big fan of the horse even though I had never seen him in the flesh. But he had a presence that came through even in black-and-white pictures in the paper. It was very exciting to get to see him race live on TV." She was watching the Derby in her den with her best friend from parochial school. "The reception was terrible and the picture was fuzzy, but we didn't care," she recalled.

Thousands of other girls across the country had also fallen for the Grey Ghost. Lulu Vanderbilt, the daughter of Alfred's brother, was one of them. A teenage student at Foxcroft, an exclusive boarding school in Virginia, Lulu had clipped out newspaper articles and put them in a scrapbook, watched the Gotham and Wood on NBC, and sent several telegrams to the smiling, dapper man who was always standing next to the horse in the winner's circle—her uncle Alfred. "My girlfriends got sick of hearing me prattle on about the horse," Lulu recalled. "I sent Alfred a telegram before the Derby."

She had planned to watch the race, but a rare chance to escape the dorm changed her mind. She was spending the day at a steeplechase race in Middleburg, Virginia. "We got out so seldom, and I was so convinced that Native Dancer was going to win that I decided to go," she recalled.

At 4:42 P.M., Ruby White, the veteran starter at Churchill Downs, pushed a button that opened the flaps to the starting gate. Out came the eleven horses. The tote board in the infield was showing the final odds: the Dancer and Social Outcast at 7–10, still odds-on after all, with Correspondent at 3–1, Royal Bay Gem at 7–1, and Straight Face at 11–1. Of the $778,556 in the win pool, almost exactly half— $386,333—was on the Dancer and Social Outcast. They had so dominated the wagering that Dark Star was 25–1 as the fifth choice of eleven.

There was immediately an incident along the rail: Ace Destroyer veered out and grazed Correspondent, squeezing Arcaro and his horse back. That allowed jockey Henry Moreno, on Dark Star, to swing in from the tenth post and take the lead without a struggle coming through the stretch the first time. Arcaro rallied quickly, jumping into second, two lengths off the lead, as he headed past the grandstand and reached the first turn. Dark Star covered the first quarter in a routine 23⅘ seconds.

The Dancer broke cleanly, without incident, and Guerin settled him off the pace, in sixth, as he passed the grandstand the first time. Some observers later suggested that he was too far back, that he had wanted to run and Guerin had restrained him, that he could have—and should have—raced nearer the front, in third or fourth. Guerin disputed the suggestion, insisting that while it may have appeared that he was holding the Dancer back, in fact, the colt was uncomfortable on the track and struggling to find his stride. In any case, the Dancer was in sixth as he moved into the first turn, in front of early stragglers such as Royal Bay Gem, Social Outcast, and Money Broker.

Al Popara, the jockey on Money Broker, wasn't pleased. Under orders from trainer Tennessee Wright to race near the front and near the rail, he was stuck on the outside and in a pack, moving at a slow pace. He later told a United Press reporter that he had wanted to remain behind Native Dancer through the first turn and then make a move, "but the pace was too slow," so he decided to "circle the Dancer," cut in front, and drop down to the rail.

A former Golden Gloves boxing champion from Hayward, California, Popara, at twenty-four, was one of the least experienced jockeys in the race. He was four years into his career, having just the year before ridden his first "name" mount, Gushing Oil. Tough and hungry, he had ridden Money Broker and other horses with success over the winter in New Orleans, then used his winnings to move his wife and four children out of a trailer and into a house. He was making his Derby debut on Money Broker but had almost lost the mount two days earlier when Churchill's stewards suspended him for ten days for rough riding. That would have knocked him out of the race in New York, where a suspended jockey was unable to take any mounts, but a suspended jockey in Kentucky could still ride stakes mounts previously contracted, so Popara was in the Derby.

He was moving Money Broker out and around Guerin on the first turn when Money Broker lugged in toward the rail and bumped

the Grey Ghost just as Curragh King, the long shot that had been racing immediately in front of the Dancer, veered out and into the
Dancer's path. The simultaneous bump and squeeze knocked the
Dancer badly off stride. "Hey!" Guerin shouted. Bill Shoemaker, riding Invigorator to the inside of the Dancer, had a clear view. "It happened right to the outside of me: Native Dancer was usually a lot
closer to the pace, but Money Broker bumped him good and knocked
him back," Shoemaker recalled years later. The chart caller for the
*Daily Racing Form* wrote that the Dancer was "roughed at the first
turn by Money Broker." Guerin righted the Dancer, pulled him back,
and veered to the outside, ending up in eighth place as he straightened out of the turn.

   The possibility of rough riding had certainly existed. Not once
in the prior seventy-eight runnings of the Derby had a horse been disqualified, so the jockeys had a license to be bold. And Churchill
Downs still hadn't installed film patrol cameras, even though the innovation was more than a decade old. The result was an old-school
free-for-all—in every race, not just the Derby. "There's more than a
bit of rough riding here; the classic phrase 'every man for himself'
seems, at times, to be the motto in the jockeys' room," James Roach
wrote in the *New York Times* that week, adding that "the jockeys are
well aware those big [film patrol] lenses aren't focused on their every
move."

   Popara's intentions would be intensely debated, as would
Guerin's response. This much was certain: with seven horses ahead
of him as he came out of the first turn, the Dancer's jockey asked his
horse to run to start making up lost ground—and run the Dancer did.
Steaming up the backstretch toward the second turn, the Grey Ghost
quickly passed four horses and closed in on the leaders. It was later
estimated that he took only 23 seconds to run this middle quarter-
mile segment of the race. "That is as fast as horses travel," Evan Shipman later wrote in the *Morning Telegraph*.

   Up front, little had changed. With six furlongs down and four to
go, Dark Star and Correspondent were still running first and second,
with Arcaro stalking the leader from a half length behind. The Master was in perfect position to strike. So was Straight Face, with Teddy

Atkinson up; the Greentree colt had moved into third, a length behind Correspondent. The Dancer was a length behind Straight Face as he moved through the second turn. The bump on the first turn had set him back, but he was just four lengths behind Dark Star now with a half mile to go.

As he negotiated the second turn, Guerin moved down to the rail to save ground; he had raced wide until now, forcing the Dancer to cover extra ground. Moving to the rail put him behind Correspondent and Straight Face, raising his chances of getting blocked off, but with so much distance still to be covered, he had time to sit back and see what developed.

Derby contenders and pretenders are separated coming out of the second turn, when they have raced a mile and start digging deep to cover the final quarter. At that point, everyone—jockeys, fans, trainers, and owners alike—discovers which horses have enough stamina to compete to the end and which don't. Fifty yards into the stretch run to the finish line, Arcaro was stunned to discover that his horse was among the pretenders. Correspondent had pulled away from every rival in his three races at Keeneland in April, but now, after racing in Dark Star's shadow for a mile, he slowed and drifted wide. He would finish fifth. Straight Face also drifted wide, his stride suddenly snagged, his chances gone. He would finish sixth. Royal Bay Gem, the third betting choice, had started his usual finishing kick on the second turn and was moving up fast on the outside, but he had too much ground to make up in too little time against horses of this caliber. He would finish fourth.

With horses fading everywhere, the race was suddenly as clear as the blue Kentucky sky. Dark Star, at 25–1 odds, with five wins in ten career starts, was in front with three-sixteenths of a mile to run. Native Dancer, at 7–10 odds, with an 11–0 record, was two lengths behind. The other nine horses were out of it. Either Dark Star would hold on for the upset, or Native Dancer, as he had so often, would swoop around the leader and win going away, realizing the defining triumph so many had foretold.

There was every reason to believe the Dancer was on the verge of winning. The Grey Ghost had won most of his races from this exact position, swooping in from the head of the stretch to pass horses who, in many cases, had credentials superior to Dark Star's. The bump on the first turn was forgotten. The Dancer was in position to take over.

Surprisingly, he gained not an inch on Dark Star for a hundred yards, through the top half of the stretch run. Moreno, who had judged the pace brilliantly until now, alertly moved his dark brown colt from the middle of the track down toward the rail, cutting off the Dancer's open lane to the finish line. Guerin had to move the Dancer yet again, swerving off the rail and to the outside of Dark Star as he tried to rally. Only then, trailing by a length and a half with a furlong to go, did the favorite begin to run.

Dark Star had little left. That was obvious. Moreno was just trying to coax his horse to the finish line. He glanced back at the sixteenth pole, saw the Dancer, and admitted later, "I was pretty scared when I saw that big grey behind me." His and everyone else's eyes were on the Dancer. The race hadn't turned out as planned, but the Grey Ghost had fluttered hearts before and come out fine, and he bore down on the leader with his trademark fierceness now, gaining ground with every step.

It was in the issue of *Life* magazine on newsstands across the country that week that the Dancer's stride had been measured at twenty-nine feet, and every inch of it was on display now as the colt closed on Dark Star. The lead was down to a length in one stride, then less than a length inside the sixteenth pole, Guerin beating a tattoo on the Dancer's flank, the crowd roaring, millions watching at home.

He was a half length behind with one hundred yards to go, then, after another step, a head behind.

Just a head to win the Derby.

Covering twenty-nine feet with every stride, the Dancer drove hard, his innate competitiveness firing him, his chances still alive.

The finish line loomed, but the Dancer took another colossal step and closed more ground, his head bobbing deliciously close to Dark Star. All he needed was another stride, two at the most.

Dark Star lunged, the Dancer made a final reach, and both crossed the finish line as millions shrieked.

The race was over.

The impossible had happened.

The Dancer had lost.

# FIFTEEN

Vanderbilt watched from his box above the homestretch, standing alongside Jeanne, Bill and Elaine Winfrey, Ralph and Blanche Kercheval, and Louis Cheri. Like the rest of the country, he thought the Dancer was in perfect position at the top of the stretch, with just one horse to pass. Like the rest of the country, he watched in disbelief as the colt failed to gain ground on Dark Star until it almost seemed too late before making his remarkable run in the final furlong.

"Did he get it?" Vanderbilt shouted amid the din as the horses crossed the finish line.

"I don't think so," Winfrey said.

Vanderbilt knew it was true. The crowd roared when it was announced that the stewards were reviewing a photo of the finish, but Vanderbilt left for the apron alongside the track, certain that Dark Star had won. He was making his way through the grandstand when the announcement came, and he grimly accepted condolences from strangers, with a nod of his head. His innate aristocratic restraint served him well now. He had won and lost hundreds of races at dozens of tracks over the years, and he knew as well as anyone to expect the unexpected, but this was hard to take. After simmering for almost two decades, his Derby dream had been dashed in two minutes.

"Alfred jumped up and left immediately, so I said, 'Well, I'll go congratulate the Guggenheims,'" Jeanne Vanderbilt recalled. "We knew them quite well. I went over to where they were sitting, but they had already left. I came back and sat down. Everyone was just stunned, absolutely shocked. It was almost incomprehensible. So close at the end! People started filtering by the box, saying how sorry they were. There was an aura of people trying to figure out how this could have happened."

Vanderbilt made it to the apron, where the jockeys were weighing out and heading to the jockeys' room to change for the next race. Vanderbilt spoke briefly to Guerin, trying to discern what had happened, and gave Al Popara a murderous stare. "If looks could have killed somebody, I would have been dead," Popara told Derby historian Jim Bolus years later. Money Broker had finished eighth, eleven lengths behind the winner, after bothering the Dancer on the first turn.

Lester Murray and Harold Walker took the Dancer from Guerin. They had watched the race from the apron, not far from the finish line, after leading the Dancer over from the barn and sending him out for the post parade. Murray sat on the ground, shank in hand, until the horses came around the far turn and headed down the stretch with the crowd roaring. Then he rose into a half-crouch and made a fist, his face flush as Dark Star held on.

"Did he get it?" the groom said, wheeling and asking Walker as the horses crossed the finish line.

"I don't think so," Walker said quietly.

Murray had been one of the stars of the week, regaling reporters with stories of the Grey Ghost. The big man with the old felt hat had become a familiar figure. Now, as Dark Star's handlers hollered and rejoiced, Murray snapped the shank on the beaten favorite. Walker led the horse back to the barn, with Murray bringing up the rear. The crowds that had surrounded them all week were suddenly gone. Murray would later swear the Dancer looked back as he walked away, seemingly confused that he wasn't getting to go to the winner's circle, where he had always gone after a race.

It was a day many would never forget, in countless ways, for countless reasons. So many Americans had never seen a major horse race, much less a Kentucky Derby, much less a Kentucky Derby with an undefeated grey favorite being hailed as the next Man O' War. And now the horse had lost as millions of fans watched, the defeat incomprehensible to many.

At the Louis Restaurant in Jamaica, a house full of customers turned away from the TV screen in disappointment. "My mother, father, two brothers, and myself, we were all rooting for Eric and Native Dancer," Costy Cavas recalled. "There was a lot of sadness when he didn't win."

Judy Ohl, the seventh grader in Mauch Chunk, Pennsylvania, was jumping up and down in her den and screaming as the horses came down the stretch. "It was devastating when he didn't win," Judy said. "I'll never forget the feeling. It seemed so unfair."

Lulu Vanderbilt, Alfred's niece, was in the crowd at the steeplechase race in Virginia when she heard the news. "They came on the loudspeaker and announced that Dark Star had won the Kentucky Derby," Lulu recalled. "I was so dumbfounded that I just sat down in a field. I was in complete shock. It was horrible. And I've talked to other people who had the same feeling that afternoon. That race just killed people."

Tim Capps burst into tears. Watching on his neighbor's TV as an eight-year-old in New Orleans, he couldn't comprehend the emotions he was feeling, but profoundly, they would lead to a career in racing. "It was kind of a riveting moment," Capps recalled. "I had no personal connection with the horse, but I was in love with him and I got so upset when he lost that I cried. After that, I started reading a lot more about horses and racing. I was on my way. Secretariat was the defining horse for later generations, but for people of my generation, it was Native Dancer. And for some reason, the image that always stands out is him losing the Derby. If you were born in the 1940s or thereabouts and follow racing, you'll never forget that day."

Ordinarily, the public is thrilled by such surprises, a champion toppling. It is human nature to root for those not expected to win, and to revel in their victories. The first half of the sports century had been littered with such moments, now burnished into the nation's memory. There was little-known Francis Ouimet's defeat of British stars Harry

Vardon and Ted Ray in the 1913 U.S. Open golf championship, the victory that turned golf into a spectator sport in America. There was the
only loss of Man O' War's career, to a colt named Upset in the 1919
Sanford Stakes. There was unbeaten Notre Dame, coached by Knute
Rockne, losing to Carnegie Tech in football in 1926. There was boxer
Jim Braddock, the Cinderella Man, struggling through the early
years of the Depression on welfare before upsetting Max Baer to win
the heavyweight championship in 1935. More recently, in 1951, baseball's New York Giants had rallied miraculously late in the season to
force a play-off with the Brooklyn Dodgers for the National League
pennant, then won the play-off on Bobby Thompson's ninth-inning
homer.

Dark Star's upset of Native Dancer was just as surprising, but it
didn't elicit the same, sweeping delight. To the contrary, where the
others had overjoyed, this depressed. "Thousands turned from their
TV screens in sorrow, a few in tears," *Time* magazine reported. *New
York Times* columnist Arthur Daley wrote, "This reporter was never
as emotionally affected by a horse race as [this one]. At the end he
felt heartbroken. Since he didn't have a pfennig bet on the outcome,
it had to be pure sentiment which moved him."

The weeping wasn't limited to press romantics. "I have never
had the defeat of any horse I did not raise myself depress me as much
as that of Native Dancer on Derby Day," wrote a Kentucky breeder
named Charles Kenney in a letter to Vanderbilt. "My wife, who is usually a stoic, burst into tears. I sure felt like joining her. [And] my reaction has been echoed by practically every man, woman and child in
the Blue Grass."

Kenney's letter was one of hundreds Vanderbilt received. Never,
safe to say, had a Derby defeat generated such emotion. "I don't believe I have ever felt so bad as the moment the Dancer lost the Derby.
I'm not ashamed that tears welled in my eyes," wrote a man from
Omaha, Nebraska. Bayard Sharp wrote, "I have never heard of so
many people who were genuinely sick" after a race.

Not everyone was "sick," of course. Those who had bet on Dark
Star and earned $51.80 for a two-dollar wager were not the least bit
sad. Neither were Harry Guggenheim, Eddie Hayward, and Henry

Moreno, Dark Star's owner, trainer, and jockey, all instantly earmarked for a place in Derby history as the purveyors of a monumental upset.

Across the country, though, there was far more sadness than elation. Why? For starters, the Dancer was enormously popular, so naturally, his defeat was disappointing. "He was just so good that you didn't want him to get beat," recalled Hall of Fame trainer Allen Jerkens, who watched the race on TV. Now he had lost, and the circumstances cast him as that most alluring of figures, the noble victim. He had faced two obstacles, many agreed, the bump on the first turn and a less-than-perfect ride from Guerin, yet had still come within a head of winning, his furious rally illustrating to a public already fond of him that, indeed, he possessed a champion's heart.

Outside of Dark Star's camp, there was the vague sense that racing's natural order had been violated, that a wrong had been committed, that the best horse not only had lost but also deserved better. Arthur Daley wrote that his sadness probably stemmed from "a bitter and brooding feeling that the best horse didn't win." Joe Tannenbaum concurred in the *Miami Daily News,* writing that Vanderbilt's colt "appeared to be the best horse in the Derby and certainly must still be rated as the potential champion of this year's three-year-old class." Momentously, even the *Daily Racing Form*'s chart caller, supposedly the most neutral man in the press box, wrote that Native Dancer was "probably best."

The postrace dissection centered on four topics: the bump, Guerin's ride, the Dancer's fitness, and Dark Star's undeniably fine performance, with the bump becoming a source of great controversy. Although Vanderbilt was gracious in Louisville after the race, the stare he gave Popara on the apron made it clear he believed Money Broker's jockey had intentionally impeded the Grey Ghost. He told the *Morning Telegraph* as much at Belmont two days later, commenting that Popara was guilty of "deliberately going and getting" the Dancer. The comment made headlines, and Vanderbilt quickly distanced himself from the issue and never again blamed Popara in public. But his inner sentiments had been revealed. "He did think Money

Broker and Popara were laying for him," Alfred Vanderbilt III said years later.

Guerin levied his own charge several days after the race, telling a United Press reporter, "I talked to Popara, and he told me his horse was lugging in and he couldn't hold him. But truthfully, I think he was lying. I don't think it was an accident."

Why would Popara have come after the favorite? Not because of some plot involving money changing hands in an attempt to orchestrate the finish. That surely happened from time to time, but in this case, it was ludicrous to suggest that a race-fixer wanting to knock off the Dancer would have identified an obscure jockey on a 45–1 shot as a willing, able, or effective accomplice.

On the other hand, it was entirely possible Popara could have "come after" the Grey Ghost as long shots often came after favorites in the early 1950s, or more accurately, as any jockey came after another in a major race. "In those days, everyone tried to get the favorite; get him out of the race," Dr. Alex Harthill said years later. "Popara certainly did that. Money Broker hit the Dancer really hard."

Eddie Arcaro seconded the idea several days after the race, suggesting that the incident, which had occurred behind him, was a typical event in a race ungoverned by the film patrol. "Sure, Popara knew what he was doing, and he did just what I would have done," Arcaro told the *Baltimore Sun*'s William Boniface. "When you are going after a big one like the Derby, you don't let any horse through the middle, especially a favorite like the Dancer. That's race riding."

A half century later, Shoemaker, who witnessed the incident, scoffed at the description of Popara's actions as "race riding"—a jockeys' term for doing what came naturally to try to win. "I suppose he thought he was race riding, but they shouldn't allow that sort of thing to go on. They don't today," Shoemaker said. "Popara didn't finish anywhere, but he caused a great horse that shouldn't have lost to get beat. If that was his idea of glory, that's too bad."

Popara vehemently denied the charge, telling the *Courier-Journal*'s Jerry McNerney several days after the race that "there was nothing intentional about the bumping." The jockey was holed up at a trailer park in Louisville, sitting out the ten-day suspension Churchill's stewards had handed him before the Derby. "I'm sorry Guerin feels the way he does," Popara said, "and I know how Guerin and Mr. Vanderbilt feel, losing the Derby by a head. I hated to see a great horse get beat."

He gave McNerney his version of what happened as he tried to pass the Dancer on the first turn. "I thought we were clear of him, but Money Broker suddenly changed stride and we bumped into him and I heard Guerin yell," he said. "It's entirely possible the bumping kept him from winning. But you know, when you have a string of wins, racing luck is bound to catch up with you."

Popara would live another forty-nine years, denying every day that he intentionally bumped the Dancer. In an interview with Bolus in 1978, he even denied bumping the favorite at all, saying he really just cut off the Dancer and forced Guerin to check the horse and take him outside. Guerin had unwittingly come close to confirming that version of the incident years earlier, when he told the United Press, "When Popara came in, he pushed me on the heels of the horses in front of me, which could have caused a terrible accident."

Whatever really happened, it was beyond the claws of review—aside from the absence of film patrol footage, no newsreel or TV camera had produced a clear-eyed view—and Churchill's stewards took no action against Popara, whom they had already sanctioned. "Everyone who saw the race is entitled to his or her opinion," said presiding steward Sam McMeekin, who otherwise refused comment.

The most infamous bump in Derby history eventually took on a life of its own, swelling to mythological proportions and stirring an unceasing debate. New York newspaper columnist Jimmy Breslin wrote years later that the Dancer "was nearly knocked down" and that "nobody who saw the race believes it was accidental." Bolus interviewed Vanderbilt in 1978 and reported that the owner said "a blind man could see" that the bump cost the Dancer the race. Annoyed by these depictions, which he saw as inaccurate, *Louisville Times* sports editor Dean Eagle wrote in a responding column that, in fact, the bump was "mild," few in the crowd saw it, and no one believed it was intentional. A consensus opinion still hadn't formed a half century after the race, and likely never would. "Louis [Cheri] just told me that everyone was on their feet, and there was a gasp because they knew something happened, but no one could say precisely what," Alfred Vanderbilt III said.

Did it cost the Dancer the race? Again, there is no consensus opinion. The Grey Ghost was certainly thrown off stride and pushed closer to the rear than Guerin wanted. "I saw it as it happened, and there was no doubt, he was impeded; Money Broker did him pretty good," Joe Tannenbaum said fifty years later. Yet there was still almost a mile left in the race, and the Dancer rallied to within two lengths of the lead by the top of the stretch, so there was time to win. "The bump was a long way from home," Allen Jerkens said. "Things like that happen in the Derby every year—even worse."

There is more of a consensus regarding the bump's effect on Guerin, who made several debatable decisions in its wake. "It probably shook Guerin up more than the horse," Vanderbilt told Bolus in 1978. Indeed, numerous criticisms of the jockey's performance slowly rose to the surface over time, with various rivals and observers second-guessing him for (a) holding the Dancer back in the first quarter mile, (b) asking for trouble on the first turn by getting caught in a pack, (c) racing up the backstretch too hurriedly, leaving little gas in the Dancer's tank for the homestretch, (d) moving down to the rail, from where the Dancer seldom charged, on the second turn, (e) holding the Dancer back yet again at the top of the stretch, postponing his final charge until it was too late, (f) getting caught behind Dark Star in the stretch, forcing him to move off the rail as he rallied, and (g) in general, giving the colt a ride consisting of so many stops and starts and ins and outs that, as one steward reportedly later said, "He took that horse everywhere on the track but to the ladies' room."

Ralph Kercheval told Bill Christine of the *Los Angeles Times* in 1989 that Guerin "panicked" after the bump. Moreno, the winning jockey, told the Knight-Ridder News Service in 1982 that Guerin "had to ease the horse up four or five different times—that was his mistake. Horses have only so many runs in them, but Guerin rode him like 'I can do anything I want.'"

Vanderbilt died in 1997 without addressing the issue publicly, but Alfred Vanderbilt III said, "I asked my father straight up about the ride one time, and he said it probably wasn't the best ride Eric Guerin ever gave him. But that was as far as he'd ever go. He didn't say it was a bad ride. He just said, 'It probably wasn't the best ride he'd ever given [the horse].' Which was very fair."

Bill Winfrey also never addressed the issue publicly, but his son Carey said years later, "My father once said to me that he felt that Native Dancer probably raced thirty or forty yards farther than any other horse in the race, which was a huge number of yards. He never said it publicly. He also admitted to me that he felt Eric moved too late in the stretch. He didn't know why he hung back. He felt that there was bad racing luck involved, that Eric gave him a bad ride and that's why he didn't win."

Years later, Guerin's own first cousin Charles Ray Leblanc was critical of Guerin's ride. "I might not oughta say this, but it was my opinion Eric rode a bad race," Leblanc said. "There were some bad judgments he made; some of the few bad judgments he made in his career. He kept trying to take the horse back in the beginning and wound up getting in trouble. He should have just let the horse run. Then when he got in trouble, I think it riled him a little bit. It's just my opinion, but he never should have got beat."

Tannenbaum said years later, "Guerin was one of the finest riders of his day, but everyone in any sport has temporary lapses. No matter how much of a pro Guerin was, and he was the consummate pro, it was still the Derby. He may have been tense. Instead of taking the horse to the outside on the second turn, he went to the rail to save ground. Maybe he was trying to save the horse after that furious run up the backside, but he should have gone to the outside and let the horse run, as he'd done in his other races."

Jerkens took a kinder view, focusing only on Guerin's failure to gain ground in the first half of the stretch, and dismissing his delayed rally as understandable. "Guerin was such a good rider and had so much confidence in the horse that he knew he could make up two lengths in a quarter mile," Jerkens said. "He had won a lot of races from a lot farther back than he was. It was incredible that he didn't make up those two lengths. What happened was the other horse kept going, and they just missed. This happens in racing."

Strangely, there was little discussion of any of this immediately after the race. In the jockeys' room, Guerin spoke mostly about the bump and told reporters the Dancer wasn't himself. "He wasn't running as well in the stretch as he was in his New York races; it may have been that he didn't like the track," the jockey said. Arthur Daley wrote that the jockey "bore a stunned and disbelieving look" and "was on his way home for a good cry." But Daley's postmortem column also offered unattributed second-guessing from a "veteran horseman" questioning Guerin for holding the Dancer back in the beginning. There was "talk," Daley wrote, "that Guerin had given the horse a slightly less than perfect ride." Things worsened from there.

Guerin would ride for another two decades, retiring after a thirty-five-year career that included 20,131 mounts, 2,712 wins, and election to the National Museum of Racing's Hall of Fame. But "because people never forget a mistake," he said years later, he was remembered mostly for losing the Derby. "Anytime anyone interviews me, it's the first question they ask: 'What happened in the Derby?'" he told the *Daily Racing Form* in 1975. He handled the criticism with class, never publicly lashing back, although he did tell the *Form* he "got a little tired of hearing about it." When he went into the Louisiana Sports Hall of Fame in 1992, he chose Popara, of all people, to introduce him at the ceremony. Guerin had long ago patched up his differences with Money Broker's jockey, who had settled in New Orleans. "They were best buddies, sitting there joking at the induction ceremony; it was water under the bridge," said Guerin's nephew, Frank Curry, who traveled with Guerin to the ceremony.

But though he was able to joke about it, Guerin never consented to the notion that his ride had cost the Dancer the Derby. He remained true to his original assessment, offered immediately after the race, that the Grey Ghost wasn't himself that day. "If he had been running his race in the first part of it, he wouldn't have been that far back; Money Broker should never have been in front of him," he told Jim Bolus in 1968. Later that year, he told Peter Finney of the *New Orleans Times* that the colt's pre-Derby training affected him adversely in the race, that he was sluggish in the early going because he had been forced to run far behind Social Outcast in their one-mile "trial" three days before the race. "He never loafed out of the gate like he did in the Derby; I couldn't get him going," Guerin said. "He was just doing the same thing he had done in that trial."

Attempts to blame a horse often sit poorly with horsemen. "Eric was not too kind after the race," Dan W. Scott said. "Every jock wants to assume it's someone else's fault or the horse's fault or he got bumped or some other jock did wrong. He said Native Dancer just wasn't himself that day. But Native Dancer was practically running over horses in the last quarter. Bill Winfrey said he had never seen a horse close that much ground as fast as he did."

History has generally dismissed Guerin's notion that the Dancer lost because he "wasn't himself." To the contrary, many believe the Dancer's greatness was, in fact, indelibly confirmed that day. His furious finish certainly laid to rest the idea—much discussed to that point—that he would have trouble racing at longer distances because Polynesian was his sire. Given the obstacles he faced, his near victory was quite a performance. Asked years later by the *Blood-Horse* to name the horse's best races, Winfrey put the Derby on the list. "Only a superhorse could have finished with the drive that he did after the trip that he had," Tannenbaum said.

"Native Dancer ran magnificently," Evan Shipman wrote in a *Morning Telegraph* column several days after the race. "Never during the two seasons that Vanderbilt's great grey has charmed and impressed the racing public has he run better, or as well. Don't let his defeat blind you to his true accomplishment, because it was remarkable, disposing once and for all the legend that he could not 'go a distance,' and attesting, as never before, to his admirable speed and courage."

Yet in Guerin's defense, there is also evidence supporting the idea that the horse wasn't at his best. Winfrey said in a 1989 interview with racing journalist Eva Jolene Boyd that he felt he didn't have the Dancer ready for the Derby, and while Carey Winfrey wonders whether his father should be believed—according to Carey, his father had suffered a series of mini-strokes, possibly clouding his memory—it is possible the Dancer wasn't in peak condition.

The other ten horses in the race had made between four and ten starts in 1953 before the Derby, but the Dancer had only raced twice, his season set back by the firing of his ankles. One of his races had been canceled and replaced by a trial, and his last workout before the Derby had also been replaced by a trial. In addition, he had apparently gotten knocked around when his train lurched to a halt on the way to Louisville, and according to Harthill, was treated with electrolytes passed through a stomach tube during Derby week. Weighing all these factors in hindsight is impossible, but the fact that the Dancer's form improved dramatically as the 1953 season progressed suggests that, as impressive as he was in the Derby, he might have fared better with more seasoning. Winfrey was a master, and the Dancer was in shape to run that day, but maybe he wasn't in peak shape.

"My own opinion, I think he had a little ankle trouble that day," Jerkens said. "His ankles had been fired and I think the track stung him. He might not have been at his very best that day."

Alfred Vanderbilt III said, "After a number of years of thinking about it, I think my father believed that a number of factors were responsible for the defeat, aside from the ride and Money Broker laying for him. I think he felt that the stars were just in the wrong constellation, that the horse wasn't quite as ready as he could have been, that he didn't run as well as he might have run, and it was all those things."

No one mistakes what happened. "The best horse got beat," Moreno, the winning jockey, told Bolus in 1978. But the best horse that day? Maybe, just maybe, it wasn't the favorite. Lost in the tumultuous debate about Money Broker, the bump, and Guerin's ride was the fact that the winner raced brilliantly and Moreno rode him superbly; that no matter why or how the Dancer was done in, Harry Guggenheim's unknown, underdog colt deserved to win.

In a wicked irony, Moreno won precisely as Guerin had won in 1947 on Jet Pilot: by taking the lead early and controlling the pace from the front. While the rest of the field was focused on Arcaro, waiting for the Master to move on Correspondent, Moreno raced just speedily enough to tire out those lacking the necessary stamina, yet just slowly enough to guarantee that his horse had enough left to hold off the Dancer down the stretch. Dark Star ran the final quarter mile in 25% seconds, two seconds faster than Citation. That strong finish enabled him to hold off the Grey Ghost's final burst. "Moreno rode a wonderful race," Arcaro said days later. "I say that because of the way he judged the pace just right."

Hayward had instructed Moreno to lay third or fourth, watch Native Dancer up the backstretch, and make a move in the final quarter, but the jockey tore up that blueprint and used his own after taking the lead as he raced past the stands the first time. He was emboldened, he told the Knight-Ridder News Service years later, when Guggenheim grabbed his boot after his prerace conversation with Hayward and said, "Listen, you do what you think is best." He heard that as a mandate to be more aggressive than Hayward had intended.

Equally important was Moreno's decision to move to the rail down the stretch. Dark Star had raced beyond a mile only once and was beginning to drift wide after turning for home. Knowing the Dancer was on the rail with a clear path to the finish, Moreno swerved back to the inside, forcing Guerin to swerve off the rail in midstretch. The ground that this cost the Dancer probably decided the race. The *Daily Racing Form* chart caller noted that Dark Star was "alertly ridden" and "won with little left"—testimony to a job well done.

Moreno was kissed several times by movie actress Marilyn Maxwell on the victory stand after the race—photographers made her keep kissing until they all got a shot of it—and asked a valet to bring him a cigarette as soon as he arrived in the jockeys' room. "I thought I had a wonderful chance all along," the jockey told reporters. "As I was going out onto the track, I got the feeling I was going to win."

Arcaro's voice was the loudest in the jockeys' room even though Correspondent had disappointed as the second choice at 2–1 odds. The Master, who had criticized the "building up" of Native Dancer before the race and then been criticized for voicing that criticism, was almost gleeful. "Well, you Native Dancer guys, wasn't I right?" he shouted to reporters. "I said he was only a fair horse and that the only thing he'd beaten was Tahitian King. If you call that a great thoroughbred, well, I don't." Continuing later with a smile, the Master said, "You just can't call a horse Citation or Man O' War until they've done what those horses did."

Guggenheim and Hayward joined Moreno in the jubilant winner's circle, where the Derby cup and a garland of roses were presented. The trainer admitted to reporters that Moreno had ignored his conservative instructions but that Dark Star "had gone to the front so handily that the boy used his own judgment and let him go. A boy has to know those things. I can't tell him. He's on his own out there."

As security guards led the owner and trainer back across the track and into the grandstand, heading for a reception for the Derby horse owners and dignitaries in Churchill president Bill Corum's office, a fan reached out and clapped Hayward on the back.

"You did it, Eddie, you did it," the fan shouted.

The low-key trainer cracked a smile. "Yeah," he said, "I guess I did."

Arriving at the crowded reception, Guggenheim immediately ran into Vanderbilt, hailed the next day by the *Courier-Journal* as "by all rights the most disappointed man at Churchill Downs." Vanderbilt had lingered briefly on the apron and then headed upstairs to the reception. He was among the first arrivals. When Guggenheim arrived minutes later, Vanderbilt stuck his hand out with a smile and said gamely, "If it had to be anybody, Harry, I'm glad it was you." Guggenheim was, after all, a family friend from Long Island and spent part of every summer with Alfred's mother at Sagamore Lodge.

"Alfred regarded Harry as one of the pillars of the racing establishment and a person of the same high standards," Clyde Roche said. "The fact that it was Harry was the reason Alfred could accept the defeat with equanimity. If it had been anyone else, I don't know."

As the two pillars of the American aristocracy shook hands, Joe Tannenbaum, the rookie Derby writer, was back at Barn 16, sniffing for scenes to include in his story. Guerin, too, was back at the barn, having showered and dressed after speaking to reporters. "I wished I'd been a photographer," Tannenbaum recalled. "Guerin was in the stall with the Dancer, talking to him. It was quite a touching scene. I wrote it. Guerin was saying, in effect, how sorry he was that the horse had lost. How very, very sorry he was."

# SIXTEEN

T he Dancer was shipped by train back to New York, with Winfrey and his wife riding up front in an overnight berth and Lester Murray caring for the horse in a special car attached to the rear. There were no famous newspaper columnists on board, as there had been on the trip down. No crowds gathered at a switching yard just to get a glimpse of the famous—and now once-beaten—grey. Only a few photographers were at Belmont to record the horse's return. But as a stew of unpleasant memories simmered, Winfrey was resolutely positive. "I have more confidence in the horse than ever," he told reporters after the Dancer was back in his stall at Barn 20 early Monday evening. What about the controversy regarding the bump and Guerin's ride? "We offer no excuse for the Derby defeat and feel he doesn't need one," the trainer said. "And I don't care to look back."

Such was the tone quickly established around the horse. Unmistakably, it came from the top. The Dancer's Derby loss would haunt Vanderbilt for the rest of his life, but other than the one slip when he accused Popara of "deliberately going and getting" his horse, he accepted his fate. "Alfred took it well," Jeanne Vanderbilt recalled. "We got on a plane and went back to New York. He was very controlled. He didn't show anything except, 'Too bad, what bad luck.' Then it was, 'Okay, let's get up and go to the barn and start all over again.'"

In a movie, the horsemen in Barn 20 would have determinedly set out to exact revenge for the Grey Ghost as inspiring music blared. But this was reality, and the men weren't neophytes who might yield to such a pitch of emotions. They were racetrack veterans hardened to the disappointment that was a constant in their sport, and they just kept getting up and coming to work, following Vanderbilt's lead. "Losing the Derby was devastating, but was my father the type to come out of it more determined? No, he was more along the lines of, 'It was a horse race. There's another next week,'" Alfred Vanderbilt III said.

The Dancer's next major race was in three weeks, actually. It was the Preakness, the second jewel of the Triple Crown, held at Pimlico, in Baltimore. Vanderbilt had once said, years earlier, that it was a race he wanted to win more than the Derby, a reflection of his many connections to the event. Baltimore was where Vanderbilt's grandfather Isaac Emerson had amassed a vast fortune, and where Vanderbilt had spent many childhood vacations and first fallen in love with racing at age ten. Later, he had managed Pimlico and served as the track's president and majority stockholder and had just recently sold his stock. And, of course, Sagamore Farm, just north of the city, was where the Dancer would retire to stud; Vanderbilt had already made that announcement, thrilling Maryland's horse clientele. "Even though Vanderbilt lived in New York, whenever I ran into him on the road, he would say, 'How are things at home?'" recalled the *Baltimore Sun*'s William Boniface.

As with the Derby, Vanderbilt had left nary a mark on the Preakness over the years, finishing third with Discovery in 1934 and fourth with Impound in 1939, and otherwise sitting the race out. Though his priorities had changed—the Derby was now the race he most wanted to win—his ties to the area remained strong, and there was no doubting his motivation, especially after the Derby.

The Preakness had been held either one or two weeks after the Derby since the end of World War II, but the Maryland Jockey Club had pushed the wait back to three weeks in 1953. Winfrey was grateful. Many of the reporters who had hung around Barn 20 all spring disappeared, their attention shifted to Rocky Marciano's heavyweight title defense against Jersey Joe Walcott, which Marciano won with a

first-round knockout. Winfrey had time to train the Dancer more purposefully than before the Derby, when things had seemed so rushed.
He put the horse through several shorter works designed to add
speed, and the Dancer responded, gaining a sharpness that hadn't existed in Louisville.

The only drawback to the long interval was that it was a little *too*
long. Winfrey didn't want the Dancer to go three weeks without racing, so he entered the horse in the Withers, a one-mile landmark on
New York's racing calendar, first held in 1874. Man O' War and Count
Fleet were among the horses that had won the event, which was
scheduled now for Belmont on May 15, two weeks after the Derby
and one week before the Preakness, fitting neatly into the Dancer's
schedule.

The announcement that the Grey Ghost would run in the Withers scared away most of the opposition. Only three other horses were
entered: Social Outcast, who had run seventh in the Derby; Invigorator, who had finished third in the Derby; and a long shot named Real
Brother. Then Winfrey and Vanderbilt scratched Social Outcast because of rain late in the week, leaving the Dancer with just two opponents. Chuck Connors of the *Morning Telegraph* warned that the race
had been reduced "to the quality of a soggy pretzel at a brewmaster's
picnic," but the public didn't mind. More than 38,000 fans came to Belmont to see the Dancer's first race since the Derby, and millions
watched on NBC.

It was the Dancer's fourth national TV appearance in twenty-
eight days, and the impact of the publicity was beginning to sink in.
"Perhaps nowhere in America is the miracle of TV more appreciated
than here on the West Coast," wrote Oscar Otis, the *Morning Telegraph*'s California correspondent, "for in this somewhat isolated [re-
gion] racing fans are avidly tuning in not only the Triple Crown
classics but also the Gillette series of races from New York on Saturdays. The latter is easily one of the most popular programs on the air."
The Dancer was becoming "the horse in the living room."

Belmont officials limited wagering on the Withers to win bets,
and all but $27,168 of the $154,909 pushed through the windows was
put on the Grey Ghost. He was sent to the post at odds of 1–20, the

legal minimum. "Those odds were staggering, quite a statement from the public about what it thought of the Derby," recalled the *Baltimore Sun*'s William Boniface. "That 1–20 wasn't just coming from all the women who said, 'Oooh, look at the pretty grey.' Dyed-in-the-wool horsemen were betting on him, too. And 1–20 said people really had dismissed the loss to racing luck."

Vanderbilt, Winfrey, and Guerin met in the paddock before the race. The Big Apple railbirds who had lost money on the Dancer in the Derby shouted wickedly at Guerin, whose ride was still being debated. Riders of other famous horses had occasionally lost their mount in such circumstances, but if Vanderbilt contemplated taking Guerin off the Dancer, he never admitted it publicly. "I wasn't there," Carey Winfrey said years later, "but I would suspect that Eric felt terrible, and Alfred and my father said, 'Don't be silly,' trying to make him feel better."

The Dancer looked resplendent in the paddock, although some horsemen noted that his "off " ankle appeared even larger than usual. Winfrey insisted again that the ankle was not a problem, explaining that a compound he was using on the ankle had bleached the skin white, merely making it more noticeable, not more troublesome. Anyone doubting that explanation was likely convinced by the Withers, in which the Dancer gave no indication that he was troubled by a sore ankle, his loss in the Derby, his trip to Louisville—or anything.

He was anxious to run, frisky through the post parade, and his hurried first step out of the gate resulted in a stumble. Real Brother shot into a clear lead along the rail, with Invigorator trailing and the Dancer in third after a quick recovery. They held their positions up the backstretch, with Real Brother two lengths in front and the Dancer just behind and to the outside of Invigorator. When Invigorator was sent toward the lead on the turn, Guerin loosened his grip and let the Grey Ghost run.

The three horses were virtually even as they came out of the turn and headed into the stretch. By the eighth pole, the Dancer and Invigorator had pulled away from Real Brother, but not from each other. Guerin refrained from using his stick, merely waving it in front of the Dancer at the sixteenth pole. The colt responded immediately and dramatically, surging two lengths ahead, then three. Guerin's gesture and the horse's response occurred right in front of the grandstand, and the crowd roared as the Grey Ghost thundered toward the finish, covering those famed twenty-nine feet with every stride. He was four lengths ahead at the wire.

Although the merits of a victory in a three-horse race are debatable, there was no doubting the quality of the performance. The Dancer's time of 1:36⅕ for a mile wasn't eye-popping, but his finish had been devastating, and the horse he pulled away from had finished third in the Kentucky Derby. "What a pleasure it is to watch a really good thoroughbred!" Evan Shipman wrote in the *Morning Telegraph*. "So sure is the Dancer's attack, so deadly in execution. The decision, when it comes, is a matter of a few strides at the most."

As he waited to receive a trophy in the winner's enclosure, Vanderbilt told reporters the Dancer would train lightly at Belmont on Monday and van down to Pimlico on Tuesday, arriving four days before the Preakness. Six other horses were set to run against him in Baltimore, including Dark Star, the surprising Derby winner; Royal Bay Gem, the stretch-running colt who had finished fourth in the Derby; Correspondent, the colt who had stalled badly in the Derby stretch after going to the post as the second betting choice; and Tahitian King. Filling out the field were Ram o' War, who had run ninth in the Derby and was owned by a Baltimore businessman; and a rangy bay colt named Jamie K., winner of just three of nineteen career starts.

Much had transpired on the Triple Crown trail since the Derby. In a stunning move, Correspondent's trainer, Wally Dunn, had changed jockeys, replacing the peerless Arcaro with Bob Summers, Correspondent's California jockey, who had never ridden in the Preakness. Evidently, Dunn wasn't happy with Arcaro's Derby ride and was turning to a jockey more familiar with the colt. Arcaro, a four-time Preakness winner, picked up the mount on Jamie K., who had recently won two allowance races in New York and, despite his poor overall record, appeared to be improving. "He might be able to beat Correspondent," Arcaro told the *Baltimore Sun*.

Five days before the Preakness, Dark Star, Royal Bay Gem, and

Correspondent—with Summers riding him—went to the post at Pimlico in the Preakness Prep, a one-mile event often used by Preakness horses as a tune-up. It was Dark Star's first race since the Derby, and he swaggered in the post parade with his ears pricked as the crowd cheered the only horse to beat Native Dancer. He was the favorite, carrying four more pounds than the other two Triple Crown horses and also Ram o' War and a pair of long shots, Country Gossip and Lord Jeffrey.

The race was a surprise, run far differently than expected. After two straight front-running victories in Kentucky, Dark Star was out-footed to the lead by Country Gossip and Lord Jeffrey as jockey Henry Moreno settled the brown colt in third going around the turn. Jimmy Combest, Royal Bay Gem's jockey, also tried a new tactic, keeping his colt closer to the lead in the early going. When Country Gossip and Lord Jeffrey predictably faltered, Dark Star, Royal Bay Gem, and Correspondent went to the front, running evenly as they turned for home. The crowd expected Dark Star to pull away, but Moreno went easy on the colt through the stretch instead of pushing him to go faster, and Royal Bay Gem nosed in front and stayed there, hitting the finish line three-quarters of a length ahead of the Derby winner. Ram o' War was third, Correspondent fourth.

To Native Dancer's legion of supporters, the surprising finish underlined the notion that Dark Star's Derby victory had been a fluke ordained by racing luck. "Native Dancer lies over anything this generation of three-year-olds has to offer, and as long as he remains racing sound, we are certain he will continue to dominate the division," *Morning Telegraph* columnist Evan Shipman wrote. "We're expecting the grey to win the Preakness with the same authority he showed in the Withers."

Dark Star's supporters argued that it was silly to ascribe any meaning to the results of the Preakness Prep, because Moreno hadn't gone to the whip in the stretch, obviously preferring to save the colt's best effort for his rematch with the Dancer in the Preakness. Either way, Charles Hatton of the *Morning Telegraph* wrote that the Preakness, "one of the most interesting in memory," would settle the argument.

The Grey Ghost arrived at Pimlico Tuesday afternoon, greeted by the usual hordes of newsmen and curious horsemen. Still known as Old Hilltop even though Vanderbilt had razed its infield hill in the 1930s, Maryland's premier track was struggling through the postwar racing boom, with crowds and betting down. But Preakness week was always a high time regardless of Pimlico's circumstances; with the nation's top three-year-olds on the grounds, the anticipation of Saturday's crowd, and spring blooming on the Chesapeake Bay, the track's humdrum daily existence was forgotten, however briefly.

The local sports public was in an expansive mood. Baltimore, a gritty port city that had long languished in the shadow of nearby Washington, D.C., was bustling with growth and optimism. A new, image-enhancing airport had opened, and a modern sports stadium had already lured a National Football League franchise, the Colts, to town, with major league baseball also reportedly on the way back after a fifty-year hiatus. (The St. Louis Browns would morph into the Baltimore Orioles by the end of the year.) The Dancer was claimed as a native son coming home, even though he had been foaled in Kentucky and raced out of New York. "The grey colt is a tremendous favorite with Marylanders," the *Baltimore Sun*'s Snowden Carter wrote, "not only because of his ability and the hard luck he encountered during the rough-run Derby, but because he will be retired to Sagamore Farm."

The colt made his first appearance on the racing strip Wednesday morning, galloping twice around a track left muddy from overnight rains. The trainers of several other Preakness horses were also out. "Look at that big horse! There oughta be a law making a horse like that give weight to my little one," said Clyde Troutt, the trainer of Royal Bay Gem, within earshot of an Associated Press reporter.

Troutt was still shaking his head about the Derby. "It was a shame for a horse like that to be beaten—just one of those unlucky breaks," the trainer said. "But he looks fitter now than at the Derby. He appeared a little drawn in Louisville."

Shortly after the Dancer's arrival, Jamie K.'s trainer, John Partridge, led his colt onto the track for the first time. Eddie Hayward, the trainer of Dark Star, called out to Partridge, "Hey, John, the grey horse is out."

"You mean his horse [Jamie K.] might get an inferiority complex?" a reporter asked.

"Sure—I got my horse on and off for that reason," Hayward said with a smile.

A thick fog hung over the track Thursday morning as the Dancer and Jamie K. went through their final workouts before Saturday's race. The Dancer covered six furlongs in 1:11⅗, an impressive time, especially with Bernie Everson never asking him to exert himself. As the colt was leaving the track, Jamie K. was just finishing a five-furlong work in 1:01⅖—not bad, either. The colt Arcaro would ride in the Preakness was a long shot, but he was tall and light-waisted and had recently exhibited a strong finishing kick; Partridge had figured out that he gave his best effort when allowed to settle gradually out of the starting gate. Teamed with Arcaro, who could provide the subtle handling required, Jamie K. might be a threat.

More rain soaked the city Thursday, but the clouds gave way to sunshine by Saturday. Although the forecast still included the possibility of rain, the Preakness, like the Derby, would be run in fine weather, on a perfect track. Winfrey arrived at the barn early and hopped on a chestnut stable horse to oversee the Dancer's morning exercise. Lester Murray removed the heavy cotton "standing bandage" from each of the colt's legs and put on lighter elastic wrappings for the gallop. Everson took him out and jogged him around the oval, asking for a harder run over the final fifty yards. The colt was then returned to the barn, and his wrappings changed again.

"How did he feel?" a reporter asked Everson.

"Real nice," the exercise rider replied.

Baltimoreans had many options to choose from in deciding what to do that Saturday. They could take in a movie, choosing among such films as *Titanic,* starring Clifton Webb and Barbara Stanwyck, and *Moulin Rouge,* starring José Ferrer. They could take a car trip to the Eastern Shore, crossing the Chesapeake Bay on the glistening Bay Bridge, which had opened the year before. They could go for a swim at Carlin's amusement park, eat a club steak for fifty-one cents at the

Oriole Cafeteria, dance to the music of Lou Mellon and his orchestra, or stay home and watch CBS's telecast of the Preakness, with Bryan Field calling the race and Red Smith, the newspaper columnist, handling the interviews.

Sunny weather and the Dancer lured more than 30,000 to Pimlico, the crowd filling the grandstand and spilling over into the infield. Politicians and lions of society mingled in the Old Clubhouse, with the dignitaries including J. Edgar Hoover, four members of President Eisenhower's cabinet, and numerous senators and congressman such as the infamous Senator Joe McCarthy of Wisconsin, who refused to pose for photographers.

The gates to the track opened at 11 A.M., and long lines formed at the betting windows before the first race at 2 P.M. After the race, the Preakness band, dressed in red coats, white caps, and blue trousers, paraded through the stretch playing a Sousa march, with five police horses high-stepping in front. The band settled in the infield and spent the afternoon playing "Dixie," Gene Autry's "Boots and Saddles," and other songs traditionally heard on race day. Favorites dominated the early races, and the betting was heated. Even though the crowd was far smaller than the record Preakness crowd of 42,000, it would wager, by the end of the day, almost $2.28 million, the most in Maryland history for a single day of racing.

The Dancer was listed in the program as a 4–5 choice, but he was 1–9 when Pimlico's new tote board blinked on before the Preakness, with Dark Star next at 2–1 and the rest of the field in double digits. The support for the Dancer would continue right up until post time: almost $700,000 was bet on the race, shattering by more than $200,000 the prior record for wagering on a single race in Maryland, and remarkably, 78 percent was on the Dancer. Surprisingly, Dark Star wasn't even the second choice, going to the post at odds of 11.3–1, slightly behind Royal Bay Gem at 11.2–1. So much was wagered on the Dancer that the tote board ran out of room to reflect the totals. In the eyes of the public, the colt was virtually a lock to win.

Guerin admitted later that the Derby was still haunting him, and he felt a sizable burden. The Dancer couldn't lose again with the public so clearly announcing it believed Dark Star's victory had been a fluke. The Grey Ghost had to win the Preakness, and for that to happen, Guerin had to furnish a smart ride over the race's mile and three-sixteenths—a sixteenth shorter than the Derby. He was operating with no margin for error.

Winfrey mentioned none of that in the paddock before the race. He had watched Guerin win dozens of races, large and small, and he still had confidence in Vanderbilt's contract jockey. The trainer pointedly offered no instructions as he helped Guerin up and onto the horse's back. Vanderbilt remained quiet as well. This was no time to imply that the jockey needed help.

Cheers rippled through the crowd as Guerin and the Dancer promenaded past the grandstand in the post parade. The band played "Maryland, My Maryland," and last-minute gamblers fought at the windows to get their bets down. Seldom had any racing crowd's allegiance been so clearly stated.

At 5:46 P.M., Eddie Blind, Pimlico's starter, pushed the button that opened the starting gate, and out came the seven horses to a roar from the crowd. Tahitian King jumped into the lead from the far outside post, with Dark Star close behind, then Correspondent and the Dancer. The first furlongs were a sprint, with Tahitian King covering the first quarter mile in 22⅘ seconds, but Guerin kept the Dancer near the front. He was determined to stay closer to the leaders than in the Derby, and not let Dark Star, in particular, get away again.

It quickly became clear that Moreno was employing the same strategy he had used in Louisville: take the lead early, control the pace from the front, and dare the field to catch him. He moved Dark Star past Tahitian King and into the lead as they cleared the first turn and headed up the backstretch. Tahitian King held on to second, with the Dancer close behind, running easily and near the rail, in perfect position to strike. Correspondent was close behind, in fourth, and Royal Bay Gem and Jamie K. were much farther to the rear.

The horses held their positions up the backstretch and into the second turn, where Royal Bay Gem and Jamie K. began to move up and Correspondent abruptly faded; he would finish last, more than twenty lengths behind the winner, and never again display the form that had helped make him the second betting choice in the Derby.

Tahitian King also gave way on the turn, lacking the necessary stamina. Royal Bay Gem, the second betting choice, was caught in a familiar trap: he had again raced too far to the rear and now had too much ground to make up. He would finish third, no factor in the stretch.

Dark Star's lead over Tahitian King was a length and a half after three-quarters of a mile. The Derby winner was in control of the Preakness as he moved through the second turn. When Guerin began creeping the Dancer closer, jockey Hedley Woodhouse swung Tahitian King wide and tried to block the onrushing grey colt, but Guerin avoided the roadblock and maneuvered into second coming out of the turn, a length behind Dark Star. Suddenly, the Preakness crystallized as a replay of the Derby. The Dancer was chasing Dark Star down the stretch. The public inhaled. Moreno, in a reprise of his brilliant Derby ride, had taken the lead with an early burst and seemingly slowed the pace just enough to leave Dark Star with a finishing kick. He would again be difficult to catch.

The two horses veered into the straightaway, the finish line looming in the distance, three-sixteenths of a mile away. Then, stunningly, just as the Dancer engaged him in a duel, Dark Star faltered. The Dancer gained ground with one stride, more ground with another stride, then nosed into the lead. Moreno whipped his colt mercilessly, trying to restart the engine, but it had no impact. Dark Star was fading. He had nothing left. "He was going along nice and easy, and boom, just like that, he stopped," Moreno said later.

The crowd roared as the Grey Ghost passed his nemesis and surged into the lead. There was, for an instant, a swatch of daylight between him and the field. It was his stretch, his race, his triumph in the offing. But then another horse, a bay, made a move behind him and began to close. Instead of pulling away as Dark Star faded, the Dancer was confronted with a new challenge. The fans strained to see the jockey's silks, or the number on the horse's saddlecloth. Who was this late-running challenger? A heartbeat passed, and then a gasp went up.

It was Arcaro!

The Master, on Jamie K., had raced easily for a mile, settling his colt's nerves as he lagged behind Royal Bay Gem. The two horses brought up the rear through the first turn, up the backstretch, and into the second turn, and no one was watching as Arcaro passed the flagging Correspondent and Tahitian King in the middle of the pack and surged beyond the Gem as well. Now, seemingly out of nowhere, Jamie K. was making a run at the Dancer.

In two strides, Arcaro was within a head of the Grey Ghost, racing just to the outside of the favorite as they passed the eighth pole. The subtext was delicious. Arcaro had complained all spring about the Dancer receiving too much acclaim, and now he was challenging the colt in the stretch run of the Preakness, seeking to upset the odds-on favorite with a 17–1 shot. A victory would do even more harm to the Dancer's standing than Dark Star's Derby surprise. Arcaro pounded Jamie K.'s flanks as they came down the stretch, and Guerin, detecting the challenge, took up his stick and pounded the Dancer, too. The situation was dangerous. The Dancer was running hard, but not too hard; his maddening habit of loafing on the lead could cost him this time with Arcaro coming after him.

The two horses ran together in the slanting late afternoon sun, casting a pair of long shadows that melded into one as they covered the final furlong. The crowd's shriek was mirrored in living rooms across the country as a TV audience later estimated at 10 million watched the Dancer try to hang on. Guerin put his stick down, then took it up again as Arcaro continued to urge Jamie K. for more. The Dancer maintained the slimmest of leads, Jamie K. pressuring him but not drawing even as the finish line neared. Arcaro needed to make up precious inches, the final fractions of the Dancer's lead.

Jamie K. kept coming . . . and failed to draw even.

Took another jump . . . and remained just behind the Dancer.

Frozen in position, running together, yet separated by inches, they reached the finish line.

The Dancer had held on.

Guerin and Arcaro stood up just past the wire, signaling to their horses that the serious running was done. Jamie K. kept digging until he nosed past Native Dancer heading into the turn. Some observers would refer to that when the two met again in the Belmont Stakes three weeks later, believing Jamie K. would have completed the upset and won the Preakness with a few extra strides. Other observers disagreed. "I thought at the time that it was Guerin's supreme confidence that made the Preakness close," recalled Joe Tannenbaum, who covered the race for the *Miami Daily News*. "Guerin didn't seem to put Native Dancer to a furious drive until maybe midstretch. Otherwise his victory may have been a little more decisive."

Decisive it wasn't—but a victory it was, and an immensely popular one. The crowd stood and cheered as the grey colt was ridden back in front of the grandstand, where Lester Murray snapped the shank on him and Harold Walker led him toward the winner's enclosure. Vanderbilt led a joyous rush to the winner's circle. "He cut it a little close, didn't he?" the smiling owner shouted to reporters as he waited for the trophy ceremony to begin.

"What was the difference between this race and the Derby?" a newsman asked.

"Well," Vanderbilt replied, "we won this one and we didn't win that one."

Guerin hopped off the Dancer wearing a huge smile, his relief apparent as he accepted congratulations from Vanderbilt in the winner's circle. Hundreds of fans rushed to the entrance of the enclosure and fanned out along the fence as track police stood guard. The Dancer stood calmly amid the tumult. The Woodlawn Vase, an ornate silver trophy standing two feet high, was presented to Vanderbilt, who posed for the win picture with Jeanne, Winfrey, Guerin, Maryland governor Theodore McKeldin, Pimlico president C. C. Boshamer, and U.S. treasury secretary George Humphrey. Red Smith arrived with a microphone and a camera crew and went down the line asking questions televised nationally on CBS.

"When did you hear Jamie K. coming?" Smith asked Guerin.

Before answering, the jockey greeted his young son, Ronnie, then fielded the question.

"I heard him coming soon enough," he said.

"Were you worried?" Smith asked.

"I wasn't," Guerin said. "We went to the front a little sooner than

I wanted. Dark Star stopped and I found myself on the lead. But he was holding Jamie K. safe at the end. He responded when I asked."

Next up, Winfrey admitted he was more worried than Guerin at the end. "The race was a little tight there, Red; Jamie K. surprised me," the trainer told Smith. Vanderbilt repeated the theme in his interview with Smith: "I didn't think Jamie K. would get that close to my horse. He's dead game and better than I thought. But I'm really proud of my horse, trainer, my jock, groom, farm, and everything else."

Vanderbilt was in high spirits. When Ralph Kercheval joined the celebration, Smith asked, on the air, if that was the man who had raised Native Dancer. Vanderbilt replied, "Yes, Ralph Kercheval raised the horse. And Mrs. Vanderbilt raised me!"

When CBS's cameras were turned off, Guerin turned and jogged toward the jockeys' room. Arcaro was waiting at the top of the stairs leading to the room. He had heard Guerin tell the TV audience the Dancer was "holding Jamie K. safe" at the wire.

"Don't try to tell me I didn't have you worried!" Arcaro shouted with a smile.

"Yes, you had me plenty worried," Guerin said. "But my horse didn't run his best race. He was doing his best, but I had to get into him with the whip. It was only the second time I've had to do that."

Later, as he showered and dressed to catch a train to New York, Arcaro told reporters he had been forced to stray from his original plan. "I had hoped to make my move at the three-eighths pole," he explained, "but Royal Bay Gem was coming up on my outside and I knew I couldn't wait. Maybe if I could have waited longer, the result would have been different. Then again, maybe it wouldn't have made a difference. Who knows?"

Outside, fans holding winning bets lined up at the windows to receive their money. "There was a huge mob," recalled Joe Kelly, then the vice president of the Maryland Horseman's Association. "The city editor of the *Baltimore Sun* had come out and bet fifty dollars, which was a lot of money, on the Dancer, and while he won the bet, he got caught in the stampede at the window after the race and his topcoat was torn. Everyone said he broke even—won the bet, tore his coat."

So much had been bet on the Dancer that his victory created a "minus pool" of $46,012. In other words, even though the Dancer was racing at odds of just twenty cents on the dollar, so much was going out that the track had to chip in more than $46,000 to ensure that all winning bets were paid.

The winning celebration continued back at the barn as the Grey Ghost cooled out. In a Preakness tradition, the Stevens catering company delivered a case of champagne for the stable hands.

"I didn't even know Jamie K.'s name until he came after us," Lester Murray said, holding a glass of champagne.

Winfrey spoke to reporters. "We had hoped he would win a little easier," the trainer said. "Frankly, I was more impressed with his race in the Derby."

Many others in the racing industry would feel similarly, that the Dancer, despite winning the Preakness, had added little to his legend. His move at the head of the stretch had been impressive, but he had wobbled to the finish line, some thought, barely holding off the charge of a horse with an inferior record. It was later estimated that Jamie K. had gained ten lengths on the winner down the stretch. A superhorse was not supposed to yield so much ground.

On the other hand, he had made a powerful move that smartly disposed of the Kentucky Derby winner at the three-eighths pole, relatively far from the finish line, yet still summoned enough strength to hold off Arcaro at the end. That was not a feat to be diminished. "He raced the speed horses into the ground, then held off a great challenge," Evan Shipman wrote in the *Morning Telegraph*. "Jamie K. had collared him at the eighth pole. If the Dancer had been any less than outstanding, Arcaro's tactics would have worked. But Native Dancer was equal to the challenge."

An hour after the race, Winfrey looked the horse over and pronounced him in "perfect" condition. "We'll van him back to New York tomorrow, and we'll run him in the Belmont," the trainer said. He needed to leave to attend a victory celebration the Vanderbilts were hosting at Sagamore Farm that night, with the Preakness trophy serving as a centerpiece. It would be a happy affair. The trip "home" to Maryland had turned out splendidly for the horse and his owner.

Vanderbilt knew the experts were right to criticize the Dancer's poor finish, but he didn't care. He had won a Triple Crown race, his first after almost two decades in racing. The thrill was incomparable, and he was grateful to those who had helped make it happen. Back in New York several days later, he pulled Bernie Everson aside after the Dancer's morning workout at Belmont and told the exercise rider to go pick out a car. Vanderbilt was buying. Everson selected a light blue Mercury Marquis.

The mood was not nearly so buoyant at Harry Guggenheim's Cain Hoy Stable. In fact, the news was grim: Dark Star had seemed fine at the barn after finishing fifth in the Preakness, leaving trainer Eddie Hayward without an excuse for the colt's failure in the stretch, but a veterinarian had examined the colt on Monday and, shockingly, discovered a "bowed" tendon in the right foreleg. Such tears in the superficial digital flexor tendon, while not a death knell, tend to heal slowly, with scar tissue replacing the torn fibers. That severely compromises the racing mechanism. Guggenheim's only choice was to retire Dark Star to stud. The horse's racing career was over just twenty-three days after he had won the Kentucky Derby. "It is a sad occasion to have to retire such a game horse," Guggenheim said. "I am very proud of his accomplishments."

In time, his Derby triumph would be known as one of racing's all-time surprises, an unthinkable upset propagated by a group of one-hit wonders. Hayward would never bring another horse to the Derby. Moreno would finish out of the money in his two other chances. Guggenheim, encouraged by the Derby success, would invest considerably more time and money in his stable, but although Cain Hoy grew into one of racing's better outfits, especially after Woody Stephens was hired as trainer in 1955, it never produced another Derby winner.

Dark Star and Native Dancer would become linked—quite an irony, as they opposed each other only three times in their careers and finished near each other only once, in Louisville. But the setting for Dark Star's victory and the arc of the rest of the Dancer's career assured their unlikely coupling as the main characters in one of racing's unforgettable dramas.

Could Dark Star have become a great rival for the Grey Ghost?

His unspectacular overall record didn't suggest it, but his last three races did. He won the Derby Trial, then led the Dancer from start to finish in the Derby and also led him through the first mile of the Preakness. In other words, he had raced in front of the favored grey for more than two miles of Triple Crown turf, faltering only after suffering a career-ending injury. "I thought Dark Star was vastly underrated," Tannenbaum said. "He had tremendous speed. Native Dancer was pounds better, and I feel he would have won the Preakness even without the injury to Dark Star, but Dark Star, in any other year, would have been a top three-year-old."

Whether he would have continued to compete at the level he exhibited in his Triple Crown races was unknown, of course. The Preakness was Dark Star's final race. The second jewel of the 1953 Triple Crown had been labeled a rematch of champions, a race that would decide who belonged at the top of the three-year-old class, but in the end, one was eliminated. Dark Star went back to the obscurity from which he had come, shipped to Kentucky to stand at Claiborne Farm. The Dancer went on, his grey coat shining ever brighter in the spotlight's glare.

# SEVENTEEN

**W**as the Dancer a horse for the ages, already assured of mention in the same breath with Man O' War, Whirlaway, and Citation? His millions of fans certainly thought so. Or did he still need to accomplish more before such high praise was warranted, as many horsemen, racing writers, and insiders believed? The debate boiled over in the three weeks between the Preakness and the Dancer's next race, the Belmont Stakes, the final jewel of the Triple Crown, which, many felt, would go a long way toward settling the argument.

The public's voice on the issue was united and strong. After making five national TV appearances between April 18 and May 23, the Dancer was as popular as any American horse that had ever looked through a bridle. The public, quite simply, had a hopeless crush on Vanderbilt's majestic, charismatic grey.

Part of the attraction, unmistakably, was Vanderbilt himself. He was a public figure in his own right, beloved by the big-city gossip columnists and sportswriters, who seldom let a day pass without finding a reason to mention him. His appeal crossed societal boundaries: the swells knew him and admired his grace and humor, and the standing-room crowd loved his passion for racing. The rich men who backed racing stables were media celebrities, and Vanderbilt was the most popular and accessible among them, the young, dashing, iconic racing man who could relate to the common fan. That he, and not another society owner, had produced the Dancer was critical.

But, of course, the horse himself was the font of the public's affection, the origin of the love story welling higher with every race. He was different, his grey coloring setting him apart. And though his blood was blue, he never took a day off, exuding an "always coming to run" work ethic that crossed his royal mien with a working-class mentality. What fan couldn't relate to a horse that procrastinated in his races, putting off his moves until the last moment before firing to the front with a rallying drive as imposing as any ever seen on the American turf?

The Dancer was somehow powerful and cuddly; attractive to women as well as men; indefatigable, yet vulnerable after the shattering Derby loss. "It was amazing: we started receiving stacks of mail," recalled John Derr of CBS radio. "It was the first time we had ever had fan mail for a horse. It came addressed to Native Dancer care of CBS in New York. Children from all over the country were falling in love. People were falling in love. I opened a letter one day from a high school girl from Kansas. She railed on about how much she loved Native Dancer, and she said, 'But you only race him on Saturday. Could you please race him twice a week?' As if we dictated when he ran."

Stacks of letters and telegrams were also arriving at Vanderbilt's Manhattan office and Barn 20 at Belmont. An attorney from Annapolis, Maryland, wrote asking for one of the Dancer's shoes, which he pledged to hang on his office wall alongside one of Whirlaway's shoes. A congressman from Maryland also asked for a shoe for "a very prominent actress." The mother of an eight-year-old with rheumatic fever asked if her child could come to the barn and meet the famous grey. Many of Vanderbilt's friends from business, politics, and entertainment also sent regards after the Preakness.

The combined viewing audience for the Derby and Preakness telecasts alone had totaled almost 28 million, and even with racing fever at a zenith across the country, many of the viewers were newcomers to the sport, without a yardstick of other champions to measure the Dancer against. They were baffled by the debate over his greatness and annoyed by the criticism of his accomplishments. He had won thirteen of fourteen starts, including eleven stakes races, by a total of thirty-two lengths. His one loss, by a head, had been dismissed as bad luck. What more did he need to do to be assured of mention as one of the greats?

He needed to do a lot, if you listened to the horsemen and newsmen who, rightly or not—and with some smugness—saw themselves as far more knowing and insightful than the public, and thus, far better judges of greatness. "There is skepticism in turf circles about Native Dancer being a really great horse, germinated by his reversal in the Derby and the heavy weather he made of it winning the Preakness," Charles Hatton wrote in the *Morning Telegraph*.

Proudly disdaining the fans' emotional assessment of the Dancer, the experts didn't disagree that he was a splendid horse and that, indeed, he might one day rate with the best. But they also felt that his credentials as a legend still lacked certain essential achievements. They were right. The Dancer had never beaten an older horse, never carried more than 126 pounds, and never won a race longer than one and three-sixteenths miles. He still had major tests to pass. Moreover, he had set only one record in his career, in the Futurity, and had seldom won any race easily, even though his rivals were of debatable quality. (Correspondent had disappeared in the Triple Crown. Jamie K. had done little before the Preakness. Dark Star had come out of nowhere to win the Derby. Royal Bay Gem was forever too late charging down the stretch.) His loss in the Derby would keep him from the ultimate equine trophy, a Triple Crown, but it was his narrow Preakness victory that really had the experts doubting him.

"The question remains: Is Native Dancer a genuine champion against top-notch competition?" pedigree expert J. A. Estes wrote in the *Blood-Horse* after the Preakness. Everyone, it seemed, was asking the same question. "Is the Dancer the super horse the experts believed him to be? Most assuredly, he didn't look it in the Preakness," Arthur Daley, one of his biggest fans, wrote in the *New York Times*. "When the great ones came on with an invincible rush ... they blasted away with a surging power that was awesome to behold. As yet, the Dancer hasn't awed anyone."

Willard Mullin, the dean of American sports cartoonists,

summed up the issue with an illustration in the *New York World-Telegram*. Man O' War, Citation, and Count Fleet were pictured sitting in a grandstand overlooking a track, arms folded, expressions haughty, a jury of dubious peers shouting "Prove it!" as Native Dancer jogged on the dirt below.

Vanderbilt and Winfrey weren't insulted by the doubts; to the contrary, they knew that, indeed, the Grey Ghost had more to prove. Arthur Daley had quoted Vanderbilt on the issue before the Derby, when Eddie Arcaro was refusing to concede greatness to the then-unbeaten Dancer. "It will be an awfully long time before we know for sure," Vanderbilt told Daley. "Greatness doesn't come in a single race or even a series of races. It comes in perspective. Sometimes you have to wait until a horse is retired before you can point a finger—politely, of course—and say, 'There's a great horse.'"

Conveniently, a chance for the Dancer to make a powerful statement was just ahead. If the Derby was America's most famous race and the Preakness was a celebrated stepping-stone to the Triple Crown, the Belmont, known as "the test of champions," was the ultimate measure of equine quality. A lesser horse could navigate the Derby's choking traffic jams and the Preakness's sharp turns and, with some luck, come out ahead, but the Belmont's mile and a half suffered no imposters. The three legendary horses in Mullin's cartoon had won the race, as had Whirlaway, War Admiral, Gallant Fox, Omaha, Colin, and Assault, all horses near the top of America's pantheon of greats.

"The function of the Belmont is to establish a champion, or to reveal the latent weakness depriving some over-praised young horse of that rare distinction," Evan Shipman wrote in the *Morning Telegraph*. "Judging by the class of its winners, the Belmont is pre-eminent among America's races for three-year-olds. [Over many years] every renewal of the race, with but two exceptions, has been captured by a high-class thoroughbred. Hurryoff in 1933 and Bounding Home in 1944 weren't much, but those two aside, the Belmont has always been the reward for outstanding merit."

The race offered a distinct crossroads for the Dancer. A defeat, giving him one Triple Crown victory in three tries, would leave many suggesting that, indeed, he was a classic example of what Shipman had called an "over-praised young horse." On the other hand, a victory in the Belmont, always a mark of distinction, would silence the doubts about his pedigree and provide a solid foundation for the rest of his climb toward greatness.

As if to emphasize what he was seeking, the pages of New York's weighty fleet of daily papers—the *Times, Post, Daily News, Herald Tribune, World-Telegram, Journal-American,* and *Morning Telegraph*—were brimming with other examples of greatness in the days just before the Belmont. The Yankees, winners of every World Series since 1949, were running away with the American League pennant again, pounding the Tigers and Indians on the road as they stretched a winning streak toward eighteen games, remarkable even by their standards. Ben Hogan, the taciturn Texan golfer with the classic swing, was dominating the U.S. Open at Oakmont Country Club near Pittsburgh. Edmund Hillary, a beekeeper from New Zealand who, with the help of a Nepalese guide, had recently become the first man to climb to the summit of Mount Everest, the world's tallest peak, was giving interviews about the experience. The Dancer wasn't in that company yet. He was still just a hugely gifted and popular horse who had somehow lost the Derby. He needed to win the Belmont, then prevail later over the obstacles of weight handicaps, travel, unfamiliar tracks, and stern opposition—the hurdles all great horses cleared—before being declared one of the best ever.

Winfrey's workout regimen was designed to build the colt up to the Belmont's twelve-furlong distance, which was a quarter mile farther than he had ever raced. He worked five-eighths of a mile on May 30, a mile on June 1, a mile and a quarter on June 5, a mile and a half on June 9, and finally, six furlongs on June 12, a day before the race. Trackside observers found little fault with any of his training. "The grey colt appears ready for the race of his life," the *Morning Telegraph* reported on the day of the Belmont.

The field of horses that would oppose him was in flux in the days before the race. Jamie K., with Arcaro up, was a certainty, and Royal Bay Gem would try again after finishing third in the Preakness and fourth in the Derby. Ram o' War, fourth in the Preakness, would also give it a shot, as would Kamehameha, a long shot owned by the King Ranch, sired by Polynesian, and named for a Hawaiian monarch from the 1800s. It appeared that those four would constitute the Dancer's opposition, but two more horses were entered a day before the race: Bassanio, fourth in the Peter Pan Handicap in his last start, and The Preem, an overmatched colt owned by bandleader Louis Prima. The Preem, winner of just one of his thirty-five career starts, had once run for a $7,500 claiming tag, and "the best thing you can say about him is that his owner blows a hot trumpet," James Roach wrote in the *Times*.

The race was being billed as a rematch of the Preakness, a virtual two-horse affair with the Grey Ghost the likely odds-on favorite and Jamie K. receiving his share of support. Arcaro's horse had raced once since the Preakness, finishing second in a six-furlong allowance race against older horses at Belmont, a performance that furthered the notion that he was a late-blooming horse on the rise. Arcaro had kept him near the front despite a fast early pace, and he had blown past a six-year-old in the stretch, then just missed catching a five-year-old carrying three fewer pounds.

The colt was owned by James D. Norris Jr., a Chicago sportsman better known as the president of the International Boxing Club, one of boxing's major governing bodies, and also as the owner of the National Hockey League's Detroit Red Wings, winner of three Stanley Cup titles. His father, James D. Norris Sr., had run the family's thoroughbred operation for years, first at an Indiana farm near Chicago, then at Spring Hill Farm in Paris, Kentucky. After breeding a top filly named Nell K. in the late forties, the elder Norris had bred the mare back to the same sire and produced Jamie K.

John Partridge, the veteran trainer who oversaw Norris's stable, had visited Spring Hill in 1951, scouting the youngsters he would soon take on. A dog's bark sent the half dozen youngsters scurrying through a field, with Jamie K. lagging far behind the others.

"That one's going to make a fine racehorse," Partridge told the farm manager, pointing to the laggard.

"You don't mean him!" the manager shouted.

He did. Partridge's insights were keen: after all, he had worked with horses for almost seven decades, since he started walking hots as a child in Detroit in the 1880s. He had worked for E. R. Bradley and other outfits along the way and had conditioned Norris's horses since the thirties, succeeding Eddie Hayward, now the trainer of Dark Star. He liked the way Jamie K. ran through the field that day at Spring Hill Farm, and he was usually right when he predicted success for a horse.

The colt had disappointed as a two-year-old, consistently breaking slowly from the starting gate, lagging far behind the leaders, and winning just one minor race for maidens. He did win the Remsen Handicap at Jamaica in October but was disqualified for drifting out in the stretch and bumping Vanderbilt's Social Outcast. He had performed no better early in 1953, continuing to break slowly and finish out of the money as Partridge and James Norris Jr. shuffled through jockeys including Dave Gorman and Conn McCreary. The elder Norris had died in December 1952, leaving his son in charge.

Finally, the colt had proved Partridge right after the trainer put Arcaro on him. Left at the gate in his first start with the Master, he had come back to beat several older horses at the wire, stunning observers. After three more races with Arcaro, including the Preakness, he was breaking quicker and racing closer to the lead, with his late charge seemingly unharmed. "Native Dancer will know he has been to the races," Arcaro told reporters shortly before the Belmont.

Winfrey was concerned. The trainer knew that Vanderbilt wanted to win at the track where he had served as president and now stabled his horses, his home on Long Island not far away. Winfrey fretted Thursday in an interview with a *Newsweek* reporter. "When you've got three come-from-behind horses in a small field," he said, referring to Jamie K., Royal Bay Gem, and the Dancer, "you just don't know what will happen."

Adding to the uncertainty, the weather soured badly on Saturday. Forecasters had wrongly predicted rain for the Derby and Preakness, and now, as if the percentages needed evening, a forecast of sun for the Belmont proved equally wrong. After a grey, humid dawn, rain fell through the morning, briefly eased, then pelted New York all afternoon, accompanied by a chilling wind. The Dodgers game at

Ebbets Field was rained out. Bassanio was scratched from the Belmont. Many fans chose to watch the race on TV rather than make the soggy trip to Queens, but 38,000 still left their homes and came out in the miserable conditions, evidence of the Grey Ghost's popularity.

Belmont officials had limited the betting to win and place wagers, wanting to avoid a reprise of the $46,000 minus pool that had occurred at the Preakness. Fifty-eight cents of every betting dollar was still put on the Dancer, who was made the heavy favorite at 9–20 odds. There was also support for Arcaro and Jamie K. at 5–2, and surprisingly, for Royal Bay Gem at 6–1. The Preem, at 122–1, attracted almost $4,000 in wagering, leading James Roach to write in the *Times* that "New Yorkers would bet on a zebra if tickets were sold."

Six horses were loaded into the starting gate at 4:46 P.M. as rain continued to fall. The Grey Ghost was in the fifth post, just to the outside of Jamie K. Surprisingly, the racing strip had held up; it was still rated fast despite the rain. Bryan Field was at the microphone for CBS as a coast-to-coast TV audience later estimated at 9 million tuned in. It was time to find out if the Grey Ghost belonged with the Yankees, Hogan, and greats from other sports.

He was the first horse out of the gate, but Guerin took him back as Ram o' War went to the lead, assuming the front-runner's role that Dark Star had commanded in the Derby and Preakness. Kamehameha moved forward and followed the leader as the field passed the grandstand for the first time, with Jamie K. running easily in third. Kamehameha soon faded, but the other two leaders held their positions around the first turn and all the way up the backstretch, with Ram o' War setting a slow pace—a half mile in 50⅕ seconds, a mile in 1:15. The Dancer was in third, racing behind Arcaro and well off the rail, with Royal Bay Gem in fourth, three lengths farther back. The Preem and Kamehameha were so far back they could barely be seen through the rain. The Preem would finish forty-five lengths behind the winner, with Kamehameha another twenty back after his saddle almost slipped off.

Arcaro had blamed the loss in the Preakness on the fact that he'd had to charge sooner than planned to fend off Royal Bay Gem, leaving Jamie K. without the energy to make up those final inches on the Dancer in the final yards of the race. Now, as if to show that he had meant what he said, the Master sent Jamie K. to the lead right on schedule, sweeping around tiring Ram o' War on the second turn and taking the lead at the head of the stretch. Instead of letting the Dancer set the pace and trying to catch him, as he had in the Preakness, Arcaro was going to make the Grey Ghost chase him.

Guerin shadowed the leader, also making a move on the turn and passing Ram o' War entering the stretch. The Dancer was less than a length behind Jamie K. as the horses moved in tandem, straightened for home, and pulled away from the field, sending Royal Bay Gem, unable to keep pace again, back toward the followers. As expected, the Belmont was down to the Dancer and Jamie K., the two best horses sprinting through the stretch as they had in the Preakness, only reversed this time, as Arcaro wanted, with Jamie K. clinging to a lead and the Dancer chasing him.

With a quarter mile to go, Jamie K. was still in front. The horses had raced the Kentucky Derby distance, a mile and a quarter, supposedly the limit of what some believed the Dancer's pedigree would support. Either the Grey Ghost would summon the necessary resolve, surge to the lead in the next 440 yards, and prove his greatness, or he would falter, giving his doubters all the ammunition they needed. There were no mitigating circumstances in play, no excuses to grasp; just a good horse and a great jockey in front of him and time starting to run out as an adoring but circumspect sports world watched.

Jamie K. was driving hard, but the Dancer gained ground as Guerin urged him on. The grey colt pulled closer with one stride, even with another, then nosed into the lead passing the eighth pole. A roar from the crowd rose, muffled in the soggy chill. The Dancer had rallied in the stretch of many of his races, and he was doing it again, his powers of acceleration fully engaged, his legs a blur. Arcaro was working Jamie K. frenetically, arms pumping as he brandished the whip, but the Dancer's lead grew from a neck to a head and even more as he neared the sixteenth pole. The Dancer had answered the challenge.

Maddeningly, he eased up again for an instant, as he so often did after finding no one in front of him in the stretch, and his surge stopped. Arcaro's horse held his ground, a head behind, and for a moment, a breathless moment, it seemed he might come back at the Dancer in the final yards. Here, truly, was a reprise of the Preakness, with Jamie K. trying to run down the Dancer as the soaked crowd shrieked.

But then, just as abruptly, as if he sensed the challenge, the Grey Ghost accelerated again, his lead steadying and even expanding. Arcaro and Jamie K. were close behind, but safely behind, unable to gain ground. The horses covered the final yards frozen in those poses, clearly separated, their positioning resolute. As they reached the finish line, almost two and a half minutes after the starting gate had opened, the Dancer was in front by a neck.

Guerin and Arcaro eased their holds and stood up in the irons after crossing the finish line. The crowd exhaled, drained by the spectacle they had witnessed—a spectacle washed of color by the miserable weather, but still as taut and uncertain as an Alfred Hitchcock film. Immediately, even as Guerin and the Dancer turned and headed for the winner's circle, there was a rush to put the race in context. Had the Dancer, to paraphrase Mullin's cartoon, proved his greatness? What was the racing world to make of him winning two of the three Triple Crown races, but by the narrowest of margins?

The answer was on the tote board, where the time of the race was illuminated: 2:28⅗. Knowing fans immediately recognized a feat creditable only to equine greatness. It was the third-fastest winning time in the history of the Belmont Stakes, just two-fifths of a second behind the record set by Count Fleet in 1943 and equaled by Citation in 1948. The Dancer had covered the last quarter mile in 24⅗ seconds and the last half in 49⅕, a remarkable burst for a horse so late in such a long race. The Dancer's time for the last half was, in fact, faster than his time for the first half. If the Belmont was, indeed, the test of champions, he had passed. Some experts would surely continue to wonder about a horse that never seemed to win going away, but there could be no more wondering about his endurance or class.

"When this one was over, there were no longer any reasonable doubts" about the Dancer, Red Smith wrote in the next day's *Herald*

*Tribune*. "Vanderbilt's grey just was too much for Jamie K. in the stretch run of one of the most stirring of all Belmonts," added Charles Hatton in the *Morning Telegraph*.

Vanderbilt met the horse at the winner's enclosure, rain dripping from his hat. He congratulated Guerin, handed the shank to Murray, shook hands with Winfrey, and stood back as a crowd gathered around the enclosure, the umbrellas occluding a view of the horse from the grandstand. It was almost 5 P.M., and the air was so chilly that wisps of fog came from the Dancer's mouth when he exhaled. It seemed closer to November than June. Vanderbilt's smile shone through the gloom. His horse was magnificent, a champion—indisputably.

CBS was going live, with Red Smith squinting through the rain as he interviewed any familiar face he could locate. "He doesn't waste any effort, that lazy so-and-so," Bill Winfrey said, referring to the Dancer's midstretch lulls. "He just does what he has to do to win, but he does it. There was never any doubt with me that he was a champion, but he surely proved himself to the others today."

Arcaro, of course, had been the most vocal of those "others," steadfastly refusing to admit that comparing the Dancer to other greats might be appropriate. But as he spoke to reporters now, beaten by the Dancer for the eighth time, he knew the time had come. "After the Preakness, I said to myself, 'I'm going to beat that grey horse the next time around,'" Arcaro said. "And I had him for sure at the head of the stretch. But then he got that neck on me, and I just couldn't get by him." The great jockey stopped, shook his head, and continued: "And if we were to have gone all the way around the track again, Native Dancer still wasn't going to let me get past him."

At last, the Master was convinced.

# EIGHTEEN

Eddie Arcaro knew he was putting himself in danger when he accepted an offer to ride Native Dancer in the American Derby after refusing for so long to join the operatic chorus of praise for the horse. "I guess I shouldn't have said so much about the Dancer," the smiling jockey told reporters several days before the race. He surely wished he had never said a word when he turned for home before 37,000 fans at Chicago's Washington Park on August 22, with the sluggish Dancer in fourth place, six lengths off the lead. "If I get beat on this horse, I'm the biggest bum alive," Arcaro had told a *Life* magazine reporter hours earlier. Now his worst fears were on the verge of being realized.

The Dancer was making his fourth start since winning the Belmont, having easily won the Dwyer Stakes on July 4 at Aqueduct, the Arlington Classic on July 18 at Chicago's Arlington Park, and the Travers Stakes on August 15 at Saratoga to run his winning streak to six races in a row, his overall record to seventeen wins in eighteen starts, and his career earnings to $677,420, fourth on racing's all-time list. His superiority among his three-year-old class was unquestioned, his place among America's racing's greats was assured, and he was expected to cruise in the American Derby, even without his regular jockey, Eric Guerin, who was sitting out a suspension. But now he was in trouble as he entered the stretch run to the finish line.

In the Dwyer, three weeks after the Belmont, he had raced with a sizable weight handicap for the first time, giving a dozen pounds to four outclassed rivals who had sat out the Triple Crown season. A holiday crowd of 35,865 bet him down to 1–20, and he hovered near the lead up the backstretch before unleashing his familiar rush on the second turn, easily taking control. A colt named Dictar chased him to the finish line without seriously challenging, although the winning margin was just one and three-quarters lengths after the Dancer's usual loafing act in the stretch. Guerin called it the colt's "easiest race," explaining that it was relatively close at the end because "he just wanted to play." Jeanne Vanderbilt accepted the trophy in the winner's circle, her husband in Europe on business.

Interestingly, the *Morning Telegraph* reported that fans in the high-end clubhouse seats warmly applauded the colt before and after the race, but that scattered fans in the grandstand, where ticket prices were cheaper, booed the Dancer. Given his overwhelming popularity, which would manifest itself throughout the summer, it was hard to know what to ascribe the discordant notes to, but the only possibilities were jealousy, general crankiness, or the belief that the horse was overrated because he seldom won easily. Whatever its source, the strain of anti-Dancer feeling never surfaced again in measurable quantities.

The colt's next race, the Arlington Classic, a one-mile event labeled as the richest race ever run for three-year-olds, figured to be far more interesting than the Dwyer. A $155,000 purse lured Triple Crown stalwarts Jamie K. and Royal Bay Gem to the track in suburban Chicago, as well as a dangerous sprinter, Van Crosby, co-owner of the track's record for seven furlongs. Away from his most ardent supporters in the East and assigned 126 pounds to 120 for the rest of the field, the Dancer encountered skepticism. Harold Simmons, the trainer of Van Crosby, said his colt had a real chance to beat the Dancer over the shorter distance. John Partridge, trainer of Jamie K., said the weight disparity should make up the inches that had separated his colt from victory in the Preakness and Belmont.

Bill Winfrey agreed with Partridge, telling reporters upon arriving in Chicago that "on cold, hard figures, Jamie K. should beat us."

But the Dancer's trainer also offered his theory about the horse in the wake of the Triple Crown season: "We have reason to believe Native Dancer does not fully extend himself once he gets to the front, and that he wins only by the margin necessary to get the job done. That was the case in the Preakness and Belmont, at least. The Classic should give us a chance to test this theory."

With 39,460 fans crammed into the track and a national TV audience watching on CBS, midwestern bettors backed Jamie K. down to 4–1 and Van Crosby to 9–2, with the Dancer at 7–10, his highest odds since the Derby. The atmosphere was electric; Chicago racing was flourishing, with the summer meetings drawing the country's best horses, trainers, and jockeys. "It was right there with New York, if not better," longtime racing official Tommy Trotter said. The Dancer was late getting saddled because of the crowd around him, throwing off the schedule for CBS's telecast. The horses were rushed to the starting gate without a post parade.

Breaking from the fourth post position on a track rated "heavy" after rains late in the week, the Grey Ghost was sixth after the first quarter, with Van Crosby setting the pace and a 19–1 shot named Sir Mango close behind. Guerin moved the colt up to third as he headed into the turn, then asked for a run. The Dancer responded as if he had heard the doubters and wanted people to know what he thought of them. His head dropped and he bolted past Van Crosby and Sir Mango, taking the lead at the top of the stretch.

Fans searched the pack for Jamie K. and Royal Bay Gem, expecting the late-runners to make their usual charges as they straightened out for home. Both were straggling near the rear, outrun and outclassed this time. It was the Dancer's day. For once, he didn't ease up after taking the lead. He pulled away steadily through the stretch, his lead growing with every stride as he passed the eighth and sixteenth poles and headed for home. The turf writers from around the country who had gathered in Arlington's press box to chronicle "the fourth jewel" of the 1953 Triple Crown broke into applause at the sight of the Dancer crushing his rivals.

His lead at the wire: nine lengths.

The racing world's response: wow.

"He never let up, did he?" a smiling Vanderbilt said to Guerin in the winner's circle.

"Not one bit, sir," Guerin said. "I think we could have spotted them twenty pounds with the way he ran today."

Arch Ward, longtime sports editor of the *Chicago Tribune* and originator of baseball's All-Star Game, wrote lavishly of the Dancer in his column the next day. "It was one of the most devastating knockout punches in the history of big-time racing," he wrote. "His closest pursuers looked as if they were in another race as the Dancer sped under the wire. He has done everything that can be asked of a three-year-old. He has beaten the sprinters, the middle-distance horses and the long-winded. He has gone to the front early. He has been hemmed in. He has come from far back. He has won on fast, sloppy and heavy tracks. Yesterday, he was at his glorious peak."

The Dancer was shipped back to Belmont and then on to Saratoga, where he had won four races in twenty-six days the year before and now was treated like a visiting potentate as he trained for the Travers. When he worked out two days before the race, all activity at the Spa ceased. Fans eating breakfast on the clubhouse porch pushed their chairs back, left their food, and went to the railing to watch. Sweepers leaned on their brooms, taking a respite. Trainers put down their stopwatches, and exercise riders on other horses stopped. Winfrey sent Bernie Everson out with instructions to cover a mile. The Grey Ghost circled the track and came through the stretch to waves of applause. "It was a moment for a horse owner, horse trainer—and exercise rider—to remember," James Roach wrote in the *New York Times*.

The Travers was memorable for what happened not during the race, but before it. More than 28,000 fans, the most in Saratoga history, filled the track. A great crowd swarmed the Dancer in the shaded paddock before the race. With little security in place and no barriers separating the horse from his public, fans came up and stroked him, petted him, spoke to him, and even plucked hairs from his tail. Winfrey became alarmed, but Harold Walker held the shank tightly and the horse remained calm.

"I'm standing there by the horse and someone comes out of the crowd and walks around Native Dancer and looks at his legs and comes and rubs his hand up the legs, and I said, 'Who is this?'" Claude Appley recalled. "Bill Winfrey came over to me and said, 'Who is this?' I said, 'I don't know who it is.' Bill went over to him and said, 'I'm sorry, you have to leave.' What it was, I think, people felt they owned him."

Security guards were called in to cut a swath through the crowd so the Dancer could get to the track for the race. "When they went to move him, they had to rein people off," recalled Daniel W. Scott III, the son of the man who had foaled the Dancer in 1950. The younger Scott was with his father at Saratoga that day. "He had become an icon, with mobs chasing him and people shouting," the younger Scott continued. "It was like the scenes with the Beatles a decade later. Native Dancer had become as popular in the sports world in 1953 as the Beatles were in music in the sixties."

Evan Shipman, covering the Saratoga meeting for the *Morning Telegraph,* devoted his column to the remarkable scene. "If there was ever any doubt about Native Dancer's popularity, it was dispelled Saturday when the record crowd greeted Vanderbilt's champion with a warmth unequalled since the brave days of old Exterminator 30 years ago," Shipman wrote. "He is the most popular thoroughbred of our time. Leaving comparisons as a racehorse out of it, we are sure Citation, Count Fleet and the others never had this . . . appeal. We have only one explanation to offer, of course, and that is television. More people have watched Native Dancer this season than have ever before seen a single horse."

The scene before the Travers had Biblical overtones, with thousands gathering to see and touch their idol and linger in his presence. The Dancer was just a horse, but the public clearly saw him as more, an alluring and profound figure. He embodied all the traits that humans attribute to a champion: stamina, grace, determination, beauty, ability, and charisma. Eleven weeks after his defeat at Churchill Downs, which had so devastated his fans and would, however unfairly, define him to some in later generations, his redemption was being fulfilled.

Vanderbilt proudly presided over the horse's triumphant summer of 1953, the Derby disappointment temporarily forgotten amid the cheers and headlines. "Dad was just so excited," Vanderbilt's daughter Heidi recalled. "He talked about the horse all the time, and you knew he couldn't wait to get to the barn. There was no mystery about how important it was to him, and how wonderful it all was." No mystery, indeed. "He was so thrilled to have bred this kind of a horse, this great champion," Dan W. Scott recalled. "And he was already commenting about how wonderful it would be to have him as a sire."

"Whenever Native Dancer was mentioned, Alfred's face just lit up," said Chick Lang, a former jockey who rose through the racing industry's ranks and became the general manager of Pimlico and a Vanderbilt confidante. "Alfred bred the horse, remember, and raised the horse at Sagamore, so Native Dancer was just a great, great validation for him and his operation. And Alfred's gratitude showed. When he spoke of Native Dancer, it was as if he was speaking of his own son who had won the Heisman Trophy."

Alfred Vanderbilt III said, "People are fascinated by horses, kids especially. Heidi and I grew up insane about horses. If I was left alone in a room with nothing to do, I played with horses. Hounds went through the bottom of the lawn at Broadhollow on fall mornings. We rode. Our father was a famous owner of horses. Horses were everything. And the most famous horse was in our family, I was young, but I remember seeing Native Dancer on TV. I remember everyone talking about him. He was the idol of all idols, and my daddy owned him."

The Travers was televised nationally on NBC, and the Dancer put on a typical show. He easily defeated four opponents as the 1–20 favorite, rallying as usual on the second turn and winning by five and a half lengths, despite giving away as much as a dozen pounds. It wasn't a race so much as a platform for his obvious superiority, barely more taxing than his workout two days earlier. "What a pleasure it is to ride a horse like that," Guerin said afterward. Winfrey confessed to reporters that he was no longer sure about his theory that the Dancer exerted himself only as much as was needed to win. The colt had won his most recent two races by a combined fourteen and a half lengths.

The chain of events that led to Arcaro's predicament in the American Derby started on the afternoon of the Travers. In the

Saratoga Special, a race for two-year-olds run earlier in the day, Guerin, on Porterhouse, and Hank Moreno, riding Turn-to, were coming down the stretch together three months after they had raced to a photo finish in the Kentucky Derby. When Porterhouse, rallying along the rail, came up on Turn-to, Moreno's horse veered in and initiated contact. Moreno immediately moved away, but Guerin's horse veered out and forced another collision at the sixteenth pole. Porterhouse went on to finish first, but stewards placed him last and suspended Guerin for ten days after determining, with help from the film patrol, that Guerin hadn't attempted to avoid the second bump and, in addition, had hit Moreno's horse in the chest with his whip.

Such suspensions were routine; even the best jockeys tangled with stewards now and then, especially now that the film patrol's cameras were watching. But this suspension was hardly routine. Guerin was scheduled to ride the Dancer in the American Derby that Saturday, but Illinois stewards said they would respect New York's ruling even though their bylaws didn't prevent suspended jockeys from fulfilling stakes-race obligations already assigned. Guerin, who had ridden the Dancer in all of the horse's eighteen races, was out of the American Derby.

The racing world wondered what Vanderbilt and Winfrey would do as the Grey Ghost boarded the Empire State Express at Saratoga and headed for Chicago, traveling in a private car as five adults and a boy—Carey Winfrey, twelve, was making the trip with his father—tended to him. Winfrey and Vanderbilt obviously wanted a top jockey, so their options were limited. There was Wee Willie Shoemaker, the young Californian leading the nation in wins. There was Teddy Atkinson, the regular rider for Greentree and its fine handicap horse, Tom Fool. And of course, there was Arcaro, the best of the best.

Before Winfrey boarded the train for Chicago, he told Vanderbilt he wanted Arcaro. Vanderbilt nodded. The Master had been the Dancer's toughest critic and rival, but he was the right replacement. He was strong enough to handle the Dancer, and his superb command of pace and tactics would give the Dancer the best chance of winning the race. Vanderbilt knew the horse's fans would howl, remembering how Arcaro had gloated after the Derby and steadfastly refused to concede that the grey deserved so much praise. The fans would take any jockey other than Arcaro, no doubt. But it appealed to Vanderbilt's arch sense of humor to put the Master on his horse after all that had happened, and it was also a sound racing decision. Arcaro was the choice.

There was only one problem: the Master had already agreed to ride Jamie K. in the American Derby, attempting yet again to knock off the Dancer. It didn't matter that he was Winfrey's and Vanderbilt's first choice. He was unavailable.

The situation simmered as the Dancer traveled all day Sunday and early Monday, attracting crowds a political candidate on a whistle-stop tour would envy. At a stop in Buffalo, New York, fans threw open his car door to see him. In Ashtabula, Ohio, a crowd of two hundred came to the station for a glimpse. Two fans in Chicago fought over a piece of cardboard he stepped on while being unloaded; they wanted his valuable footprint. Marshall Smith and Howard Sochurek, a writer and photographer for *Life* magazine, were making the train trip with him, preparing a major story.

As the Dancer rode the rails, a fateful twist occurred; the racing gods, it seemed, were intent on making sure the marriage of the Dancer and the Master came about. Jamie K., with Arcaro up, raced dismally in a prep event at Washington Park five days before the American Derby, finishing fourth, nine lengths behind the winner, Sir Mango. The Dancer's Triple Crown rival had finished tenth, fifth, second, and fourth in his recent races, sharply off the form he had shown in the spring. James Norris decided to pull his horse out of the American Derby. Norris lived in Chicago and didn't want the horse laying an egg at home.

Arcaro was available.

John Partridge met Winfrey with the news when the Dancer arrived at Washington Park on Monday afternoon.

"We're out of it, Bill—and Arcaro is available to you, if you want him," Partridge said.

"We can sure use him," replied Winfrey. "Although Guerin knows the horse and is used to him, Arcaro is a pretty good substitute, don't you think?"

Arcaro's agent, Bones LeBoyne, was also on hand to meet Winfrey, and a deal was quickly struck. "Eddie knew what he was getting into, but it's worth noting that he took the chance anyway," *Daily Racing Form* columnist Joe Hirsch recalled years later. "He knew that there was going to be heat and that he would feel it. Not every jockey would have signed on for that. But Eddie was one of a kind."

Lester Murray was skeptical, to say the least. The Dancer's groom was a great believer in the horse's intellectual powers, which, Murray felt, seemed to border at times on what a human might possess.

"You got a new boy and you ain't gonna like this," Murray mumbled as he settled the horse in the stall after the long trip.

Years later, Mary Appley, the wife of Claude, recalled, "Lester was extremely upset about Arcaro coming on. Lester knew what Geurin could do. It was like letting your kid go with a different baby sitter. Lester very much related to the horse that way, like a child. He treated the horse like a diamond ring and he didn't want anything to change. He said to me, 'I don't know, Miss Mary. I don't know about this new boy.' Eddie Arcaro was a 'boy.'"

The public's reaction to Arcaro's hiring was predictable. Telegrams, letters, and phone calls poured in from fans urging Vanderbilt and Winfrey to change their minds and choose any jockey other than the Dancer's most vocal critic. The owner and trainer weren't swayed. They had the man they wanted. After Everson jogged the Dancer on Wednesday morning, Winfrey scheduled a serious workout for Thursday morning with Arcaro up. The jockey and horse needed to get acquainted.

Never, perhaps, had a routine workout attracted so much attention. Reporters swarmed the Dancer's barn at dawn, spoke to Winfrey and Murray, and waited for Arcaro, who soon arrived wearing khakis and a dark polo shirt. Winfrey gave the Master a leg up and asked him to cover five furlongs in 1:05—an easy pace. Under a bright sun, Washington Park came to a standstill when Arcaro and the Dancer made their move, much as Saratoga had frozen during the Dancer's work before the Travers a week earlier. Marshall Smith later reported in *Life* that the racing secretary's office emptied, exercise riders stopped to watch, and "the backstretch was lined solid for almost a quarter mile with racetrack people."

Arcaro covered the five furlongs in exactly 1:05, proving that the old-timers might be right when they said he had a stopwatch in his head. Reporters surrounded Arcaro afterward, but the Master downplayed the significance of his first ride on the Grey Ghost. "It was just a workout, and actually, I just sat there and he moved along; I think Mr. Winfrey was breezing the jockey more than the horse," he said.

The Master fielded numerous questions about all aspects of his pending ride. How did the Dancer compare to Citation? "Come on, all I have done is work him out once," the jockey said. Why had he been so critical of Vanderbilt's horse? "He was a great horse all along; all I meant was he would have to show me he was the greatest before I rated him that way," Arcaro said. "Now I'm on the spot where I hope he does show me—it's money out of my pocket if he doesn't."

The loss of money wouldn't mean nearly as much as the blow to his reputation, of course. If he failed to win after Guerin had guided the Dancer to seventeen wins in eighteen starts, it would be "a terrible blot on Eddie's record," the *Chicago Tribune*'s Maurice Shevlin wrote. The pressure was getting to Arcaro by Friday night. "I wanted to ride this horse a couple of days ago, but now I'm not so sure," he told Marshall Smith of *Life*.

It was unlike Arcaro to doubt himself, but there was a mitigating circumstance: the jockey was injured, having wrenched his ankle in a fall and then watched it swell to the point that he had to cut a hole in his boot to relieve the pressure and continue to ride. Arcaro hadn't spoken publicly about the injury, and few outside of his inner circle knew, but *Morning Telegraph* reporter J. J. Murphy broke the story a day before the American Derby. "Eddie has put a blackout on information regarding the injury, but we feel the story should be told," Murphy wrote. "He's been undergoing day-long and night-long treatments, with considerable pain involved, to keep the swelling down. There hasn't been a moment between races in the past week that his valet hasn't wrapped the ankle in hot packs with cellophane covering, and given it massages."

Arcaro canceled all of his mounts on Friday to rest the ankle, but the pain was still so severe on Saturday morning that he asked to have the ankle X-rayed, according to the *New York Times*. Presumably, he would have pulled out of the race if the X rays had revealed a broken bone. He kept the mount but was obviously still in pain. Years later, Carey Winfrey recalled Arcaro taking a shot of novocaine before the race. "I vividly remember Eddie being very worried about riding with no feeling in his leg," Carey recalled.

Bernie Everson took the Dancer out for a brief jog on the morning of the race, then brought him back to the barn and turned him over to Murray. The groom was palpably nervous about the challenge the horse would confront later that day.

"You know it's different this time, don't you," the groom said as he wrapped stall bandages on the Dancer's legs for the horse to wear until post.

Murray's concerns were well founded. Though the Dancer was as predictable as the sunrise in some ways, never failing to turn on his motor in the stretch for a winning run to the finish line, he was also occasionally distrustful of strangers and, like many horses, wary of changes in his routine. As Murray saw it, the change from Guerin to Arcaro wasn't to be dismissed; eighteen races with the same jockey had established a routine in the horse's mind, and there was no telling how a horse as headstrong and intelligent as the Dancer would respond.

"You gonna be okay, Daddy," the groom said as he worked in the stall, using a nickname he had pinned on the Dancer in the spring after the Vanderbilt barn cat named Mom had delivered her litter of grey kittens. But Murray's voice lacked its usual conviction.

The American Derby had a long and glorious history. It had been one of America's most important races late in the nineteenth century, more prestigious than the Kentucky Derby. E. J. "Lucky" Baldwin, the famed California pioneer and horse owner, had supposedly once said he would rather win the American Derby than become governor of California. (He won it twice with Isaac Murphy, the legendary African American jockey.) The Triple Crown events had surpassed it and all other three-year-old races in importance, and other second-tier events such as the Arlington Classic had larger purses, but it was still the culmination of the summer racing season in Chicago. Whirlaway and Citation were among the race's recent winners.

Vanderbilt had entered a horse in the American Derby only once before, finishing second with Discovery, behind Cavalcade, in 1934. Although he now had the favorite, his horse's path to the winner's circle appeared anything but easy once the field and weights were set. The Dancer would carry 128 pounds, more than any American Derby winner had carried. The seven horses opposing him in the one-and-an-eighth-mile race would carry from eight to fourteen fewer pounds. Sir Mango, second behind the Dancer in the Arlington Classic and winner of the prep race in which Jamie K. had faltered five days earlier, would carry 114. "He is ready for the race of his life," Sir Mango's owner, Harry Eads, said. A stakes-winning English gelding named Stan, making his dirt track debut after a career on grass, would carry 117. Landlocked, recent winner of two stakes races in New Jersey, would race closest to the Dancer at 120 pounds. Van Crosby, at 114, was expected to set the early pace, and a second Vanderbilt colt, Beachcomber, would also run at 114, coupled with the Dancer as a betting entity.

The Grey Ghost was the class of the field, but the weight differentials and the ballyhoo over the jockey change produced an air of uncertainty all day Saturday. The third-largest crowd in Washington Park history gathered in a broiling haze. The fans were there not only to bet on the Dancer, who was sent to the post at 1–5 odds, but also to see for themselves how Arcaro handled one of his most devilish assignments.

As expected, hundreds gathered around the paddock and let the Master have it when he appeared in Vanderbilt's cerise and white silks, last worn by Arcaro when he rode Social Outcast in the Wood Memorial. The fans booed him, hurled invectives, stood on the rail and shouted that he had damn well better win. Arcaro's expression was grim. These were circumstances as harrowing as any he had experienced, quite a statement for a jockey who had started 16,274 races over twenty-two years and won 3,214. None of that mattered now. If he didn't win, he would never hear the end of it.

The horses were sent to the post at 4:59 P.M., with the Dancer in the no. 4 stall. He broke cleanly and dropped off the lead as Sir Mango, with a local jockey named Dave Erb riding, zoomed to the front from the far outside post as the pack headed for the first turn. Arcaro planned to follow Guerin's usual strategy: race close to the front, but in the shadow of the leaders, until the second turn, then let the Dancer loose and hold on.

Whatever hopes Arcaro had of a routine, uneventful ride soon evaporated. Passing the grandstand the first time, the Dancer refused to do what his jockey asked. It was as if he knew Arcaro had doubted him and wanted to make the jockey suffer. Arcaro asked him to press closer to the front as they entered the first turn, but the Dancer languished near the rear, in front of only one horse.

Arcaro shouted at the horse as they came out of the first turn and headed up the backstretch, then shook the reins to try to convince him to run. Unmoved, the Dancer continued to lag behind, refusing to put out as he briefly slipped into last—last!—place, ten lengths off the pace. Arcaro, becoming desperate, shook the reins again, and the Dancer finally responded with a token effort, accelerating past a few laggards and moving into fourth on the second turn. But then he stalled again, his stride shortening. The crowd roared. Sir Mango was two lengths ahead of the pack. The fans were beginning to envision an upset.

Later, Arcaro would admit he was worried when the Dancer stalled on the second turn; maybe the colt just wasn't going to run for a jockey other than Guerin. He was in fourth as he turned for home, in no way resembling the likely winner. Arcaro, who had moved to the rail to save ground, swerved back to the middle of the track to find an open lane and running room. The leaders were racing inside of him, with Sir Mango a head in front of Landlocked and a 27–1 shot named Precious Stone. Arcaro was in trouble.

But then suddenly, without urging, the Dancer turned it on. Arcaro didn't shout at him, strike him, wave the stick, or shake the reins. The horse decided on his own to start moving, as if he had suddenly realized that time was running out. Back went his ears, down went his head, and off he went. The leaders never had a chance.

With just a few gargantuan strides, the Grey Ghost passed Precious Stone and Landlocked and zoomed past tiring Sir Mango as he reached the eighth pole. Suddenly, there was only dirt in front of him and cheers raining down. The Dancer pulled farther away with every stride, taking control, leaving the others behind.

Just like that, Arcaro was saved.

Before the Belmont, when the Dancer's greatness was still being debated, Arthur Daley had written in the *New York Times* that when great horses "came on with an invincible rush . . . they blasted away with a surging power that was awesome to behold." Here was such a rush, a champion demolishing his opponents in a matter of moments after having given them reason to believe they could win. The Dancer powered to the finish and hit the wire two lengths ahead of Landlocked, his time just one-fifth of a second off the track record, held by a horse who had carried ten fewer pounds.

"We could have broken that track record easily," Arcaro told Vanderbilt after the race, referring to the Dancer's meandering in the early going.

The owner accepted the trophy, the *Chicago Tribune* reported, "in the manner of a New York Yankee winning a baseball game, or a Notre Dame halfback after a football victory—it was old stuff." The *Tribune* also noted that famed New Orleans high roller Diamond Jim Moran was in the crowd and had proclaimed the Dancer "the greatest of 'em all," even though he had placed a losing twenty-dollar bet on Landlocked that was "as wrong as sin."

Lester Murray was beaming when he took the horse from the Master. The Dancer's groom had been more nervous before this race than the Kentucky Derby, fearing how the horse would respond to the jockey change.

"You the champ, Daddy," Murray said into the horse's ear. "You show these people."

Arcaro's relief was obvious as he smiled broadly in the winner's circle. Despite the must-win pressure and his sore ankle, the Master had performed brilliantly as a relief pitcher, keeping the Dancer off the early pace, saving ground along the rail, and then finding a lane for the Dancer to uncork his finishing kick. The horse had resisted orders and acted on his own, but everything had worked out.

What did Arcaro think now of the famous Grey Ghost? His opinions were, to some reporters, more newsworthy than the outcome of the race. The writers crowded around Arcaro in the jockeys' room.

"I guess Native Dancer is about everything they said he is. He had plenty left. He's one hell of a horse," the jockey said. "He handled himself perfectly, but going down the backstretch he didn't seem to be doing much. He still didn't do much at the half-mile pole. Then all of a sudden he started to roll, and that was it. Apparently he likes to make his move when he sees fit. But man, does he make up ground when he decides to move."

Was he worried to find himself in fourth place turning for home? "I was worried because I didn't know much about him," Arcaro said, "but he got me over that worry fast—as soon as he hit the stretch. Then he had sheer power. I never hit him, just waved my stick a few times. I wanted to keep control because I'd been warned he might take it easy after getting into the lead. It wasn't necessary to strike him. When we hit the wire he was loafing along and winking at the photographers."

How did the Dancer compare with Citation? That was the opinion everyone wanted to know, and accounts of Arcaro's response differed. Marshall Smith, in *Life*, wrote that Arcaro said, "The best horse I ever rode was Citation." Neither the *Chicago Tribune* nor the *New York Times* used such a quote. The *Tribune* reported that Arcaro said, "It's difficult to compare them. Citation was easier to ride. He responded quicker when I asked him." The *Times* didn't mention the issue. Whatever he said, he obviously still favored Citation. But the Dancer had impressed him. After publicly doubting the colt for more than a year, he never again voiced a hint of criticism.

After the race, an Associated Press reporter tracked down Guerin, who was sitting out his suspension at home in New York.

"Boy, do I feel low," Guerin said. "I hope no one feels as low as I do today."

Why didn't he travel to Chicago to see the race?

"Watch the Dancer out there with someone else riding? Man, that would make me feel even worse."

The jockey said he had been confident Arcaro would win, but added, "The Dancer and I, we like to win together."

Given the Dancer's supreme intelligence ("he knows it's a race day as surely as Winfrey does," Evan Shipman had written), which some observers believed was his greatest asset, even greater than his physical gifts, it was easy to ascribe to him the same feeling: that he preferred to win with Guerin. The reality, of course, was that no one knew what he was thinking or what motivated him. But as he headed back to the barn after winning the American Derby, having tortured Arcaro before letting him off the hook, it was hard not to perceive a sense of satisfaction in the lively bounce in his step and the happy bob of his head; hard not to feel that he hadn't delivered his version of a response to Arcaro, the equine translation of that most basic of human epithets: "Take that, you little s.o.b.!"

# NINETEEN

D espite a seven-race winning streak and career earnings of $743,820, the fourth-highest total ever, the Dancer wasn't alone at the top of the American racing world after the American Derby. In fact, hard as it was to believe, many experts didn't even feel he was the best horse in training. Tom Fool, a muscular four-year-old bay owned by the Whitney family's Greentree Stable, was regarded by many horsemen as superior, having won eight straight races during the year, at distances from five and a half furlongs to one and a quarter miles, while setting records, carrying up to 136 pounds and ceding vast amounts of weight.

Bred in Kentucky and sold privately to Greentree for an amount widely believed to have been $25,000, Tom Fool had won five of seven starts as a two-year-old in 1951—losing the Hopeful Stakes to Vanderbilt's Cousin—and ended the year as the nation's top juvenile. He missed the Triple Crown the next spring because of an illness, but recovered in time to establish his dominance among his class by the end of the year. Now he had blossomed into a full-fledged star at four, becoming the first horse since 1913 to sweep New York's handicap Triple Crown—the Metropolitan, Brooklyn, and Suburban, run through the spring and early summer. He wasn't as well known from coast to coast as the Dancer, having raced only in New York and not as often on national TV, but he was equally gifted and, indeed, quite possibly superior.

The idea of pitting the Grey Ghost against Tom Fool had gained momentum through the summer, starting out as little more than an interesting topic to debate—"Can Vanderbilt's colt beat Tom Fool?" columnist Nelson Dunstan had asked in the *Morning Telegraph* in June—and making more and more sense as the two horses ran out of opposition in their respective divisions. Tom Fool's two starts at Saratoga in August had been little more than exhibitions, with just one horse opposing him in each event and the track not accepting any bets. Obviously, the owners and trainers of the other top handicap horses didn't want to take him on anymore. Similarly, after the Travers and American Derby, it seemed the Dancer was just about out of three-year-old opposition. Both horses needed a challenge. Bringing them together was a natural.

Vanderbilt loved the idea. The public wanted it, and it would be good for the sport. Jock Whitney, who co-owned Greentree with his sister, was also in favor. The two men had much in common, although Whitney was seven years older. Both had inherited large family fortunes, taken over racing stables from their mothers, and been elected to the Jockey Club while still in their twenties. "They had great respect for each other," Jeanne Vanderbilt recalled. They also wielded enormous influence in racing, especially in New York, so it was no surprise when the Westchester Racing Association, which operated Belmont, announced in July that it was changing the conditions of the Sysonby Mile with the idea of bringing the Grey Ghost and Tom Fool together.

Previously run as a traditional handicap in early October, with weights assigned by racing secretary John Campbell, the Sysonby was being changed to a "weight-for-age" event in late September, with the purse rising from $20,000 to $50,000. Tom Fool and all four-year-olds would carry 126 pounds. The Dancer and all three-year-olds would carry 119 pounds. Vanderbilt and Whitney nominated their horses to run in those conditions, "and if all goes well and both horses are right, there is no doubt they'll meet," Vanderbilt told reporters.

Not since the ballyhooed match race between War Admiral and Seabiscuit, which Vanderbilt had staged in 1938 when he was running Pimlico, had a possible meeting of champions so intrigued the racing world. Talk of Tom Fool and the Dancer dominated conversations through the early fall, with opinions in the nation's barns, grandstands, and press boxes divided, as might be expected, into two camps—those who thought Tom Fool would win and those picking the Dancer.

There was no doubt which camp was larger. The Greentree star was older, more experienced, and more dominating, usually leaving his opponents far behind before reaching the finish line, unlike the Dancer. The Dancer was the people's choice, but more experts thought Tom Fool would win. *Newsweek*'s John Lardner picked him "on the principle that weight-carrying is one of Tom Fool's special talents." Calumet's Plain Ben Jones agreed, telling Grantland Rice that "Vanderbilt should keep his horse away from Tom Fool—if he don't want to get licked." When the *Daily Racing Form* asked veteran race-caller Clem McCarthy to "visualize" a meeting and write a column about it, McCarthy picked Tom Fool to win by a length.

The most telling support for the Greentree four-year-old came from Evan Shipman, the insightful *Morning Telegraph* columnist who had written so glowingly about the Dancer all year. "We do not hesitate in picking Tom Fool to win," he wrote in a September 9 column, "and this selection, we will add, is that of all the horsemen with whom we have discussed the race, while the preference of the general public veers strongly in the other direction. As we see it, Tom Fool is a great horse, and we have the proper respect for the adjective. He has as much speed as any horse we have ever seen at all our popular distances. He can carry crushing weights, and he has admirable consistency. Native Dancer is not to be faulted on any of these counts, but it is a question of degree. Native Dancer is versatile, courageous and fast, nor do we think that we have ever failed to pay full tribute to those qualities. Nevertheless, we have seen Tom Fool do things of which we do not believe Native Dancer, good as he is, is capable. It will take direct evidence to convince us that we are wrong."

The Grey Ghost wasn't without his supporters among experts. Guerin, admittedly biased, told reporters after the Dwyer Stakes in July that the rare weight advantage for the Dancer would prove decisive. The *Baltimore Sun*'s William Boniface also thought Vanderbilt's horse would win. "In all the match races I had seen, the come-from-behind horse won," Boniface recalled years later. "Seabiscuit was a plodder, War Admiral was the speed horse, and Seabiscuit won. That's why I liked Native Dancer over Tom Fool. Tom Fool was flashier, the one that dominated races. But Native Dancer was the workhorse."

*Newsweek*'s Lardner interviewed Winfrey and Greentree trainer John Gaver in early September, with the race some three weeks away.

"We're giving the grey horse seven pounds," Gaver said. "Can we do it? I don't know. The Dancer is all power. Nobody knows yet how fast he can run if he has to."

"Those big, wide turns at Belmont are made to order for Tom Fool," Winfrey said. "He is much cleverer than my horse. He can turn on a dime. And the race is one mile, which has always been Tom Fool's best distance."

The countdown was on.

The Dancer was dealing with a sore left front foot, discovered shortly after the American Derby, but although it had hindered his training, it wasn't expected to interfere with the race. Dr. William Wright, Vanderbilt's veterinarian, had trimmed a pair of small stone bruises from the bottom of the foot in late August, and the area was expected to be trouble-free once the foot "grew back." Winfrey was optimistic after the Dancer galloped at Belmont on September 7. "He seemed first-rate this morning," the trainer said. "We let him gallop out a bit, and he moved into it comfortably and looked well. I guess, and hope, that we located the trouble and caught it in time. As soon as it appears certain the tenderness has left the two spots we cut out, we'll breeze him. That ought to be in the next couple of days."

The colt was in a playful mood after another gallop the next morning, hamming it up for photographers and trying to unseat Everson, but there was lingering soreness in the foot the next day. The race was just sixteen days away, and the Grey Ghost still wasn't in serious training; he hadn't breezed since late August. It was going to be difficult to have him in top condition for the Sysonby.

After thinking the situation over for a night, Vanderbilt issued a statement on September 12: "After Native Dancer's last workout, the injured hoof showed that it had not healed sufficiently from the removal of the bruised parts and that it would be approximately a week before it would be safe to continue full training. Inasmuch as the Sysonby is only two weeks away, it will be impossible to have him at his best for the race. It would not be fair, either to the horse or to the public, to run him when he is not at his best. So we feel we must announce that Native Dancer will not run in the Sysonby.

"It's just a matter of time. If the Sysonby was a week later than it is, we would not have to issue a statement today, as there would be a good chance that he would be ready for the race."

Race-goers everywhere were disappointed, and especially those in New York. The Westchester Racing Association had gone to great trouble to bring the two horses together in the Sysonby, but now only Tom Fool would run. There was, however, still hope of getting the horses into the same starting gate. The Pimlico Special, another weight-for-age event that Vanderbilt had inaugurated when he was running Pimlico, loomed as a possibility. Vanderbilt and Winfrey said they would probably run the Dancer in the Jockey Club Gold Cup, a two-mile race at Belmont on October 10, then ship him to Pimlico for the Special on October 24. Gaver said he wouldn't run Tom Fool in the Gold Cup—his horse had never raced more than one and a quarter miles, so two miles seemed like a stretch—but the Pimlico Special was, indeed, in his plans. The news struck like a thunderbolt in Baltimore: the race of the year, if not the decade, would apparently take place there.

But then came a second announcement from Barn 20, one week after the first, quashing plans for the new "dream race." On September 19, Winfrey told reporters that Dr. Wright had discovered more bruises on the bottom of the Dancer's left front foot, and although they were small, they had to be cut away. That meant more time off from serious training, and since the Dancer had already accomplished so much, he was being retired for the year. Vanderbilt had made the decision. The Dancer's three-year-old season was over.

The racing press and public were profoundly dejected. The *Thoroughbred Record* called it "a stunning disappointment, almost a personal blow." The Grey Ghost's fans were speechless. Tom Fool's fans smiled, believing that Vanderbilt, contrary to his reputation as a sportsman, was ducking the older horse; speculation was so rampant that the *Morning Telegraph* reported that the Dancer's retirement for the year had "stirred up controversy." Vanderbilt added to the frustration when he told reporters that the Dancer could probably have continued to race with bar plates protecting his injured foot if he had been "just another colt," but since the horse was a star with higher standards to uphold, he was being shut down altogether.

Vanderbilt surely was willing to run a healthy Dancer against Tom Fool, but he was uncomfortable with the pressure to run. According to his son years later, he was influenced by his memory of the famed match race between War Admiral and Seabiscuit, which Vanderbilt had promoted at Pimlico in 1938. "Dad told me he always felt bad about the way he 'kind of trapped' [War Admiral owner] Sam Riddle into running," Alfred Vanderbilt III said. "He felt that War Admiral wasn't in shape for the race and wouldn't have run if the pressure hadn't been so fierce. I think that's why he didn't want to commit the Dancer; why the sore ankle was a good reason to retire him for the year. He knew he could never duck a match race even if he needed to, having promoted the greatest one of all himself."

Days after the Dancer was shut down for the year, Jock Whitney announced that Tom Fool would be permanently retired at the end of his four-year-old season. He would race in the Sysonby and Pimlico Special, then embark on a new career as a stallion at Greentree Farm in Kentucky. The dream race between Tom Fool and the Dancer would never occur, a victim of injuries, timing, and happenstance.

Without the Dancer to challenge him, Tom Fool easily won the Sysonby and Pimlico Special to end his season unbeaten in ten starts. Only two horses opposed him in the Sysonby, and he won so handily that jockey Teddy Atkinson was easing him through the stretch. He also had only two horses to beat in the Special, and he won by eight lengths, setting a new track record for one and three-sixteenth miles.

There was little suspense when the sport's end-of-the-year honors were announced in December, as voted on by various panels of racing secretaries and writers. The Dancer was the champion male three-year-old. Tom Fool was the champion male handicap horse.

They were the only candidates for overall Horse of the Year honors, but the balloting wasn't close. Tom Fool won all polls easily, almost unanimously.

The voting results were hard for some of the Dancer's fans to fathom. The Grey Ghost had won nine of ten starts, two-thirds of the Triple Crown, and $513,425 in 1953. He ranked fourth on the sport's all-time earnings list. He had lost one race in his life; Tom Fool had lost nine. How could Native Dancer not be the Horse of the Year? On the other hand, Tom Fool had, indeed, accomplished more in some ways in 1953. He had carried 130 or more pounds in four starts; Native Dancer never carried more than 128. He had won every time out, whereas Native Dancer had lost the Derby. And he had often dominated, winning many races by sizable margins; Native Dancer had often needed to rally in the stretch. The public loved the Dancer's sense of drama, but racing insiders were more impressed with Tom Fool. John Turner, the director of racing at Pimlico, told the *Daily Racing Form* that Tom Fool as a four-year-old was the best horse he had seen in twenty-five years.

Interestingly, when various panels of experts almost a half century later were asked to rate the best horses of the twentieth century, the Dancer always finished ahead of Tom Fool, the Greentree colt being penalized in the long run for not winning a Triple Crown race or winning at any distances longer than one and a quarter miles. Tom Fool was the experts' choice at the time, but the Dancer was judged superior in the end.

"Native Dancer and [1979 Kentucky Derby and Preakness winner] Spectacular Bid are the two greatest horses I have ever seen; they did things even the Triple Crown winners never did," Joe Tannenbaum said. "Native Dancer's victorious races were awesome. He had an all-conquering run once Guerin let him loose. He gave the impression that if there was a brick wall in front of him, he would just run right through it to finish first. He had a charisma when racing that made you think that if you didn't know who he was, just by watching him you'd say, 'There goes a champion.' His stride, his drive, his nerve, everything about him was exceptional. It was almost like he shouldn't even be running against other horses, he was so much in a class by himself."

A race against Tom Fool would have provided the ultimate test for him, but it never happened. The horses were on the track together only once, when they paraded through the stretch on Red Cross Day at Belmont in early November 1953. The fans cheered and longed to see them loaded into the starting gate and sent running, but instead they went their separate ways, Tom Fool to a stud career and the Dancer to Sagamore Farm, where he would spend the winter recovering from his injury and prepare for 1954. The question of which would have won, had they raced, became one of racing's great mysteries, endlessly debated, never resolved.

# TWENTY

W hen the Dancer made his stakes-race debut as a four-
year-old in the Metropolitan Handicap, a mile race at
Belmont, on May 15, 1954, it was clear he was no longer
just a champion with a large following. He had become a cultural landmark, his renown stretching beyond racing's boundaries into
crevasses and corners of the country that racing had seldom reached.
*Time,* the nation's foremost newsmagazine, had assigned a reporter
to trail the colt and prepare a cover story. *TV Guide,* a weekly magazine devoted to the new medium, had named him one of the three
most popular TV figures of 1953, along with comedian Arthur Godfrey and host Ed Sullivan. Millions of viewers, as many as watched the
Triple Crown races, were expected to tune in to CBS's national telecast of the Metropolitan, with Bryan Field calling the race.

The Dancer hadn't raced in a major event in nine months, and
more than 39,000 fans came to Belmont on a cloudy Saturday afternoon to watch him run. His prolonged absence forged an insatiable
curiosity before the race, similar to the scene before the Dancer's
1953 debut in the Gotham Stakes. Hundreds of fans swarmed the paddock to get a closer look at a colt now standing 16.3 hands high and
weighing 1,250 pounds, truly a grey monster in his racing tack. Old-
timers couldn't recall a larger crowd around Belmont's saddling shed
and walking ring.

The riding tack was brought in and the Dancer reared magnificently when Winfrey tightened the cinch belt around his waist, drawing a gasp from the crowd, but the horse was composed again within
moments, seemingly waiting to be led to the track. "He's the coolest
horse I've ever seen," Winfrey said to a reporter. "He knows when it's
time to race, and he anticipates it. But none of this bothers him in the
least."

Blue-coated security guards had to cut a swath through the herd
to get the Dancer and his eight rivals to the track for the race. A wide-
eyed stew of horsemen and racing officials huddled inside the ropes,
fixated on the colt.

Other champions had raced to the forefront of the American
public's consciousness before, but never, safe to say, had one become
such a popular figure, such a hero to so many. Television was partly
responsible, of course. The Dancer's career was the first of equine
distinction to have unfolded live in living rooms across the country,
and it did so just as the powerful sense of intimacy that TV generated
was being realized, with viewers feeling, however irrationally, that the
actresses, newsmen, athletes, and horses they saw on the screen
were so familiar they were almost part of the family. Fans drawn to
their sets by the spectacle of racing and the phenomenon of the
medium had watched the Dancer win and lose and win and win, always dramatically, with a closing rush, and had become as attached
to his races as they were to the other programs now dictating their
nighttime routines, such as *Dragnet,* the police drama starring Jack
Webb, *I Love Lucy,* and Sullivan's New York–based variety show. The
Dancer was, in a sense, like Godfrey and Sullivan, the star of his own
show, and what a TV classic it was, faithfully incorporating danger,
suspense, and, with one unforgettable exception, a happy ending.

Tom Gilcoyne, a marketing executive from New Jersey who
later became the historian at the National Museum of Racing in
Saratoga, had followed racing since the 1920s and seldom seen such
hysteria over a horse. "Native Dancer and Milton Berle made TV popular," recalled Gilcoyne, who saw the Grey Ghost in person in the Futurity, Withers, and Belmont and otherwise followed him on TV. "He
gathered up the sorts of fans who had never been to a track and

brought them to racing. He was different, a grey. You could really watch him during a race. It wasn't just a bunch of bays and browns running around. You could pick him up on the TV screen and follow him, and when he made his surge, you surged with him. People cheered him like they cheered their heroes on the football field."

It wasn't just the power of the medium, however; the "message" in the Dancer's races—his winning qualities—was also essential to his popularity. There were reasons why he had become America's horse instead of Tom Fool as the public debated their respective merits. The two were equally gifted, exemplifying the thoroughbred breed at its finest with their power, speed, and heart, but the Dancer was more idiosyncratic, exuding the smoky allure of a legend. He preferred to take the harder road—coming from behind instead of dominating, relaxing in the stretch instead of pulling away—yet no matter how hard he made it on himself, he always prevailed. He also had a distinct personality: he was a cutup around the barn in the mornings and had been labeled "a lazy so-and-so" on national TV by Winfrey, yet as Evan Shipman had written, he was the consummate professional, always knowing when it was time to stop fooling around and go to work. Hard-core race-goers loved his class. Casual fans loved his coloring and individualism. Everyone, it seemed, loved being on his side.

"No one has ever quite documented how or why the legend of a champion grows," *Time* wrote of the Dancer. "The present has its press agents as the past had its poets. (Was Achilles really that good, or did Homer just make him seem so?) But a legend's feats endure because of what he adds: an undying spirit of competition, an ability to inspire awe, a willingness to gamble on losing, the guts to lose and rise again, an elusive mixture of spirit and showmanship. Whatever it is called—flair, class, style or what Hemingway once termed 'grace under pressure'—it is the quality that breeds sport legend."

The Grey Ghost had it. Jock Whitney, sending out the dangerous Greentree gelding Straight Face to try to beat the Dancer in the Metropolitan, gazed at the grey favorite being saddled in the crowded paddock before the race. "If anyone beats him, I hope it's my horse," Whitney mused, then reconsidered and corrected himself with a wan smile: "It's strange, but I hope the Dancer wins." The comments were overheard by the *Time* reporter, who later printed them. Even the opposition was rooting for Vanderbilt's champion.

The Dancer's return to the races was welcomed by a racing public looking for action. The 1954 Triple Crown season was under way, the Kentucky Derby already run and the Preakness coming up, but it was a pale imitation of the 1953 drama featuring the Dancer, Dark Star, and Jamie K. A tough little grey named Determine had won the Derby, but his owner, Andy Crevolin, had shipped him back to California rather than run him in the Preakness. None of the three-year-olds had the makings of a star, and with Tom Fool at stud, every other horse seemed pint-sized compared to the larger-than-life Dancer.

The Grey Ghost was more exciting just preparing to race than the others were at full speed. The colt had actually made his 1954 racing debut eight days before the Metropolitan in a weekday afternoon allowance at Belmont, "and as he stood in the stall with his handlers before the race, he was so massive and rock-like that he could have been hewn from New Hampshire granite," Evan Shipman wrote. "Immobile, he was as weighty as a monument. But he did not remain immobile for long. Twice, he reared majestically while Les Murray clung to the shank. His eye, usually so calm when action was imminent, was wicked and fiery, like that of a seed bull."

Now, there was a racehorse.

The Dancer had spent the winter under Ralph Kercheval's care at Sagamore Farm instead of traveling with Winfrey and the rest of Vanderbilt's horses to California; he had then rejoined the stable at Belmont in March and trained under Winfrey until now. Winfrey and Vanderbilt had chosen the obscure spot to prep him for the Metropolitan, and 21,792 fans came to Belmont to see him shake off the rust that had accumulated during his long layoff. John Campbell, the respected New York racing secretary, had assigned him 126 pounds, five more than Laffango, an old rival, and from twelve to eighteen pounds more than the rest of the field, mostly fringe four-year-olds. The race, titled the Commando Purse, was just six furlongs, the shortest distance the Dancer had raced since the spring of his two-year-old season.

Even though the late-running Dancer was better at longer distances and there was a chance he could get caught in traffic and not have time to rally, the bettors, predictably, leaned heavily on him, backing him down to 3–20 odds by post time. Justifying the support, the colt raced as if he had never stopped, following his familiar blueprint of "rating" near the lead until the turn, then accelerating and zooming to the lead as he straightened for home. Showing no signs of the foot injury that had ended his 1953 season, he reached the finish line slightly more than a length ahead of Laffango, who was a neck in front of a colt named Impasse. It wasn't an overpowering performance and the winning time of 1:11⅘ was modest, but "there is no way of knowing how fast the Dancer might have gone had he been urged," the *Morning Telegraph* reported. "Guerin never touched him with his stick and had only to move his hands to take command, then scrubbed intermittently through the final furlong as the rivals behind him struggled desperately under whip, hand and heel."

His season was under way, and what a season of possibilities it was. Vanderbilt and Winfrey had charted a course for him unlike any ever outlined for a top American horse. First, the Dancer would try to emulate Tom Fool and win New York's Triple Crown of handicap races—the Metropolitan, Brooklyn, and Suburban—along with the Carter Stakes at Aqueduct. He would then be shipped across the Atlantic Ocean and race in major events in England and France through the summer and fall. He had already been nominated for the King George VI Stakes and Queen Elizabeth Stakes, run in July during the Royal Meeting at Ascot, the historic racecourse near Windsor Castle in England. There was talk of entering him in the Prix de l'Arc de Triomphe, France's most important race, at Longchamp in Paris. The trainer of Vanderbilt's small British division had told reporters he was expecting the horse in Newmarket that fall. The thinking was that the Dancer was likely to exhaust his competition in America, so why not try to conquer a new world? If any horse could, it was the Grey Ghost.

America's handicap division was indeed weak, with few horses seemingly capable of beating the Dancer. Royal Vale was a threat—the British-bred five-year-old had given Tom Fool several scares the year before—but he hadn't raced at the same level in recent months.

A sprinter named White Skies would be dangerous at seven furlongs, but the Dancer would seldom, if ever, meet him. Jamie K. was still around but had never realized the promise shown in the Preakness and Belmont the previous year. The Phipps family's Level Lea had emerged as a late-blooming three-year-old the previous fall, and Vanderbilt's second-string four-year-olds, Social Outcast and Find, were improving, but it was hard to envision any of them beating the Dancer.

Straight Face, at age four, was a mystery. He had finished sixth behind Dark Star and the Dancer in the Kentucky Derby the year before, hindered by ankle and leg injuries suffered during the prep season in Florida. Greentree trainer John Gaver had taken him out of training after the Derby to have his ankles fired, and he had ended up missing the rest of the year. Returning, sound, in 1954, the horse had won two allowance races in Florida in January, then finished out of the money in major races such as the Santa Anita Maturity, Widener Handicap, and Gulfstream Park Handicap. But just when it appeared he was destined to disappoint, he had come within a fifth of a second of the Pimlico track record for nine furlongs in winning the Dixie Handicap. That was his most recent race, a week earlier. It would be interesting to see which Straight Face showed up in the Metropolitan.

That the Dancer would be assigned the highest weight in the race was a given, but how much weight was a fair handicap? Speculation had swirled at Belmont as John Campbell mulled his decision, announced six days before the race. Grey Lag had carried 133 to victory in the Metropolitan in 1923, ceding twenty-six pounds to a rival. Devil Diver had carried 134 in 1944. Tom Fool had carried 130 the year before, giving three pounds to Royal Vale. Some believed the Dancer might be assigned as many as 135, but Campbell ultimately settled on 130, two pounds more than the Dancer had ever carried, and the same weight assigned Tom Fool the year before in the Metropolitan. Campbell told reporters the Grey Ghost hadn't yet shown he was as good as or better than Tom Fool, so he shouldn't have to carry more weight. The *Morning Telegraph*'s Nelson Dunstan labeled the assignment "eminently fair."

In the end, Royal Vale and White Skies weren't entered in the

Metropolitan, and Find was scratched. The second-highest weight in the field fell to Straight Face, at 117 pounds, thirteen fewer than the Dancer. Jamie K. was at 110, getting twenty pounds from a horse he had almost beaten on the same track a year earlier. A four-year-old named Count Cain was getting twenty-three pounds from the Dancer, and a five-year-old named Flaunt was getting twenty-four. The Dancer would race at quite a handicap, finally facing the test many experts had wanted to see when he was forced to the sidelines in 1953. Could he carry crushing weights and beat quality opposition under a severe handicap? Vanderbilt himself had said the colt "still had things to prove," and the Metropolitan loomed as a worthwhile opportunity, even without Royal Vale and White Skies.

In the minutes before the race, the bettors made the usual rush to put their money on the Dancer, knowing they would get little in return if he won. Of the $210,712 in win bets pushed through the windows, 53 percent went with the Dancer, lowering his odds to 1–4 by post time. That made it twenty races in a row in which he had left the starting gate as an odds-on favorite. Only in the first race of his career, at Jamaica in April 1952, had he been more than even money.

Straight Face was the second choice at 7–1, the only other horse to garner much support, and it seemed he was resolved to justify the fans' faith when the starting gate opened at 4:19 P.M., with the track rated fast and Bryan Field at the microphone for CBS. Breaking alertly from the seventh post with jockey Teddy Atkinson dressed in Greentree's pink silks with black-striped sleeves, Straight Face immediately shot into the lead and dropped toward the rail. A trio of long shots gave chase up the backstretch along with Impasse, the third betting choice at 9–1, but the pace was fast, a quarter in 23¼, and Straight Face quickly opened daylight on the field.

The Dancer was sluggish. He broke sharply, but Guerin took him back as usual and the colt slowly drifted toward the rear, seemingly not in the mood to run. As the pack separated into two four-abreast waves of horses chasing the leader, with the Dancer and Magic Lamp at the back of the rear quartet, Straight Face hurtled ahead, covering the second quarter mile in 22⅘ seconds. Atkinson glanced back as he neared the turn, obviously trying to locate the

Grey Ghost, but the grey colt was beyond the jockey's view: there were too many lengths and too many horses between them. Atkinson turned back and asked for more from the gelding. His tactics were apparent: he was going to try to steal the race from in front, building a lead so large that the Dancer couldn't erase it down the stretch. "My goal," Atkinson said later, "was to put as much ground as possible between my horse and Native Dancer."

Shockingly, Straight Face was ten lengths ahead of the Dancer halfway through the race, running about as fluidly and fast as a horse could run as he angled into the turn. A colt named Jampol tried to move up and run with him but quickly faltered and dropped back. Count Cain suffered the same fate when he tried to mount a charge. Straight Face's lead grew to four lengths on the turn. Atkinson glanced back again, still trying to locate the horse he knew would come after him, but he still couldn't find the grey favorite. Where was the Dancer? Fans at Belmont and across the nation were shouting the same question. Vanderbilt's horse had made up ground in the stretch before, but he was testing his limits here.

Quietly, from deep in the field, the Dancer started to make his move on the turn. Without urging from Guerin, he lowered his head, picked up his stride, and shot ahead of the laggards, jumping into fifth place. Jampol and Count Cain were still in front of him when Atkinson looked back the second time, blocking the jockey's view, but the savvy Atkinson didn't need to see the Dancer to know the challenge was coming. Atkinson turned back around and smacked Straight Face with his stick, desperate for the effort he felt would be needed to maintain the lead to the wire. The horse passed the quarter pole just before straightening for home, having covered the first three quarters in a blazing 1:10⅕. His lead was three and a half lengths as he hugged the rail, in perfect position for the stretch run.

Guerin moved the Dancer wide to avoid traffic as he rallied. The colt was still in fifth as he passed the quarter pole, seven lengths behind the leader. There were three horses between them, and the Dancer almost casually swept around them all as he came out of the turn and straightened for home, moving into second place as he charged past Impasse. He was still five lengths behind Straight Face, and it hadn't taken much for him to put the others behind him, so Guerin reached back and struck the colt four times, eliciting gasps from the fans who had never seen the Dancer's jockey get so tough with the horse. "I called for him on the turn and he didn't answer with all that he had," Guerin said later, "so I had to call for more, and he came on with his answer then."

Two hundred yards to go, one horse ahead of him, the Grey Ghost careening down the middle of the stretch. His legs blurred as he picked up his pace, spotting Straight Face along the rail and feeling Guerin's stick on his side. A challenge had been put down, and the Dancer picked it up, his intense competitive urge engaged. He veered sharply across the stretch, toward Straight Face. Even the lay fan could see what he had to be thinking: "If I'm going to beat that damn horse over there, I'm going to beat him like a champion, eye-to-eye, where he can see me and hear me and feel my superiority." It wouldn't be any fun beating him from a distance, in the middle of the track.

He started gaining ground, cutting the lead to four lengths, then three at the eighth pole as the crowd's roar swelled. "He still had a ton of ground to make up; it looked like it was going to be impossible for him to get up to the lead, but he kept coming," recalled Hall of Fame trainer Allen Jerkens, who was at Belmont that afternoon. The lead was down to two lengths, then one just inside the sixteenth pole, with the Dancer now hovering next to the leader. The grandstand was in an uproar, the crowd hoarsely imploring the Dancer to keep charging. Atkinson, sensing the challenge he had known would come, pounded Straight Face with the stick, once, twice, three times with a violent right-handed spank. The Greentree colt had raced magnificently— and been ridden magnificently—for more than seven furlongs, but there was little left to give.

Guerin had always ridden the Dancer with supreme confidence, knowing he could wait until deep into races to make a charge because the colt's finishing kick was so strong. That confidence might have cost the Dancer in the Derby, when Guerin hesitated, perhaps fatally, at the top of the stretch; but since then, the jockey had all but perfected his use of the powerful racing machine underneath him. The zenith of their understanding occurred in the final furlong of the Metropolitan, with the finish line approaching, the crowd shrieking, and the jockey on the horse in front of him furiously pounding away. Guerin, cool amid the hysteria, put his stick away. He had seen and felt enough. The Dancer was still running second, within a head of Straight Face inside the sixteenth pole, the issue supposedly in doubt, but Guerin's hands went down. The gesture, as simple as it was stunning, spoke volumes. The horse could take it from there. And the jockey knew the horse could take it from there.

The Dancer had made up seventh lengths in a quarter mile on a fast horse carrying thirteen fewer pounds—a move that almost defied belief. Starting from ten lengths behind on the turn, he had circled the field and run down a leader racing furiously on the rail. Anyone who had doubted him—and goodness knows how many doubts had been voiced along the way—would have to keep quiet now. With his jockey motionless, trusting him to complete what had been started, the colt pulled even with Straight Face with fifty yards to go. "The horse's finish was superb, a spectacle of power; he was in perfect balance, with perfect equilibrium at all times," Evan Shipman would write. The next jump put the Dancer in front by a nose. There was no doubt now. As the finish line approached, the Grey Ghost cocked his head to the side almost imperceptibly, glancing at Straight Face, seemingly seeking a nod from his opponent that the better horse had won. Then he took another step and reached the wire. The fans were jumping and shouting, lost in a delirium. The Dancer had pulled it off.

The stewards immediately called for a photo to check the finish, but that was just a formality. The limp crowd and exhausted jockeys knew that the Dancer had reached the wire first. "He was so far out of it, it was incredible," *Daily Racing Form* columnist Joe Hirsch recalled almost fifty years later. "But he closed ground unbelievably! That was a very fine Greentree horse, and Native Dancer beat him right at the end. It was amazing that he could get up there, but he did. It remains, to this day, one of the greatest races I have ever seen."

Vanderbilt and Winfrey rushed from their box seats to the winner's enclosure to greet Guerin. The enormity of the performance was quickly sinking in. The Dancer had covered the final quarter in under 24 seconds and the mile in 1:35½—three-fifths faster than Tom

Fool's time in the Metropolitan the year before and just two-fifths off Belmont's track record for a mile, set by Count Fleet in 1942 while carrying thirteen fewer pounds. It was a performance that left no wiggle room for doubters. Turf writers didn't need to pause and reflect before passing judgment. "Magnificent; a dangling Pearl White never produced more suspense than the famous grey in the final half-mile," wrote Pat O'Brien in the *Blood-Horse*, referring to the silent movie star who was always being rescued from train tracks just before the train ran over her. James Roach, in the *New York Times*, called the race "a five-star thriller," and Shipman called the Dancer's finish "one of the greatest final quarters ever run on the American turf."

Almost a half century later, jockey Teddy Atkinson recalled the stretch run vividly, smiling and shaking his head. "Straight Face was a very good horse, and especially good that day," he said from the home in Virginia to which he had retired. "But Native Dancer was always at his best when he was trailing like he was. He was so far back that day that he really had to come on. I thought that maybe I had opened up enough of a lead, but I was wrong."

When reporters surrounded Guerin after the race, he just smiled. "Was I scared? Damn right I was, right down to the last fifty yards," he said. "I wanted to start moving up at the half mile pole, but he wouldn't go. Then he made up his mind to go. It was like always. You can try to explain to another rider how good it is, how strong he feels and what it's like to ride him, but you can't; a guy just had to ride him to know."

Harold Walker and Lester Murray led him away, toward Barn 20, with Murray chattering as he gripped the horse's tail.

"Come on, Daddy, and I'll do you up nice," the groom said. "You got a nice night coming after that."

An hour later, after the horse had cooled down and been bathed and fed, Murray stood outside stall 6 and spoke to several reporters.

"He run every time," the groom said, unable to suppress the pride welling inside him. "He make you think he isn't gonna go, and he always go. He don't need someone telling him when it's time. He knows."

The Dancer abruptly looked up, as if he had heard the compliment. Murray and the horse had been together for two years now, and anyone who spent any time around them could see that their connection was almost kinetic.

"You like that, huh," Murray said. "You listening."

The Metropolitan, it turned out, was the most important of the year. The miracle comeback ultimately convinced Horse of the Year voters that the Dancer deserved the sport's highest honor in 1954. It also convinced the editors of *Time* that he was a public figure of the highest distinction. An illustration of the Dancer, in profile, made the cover of the issue of *Time* dated May 31, 1954, above a headline reading, "Native Dancer: A little heartbreak, then a burst of glory." The colt's light grey face was set against a luminous backdrop of blue sky, a horse farm pasture, and two strips of Vanderbilt's cerise and white silks.

The sight of a horse's face on the cover surely shocked some of *Time*'s readers accustomed to pictures and portraits of prominent, serious-minded figures from business and national and international affairs. Others who had made the cover in the previous year included Earl Warren, chief justice of the U.S. Supreme Court; Allen Dulles, head of the Central Intelligence Agency; Queen Frederika of Greece; Chou En-lai, premier of the People's Republic of China; and just the week before, Texas millionaire Clint Murchison. Now added to that roll call: the Grey Ghost.

"There were people who collected autographed covers of *Time* magazine, and after Native Dancer was on the cover, we suddenly got fifteen or twenty in the mail asking for them to be signed," Bill Winfrey's son Carey recalled. "We put them on the ground in his stall and got Native Dancer to stand on them, and then sent them back 'autographed.'"

The magazine's two-thousand-word article (printed without a byline) detailed the Dancer's career and personality as well as those of Vanderbilt and Guerin, and also took readers minute by minute through the Metropolitan drama. "The Big Grey reigns as popularly chosen monarch over a domain that has grown into the nation's biggest spectator sport," the article reported.

The wording on the cover—"a little heartbreak, then a burst of glory"—referred to what the editors saw as the Dancer's racing blue-print: he temporarily broke his fans' hearts with his agonizingly slow starts, then mended them with his mad rushes to glory down the stretch. But the wording was even more appropriate as a summary description of the Dancer's career, which, after the Metropolitan, now stood at twenty victories in twenty-one starts, with the past ten races all successes. The Derby had been his heartbreak, but the ensuing burst of glory had elevated him to the pinnacle where he now stood, hailed as one of America's most famous athletes, the hero of racing's golden age, his status papers stamped in ink in the wake of his great-est escape.

# TWENTY-ONE

On the very day the Dancer's issue of *Time* magazine reached newsstands across America, the horse was declared lame after a morning workout at Belmont. Battling what appeared to be a mild case of soreness in his right front foot, he was twelve days removed from the Metropolitan and four days away from a rematch with Straight Face in the Suburban Handicap when he came out of a three-furlong breeze in obvious distress. Bernie Everson jumped off his back as he pulled up, unsaddled the limping colt, and walked him back to the barn. After an examination, Winfrey announced the Dancer would miss the Suburban. "He seemed fine this morning, so we tried him out with a breeze—you saw the results," the trainer told reporters.

The first sign of foot trouble had come several days earlier, after an excellent mile workout on a quiet Sunday morning. The Dancer cooled out nicely but appeared to miss a step as he entered his stall. Winfrey had him led back out for an examination and detected that the foot was, indeed, tender, but X rays showed no breaks and Winfrey lightheartedly dismissed the problem as "a sore tootsie." The Dancer resumed training after taking a day off, walking for an hour on Tuesday and galloping two miles on Wednesday with Winfrey riding just ahead on a pony, monitoring every step. There was no sign of soreness, so the ill-fated breeze was scheduled for Thursday. "It goes without saying that we're disappointed," Vanderbilt said afterward.

Another set of X rays was taken, again indicating no broken bones. Vanderbilt's vet, Dr. William Wright, settled on a complicated-sounding diagnosis: a bruised digital cushion with a secondary inflammation of the bursar between the navicular and coffin bones. Lay term: a bruise similar to the injury to the Dancer's other front foot that had ended his 1953 campaign after the American Derby.

This latest injury had probably occurred during the horse's spectacular rally in the Metropolitan, when his feet were asked to absorb the awesome thumping of his 1,250 pounds being hurled to the ground with a violence seldom seen from a thoroughbred. The possibility of a wicked irony surfaced with a "tootsie" problem having stopped the Dancer twice in nine months. It could be, now that he had matured from an equine teenager into an adult, that his immense body and powerful racing mechanism—the very assets that made him great—generated too much force, more than his feet could handle. "He is so heavy and hits the ground so hard that that may have caused the bruising," Winfrey told the *Blood-Horse*.

The only antidote was rest. Amid whispers that he might never race again, the Dancer was taken out of training, much to the public's dismay. Straight Face rolled to a four-and-a-half-length victory as a 7–5 favorite in the Suburban before a Memorial Day crowd of 56,736, New York's largest racing crowd in five years. Hundreds of get-well cards arrived at Barn 20 and Vanderbilt's New York office, and the Dancer embraced the "downtime" with his trademark charisma. As Vanderbilt's other horses trained and raced out of Barn 20, the "lazy so-and-so" ate lavish hay "brunches" while soaking his sore foot in a hot bath, then slept standing up with the foot in a poultice wrap. It didn't take much imagination to envision him winking and saying, "Beats working for a living."

The foot improved enough for the colt to resume training in early July. Obviously, his summer trip to Europe was out, as was the New York handicap Triple Crown, but there were numerous other races on both sides of the Atlantic that he could win before being retired at the end of the year. Winfrey worked to have him back into racing shape as quickly as possible. The colt was breezing at Belmont by the end of July, his foot seemingly healed, and was shipped to Saratoga along with Find, Social Outcast, and the other Vanderbilt horses that would run at the Spa that year. The plan was to run him either in the Saratoga Cup, a one-and-three-quarter-mile weight-for-age event near the end of August, or the Whitney, a straightforward Spa handicap in which he would surely be assigned a crushing weight.

If all went well in August, the colt would probably then travel to France to race in the Prix de l'Arc de Triomphe in October. Vanderbilt was optimistic enough about that possibility to take Winfrey with him on a trip to Paris in July to inspect Longchamp and gauge the challenge the race would pose. They were encouraged. The Dancer would have to race in a clockwise direction for the first time, and also race on grass for the first time, but Winfrey and Vanderbilt had long suspected the Dancer would be murderous on grass.

Back in America, the horse trained sharply at Saratoga in early August, and Winfrey and Vanderbilt decided to give him a prep race before returning him to stakes competition in the Whitney or the Saratoga Cup. They picked out the Oneonta Handicap, an obscure seven-furlong sprint on August 16, as the place for him to shake off the rust that had gathered since May. Saratoga handicapper James Kilroe assigned him 137 pounds, by far the most he had ever carried, but even with that massive handicap, he drew only two opponents. One was another Vanderbilt horse, seven-year-old First Glance. Joe W. Brown's three-year-old Gigantic was the other.

With so few horses entered and the Dancer certain to attract virtually every dollar wagered, Saratoga elected to run the race without taking bets, essentially transforming it into a public exhibition. More than 14,000 fans came to the Spa on a muggy Monday, lured by the increasingly rare chance to see the Dancer race. A brief downpour left the track rated sloppy, with puddles on the turns and rivulets in the stretch. The heavy air didn't dampen the crowd's enthusiasm. After Lester Murray walked the Dancer from the barn to the paddock (Murray was celebrating his sixty-fifth birthday, so Winfrey let him handle Harold Walker's customary chore of leading the Dancer on race day), some 2,000 fans surrounded the horse as he was saddled underneath the Dutch elm in the paddock. He was giving eighteen pounds to First Glance, winner of the Wilson Handicap at Jamaica earlier that summer, and thirty pounds to Gigantic, winner of the Swift Stakes at Belmont in May. The Dancer figured to win easily, but he had been out of action for three months and the other two were capable horses. Who knew what would happen, especially with such a severe weight disparity in play?

The crowd cheered the Dancer's appearance on the track and applauded him through the brief post parade. There was a hush when the horses were loaded into the starting gate on the backstretch, then a roar as they were sent running. The Dancer was first out of the gate, but Guerin quickly dropped him back, following the usual blueprint. First Glance jumped into the lead by a couple of lengths over Gigantic, with the Dancer in third, another couple of lengths back. They held those positions through the short run up the backstretch, then angled into the turn. "Gigantic will be able to tell his grandchildren he was ahead of Native Dancer after three furlongs," James Roach wrote later in the *New York Times*.

The Dancer started to roll on the turn. It was a familiar sight. Down went his head, out went his stride, and away went the opposition. He quickly passed Gigantic, then pulled even with First Glance, gaining ground with every stride. He shot past his stablemate at the quarter pole, taking a clear lead. So much for any chance of a real race developing.

Guerin waved his stick in front of the Dancer's right eye a couple of times, seeking to keep the colt from easing up in the stretch. The threat worked. The Grey Ghost charged ahead purposefully along the rail, the 137 pounds on his back seemingly no hindrance. "He ran as if he had no more than a feather-stuffed pillow on his back," Roach later wrote. The crowd stood and cheered as his lead widened to two lengths, four, six, even more. Guerin waved the stick again in the final furlong, and the Dancer raced hard to the finish. He was nine lengths ahead of First Glance at the wire, thirteen up on Gigantic.

Though just a betless weekday exhibition, the race had given fans a glimpse of the Grey Ghost at his finest. His time of 1:24⅘ was impressive, especially considering the weight he had carried over a sloppy track. (A horse carrying twenty-one fewer pounds over a fast track had set Saratoga's seven-furlong record of 1:23.) He was so decisive when he moved and so fluid and dominating in the stretch that it was hard to watch other horses after observing him. Even the best couldn't compare with Native Dancer at the peak of his powers.

The Oneonta's tiny purse of $3,270 raised his career earnings to $785,240, fourth on the all-time list behind Citation, Armed, and Stymie. A few more major victories would make him the sport's all-time money-winner, and Vanderbilt's plans for getting him to that goal became the focus after the colt had cooled out without soreness in his foot. What was next? Vanderbilt said it was more likely that the Dancer would run in the Saratoga Cup than the Whitney, for which he had already been assigned 136 pounds, but no firm decisions would be made for a few days. "We should know more in a day or two," Vanderbilt said.

The colt resumed training, stopping traffic with his daily appearances at the Spa. He galloped one day, worked nine furlongs with Social Outcast the next, then galloped again. Vanderbilt settled on the Saratoga Cup as his next race, preferring not to make the horse carry 136 pounds. The victory in the Oneonta, dismissed by many as hollow, assumed a brighter cast when First Glance raced to a victory against a field of top sprinters a few days later. In hindsight, the Grey Ghost had destroyed a quality older horse under severe handicap conditions. Even though he had raced only three times in 1954, he was, it appeared, in midcampaign condition.

Six days after the Oneonta, the Dancer worked ten furlongs in a slow 2:11 on Sunday, August 22. Winfrey and Vanderbilt watched the exercise, which Winfrey later termed "completely satisfactory," and Vanderbilt left to attend a Jockey Club–sponsored roundtable, an annual Saratoga event at which panels of horsemen, officials, and journalists discussed racing topics. Winfrey remained at the barn to monitor the Dancer, then ate breakfast with several writers before heading over to the roundtable. When the panel broke briefly for lunch, Winfrey pulled Vanderbilt aside and gave him the bad news he had somehow kept to himself all morning: the Dancer had taken several bad steps while cooling out after his workout. He was lame again.

The roundtable soon reconvened, and Vanderbilt found himself sitting at a table with several writers and Robert Kelley, the New York tracks' director of publicity. Only Vanderbilt and Winfrey knew about the Dancer as yet, but Vanderbilt grabbed a pen, scribbled four letters on a piece of paper—N.D.N.G.—and gave the note to Kelley before leaving to huddle with Winfrey. Kelley read the cryptic note to the others, and everyone in the room immediately grasped its meaning: N.D.N.G. stood for "Native Dancer No Good."

Within minutes, Vanderbilt and Winfrey convened a press conference in a small office adjoining the president's room at the Spa. They had a sad and stunning announcement to make.

The Dancer's career was over.

"He pulled up fine after the work and he was fine walking off the track," Winfrey said, "but after ten or fifteen minutes of walking outside the shed, he took a few bad steps. He was beginning to favor the right front foot. I imagine he would have become quite lame if we had continued to walk him, so he was put in his stall. It was quite surprising. He certainly didn't feel any pain while he was working. Bernie didn't feel that anything was wrong. There was no inkling of trouble. We thought we had a completely recovered horse.

"So far as I can see, it is a recurrence of the recent injury. Since this happened after the Metropolitan and we gave him time [off] then, but the trouble has come back after appearing to be cured, we have decided that the only thing to do is to retire him now. If he was just another horse—say, if he was First Glance—we would probably try to go on with him, but since he's Native Dancer, there doesn't seem to be any point in not retiring him now."

Vanderbilt explained, "He was going to stud next year, anyway, and we just don't have enough time left this year to stop him now and start again."

The announcement seemed abrupt to some. If there was any chance the injury wasn't serious and wouldn't take long to heal, why not wait it out and at least give the Dancer a chance to come back in the fall? "I think Mr. Vanderbilt was of the feeling that the horse was going to be carrying a great deal of weight, and perhaps he said, 'I just don't want to see that,'" recalled Tommy Trotter, then an assistant racing secretary in New York. "Sam Riddle retired Man O' War for the same reason. Most of the races available for Native Dancer were handicap races, as opposed to weight-for-age races, and I imagine that had a great influence on Mr. Vanderbilt's decision."

Costy Caras, who worked at the *Daily Racing Form,* suggested that protecting the horse's reputation was also a factor. "I don't know that the horse was badly hurt, but he was hurt to the extent that he was no longer the number one racehorse in the country," Caras recalled. "He had gone out with Social Outcast one morning after the Oneonta and had some problems and couldn't catch Social Outcast. When Native Dancer couldn't catch Social Outcast, it was time to retire him."

Whatever its rationale, the retirement was final: Vanderbilt was not the type to change his mind after making such an important decision. The news rocketed through the sports world that Sunday and made headlines in Monday's papers across the country. Horsemen and others in the racing industry were phlegmatic; as sorry as they were to see a horse of such caliber retired, these things happened in racing. The Dancer's millions of fans took it much harder. For many, it was almost as if they had experienced a death in the family. The Grey Ghost had introduced them to the majesty of horses and the thrill of racing. Now their favorite racing "show" was being canceled. Other champions would surely come along, but the Dancer would always be the first.

"His retirement leaves a void that may not be filled for a long, long time," Evan Shipman wrote in the *Morning Telegraph.* "Champions, by definition, are rare, and Native Dancer was a true champion. Thanks to TV, he was known to millions, a public that had only dimly been aware of other greats such as Man O' War, Citation and Count Fleet. The impressive grey was an ambassador for the sport to those who had never seen a race, and whose knowledge of horseflesh, in this era of the automobile and the airplane, was limited to his brief and shadowy appearances on the screen. This medium, however, for all its limitations, did in his case project a compelling 'personality,' his enormous popularity due to the intangible of equine character as much as to his almost unbroken string of victories.

"Horsemen may argue concerning the exact place Native Dancer should occupy in the hierarchy of distinguished American thoroughbreds, but anything they say, pro or con, is quite beside the point to the colt's host of uncritical worshippers. They, for their part, are convinced that this is what a horse should be; this is the ideal. And no matter how it was arrived at, that intuitive conclusion may be correct."

Amazingly, there were those who still questioned claims to greatness made on the Dancer's behalf, refusing to bestow such high praise on a horse who had set few records and seldom won easily. But the argument was moot at this point, seemingly sustained more by jealousy and general contrariness than any hard evidence. The Dancer's record was beyond criticism. He had started twenty-two races and won twenty-one, bettering Man O' War's career performance of twenty wins in twenty-one starts, and missing perfection by a head in the Kentucky Derby. He had carried 137 pounds as if it were a pillow. Seventeen of his victories had come in stakes races. Overall, he had beaten 137 of 138 opponents over some twenty-four miles of racing, averaging thirty-seven miles per hour during a career in which he competed on eight tracks in four states. He had nothing left to prove.

"It is safe to say that Native Dancer's place among the famous horses of the American turf is secure," wrote *Morning Telegraph* columnist Nelson Dunstan, who had been among the less willing to confer such greatness during the Dancer's career. "Time and again we have seen lists of the '20 greatest American horses,' and invariably the list includes Hindoo, Sysonby, Man O' War, Exterminator and the undefeated Colin. We have no quarrel with the veterans but contend that the list must be brought up to date with Count Fleet, Citation, Assault, Tom Fool and Native Dancer. The grey's record of winning 21 of 22 starts speaks for itself."

Such a horse couldn't leave for the breeding shed without taking a final bow—on TV, of course—and a "farewell" appearance was scheduled. It was a spectacle. Six weeks into his retirement, the Grey

Ghost was paraded through the stretch between races at Belmont on a sunny October Saturday redolent of summer. Thirty-three thousand fans were at the track, and millions across the country were watching on TV. Shortly after 4 P.M., just as CBS was beginning its coverage of the Woodward Stakes, the Dancer walked to the second turn and began jogging down the stretch toward the finish line. "Ladies and gentlemen . . . Native Dancer," Fred Caposella intoned over the public-address system, not that a horse who had been on the cover of *Time* needed an introduction.

He looked fit as he passed in front of the grandstand in the regal, upright pose he had cast in his post parades, eliciting a standing ovation from the crowd. His hair was braided, his step was lively, and Guerin was on his back dressed in cerise and white. Many other champions had seemed old and diminished in their valedictory saunters across the track, but this moment was underscored with raw temptation. The Dancer did, indeed, appear quite capable of running in the Woodward, and he would surely have handled the field with ease, even with a slight bulge in his belly, the first effect of retirement.

Intuitive to the end, the colt almost seemed to grasp that this was his final run through the stretch. He raced fifty yards past the finish line, resisting Guerin's gentle tugs, not wanting to stop. The crowd, too, kept cheering as he was finally halted, turned, and directed to the winner's enclosure, where George D. Widener, the head of Belmont, presented to Vanderbilt and Winfrey a silver plaque listing the Dancer's victories. Everyone shook hands as the horse eyed the crowd. Guerin excused himself—he had to ride another horse for Vanderbilt in the Woodward—and soon Harold Walker led the Dancer down the track, headed for the barn. Lester Murray placed a reassuring hand on the horse's flank as they walked. The Dancer's groom was unabashedly crying, his vision blurred as he helped the horse through an opening in the rail and beyond the view of the fans in the grandstand; as hardened as he was to the cycle of horses passing through the barn, Murray could barely stand the idea of the Dancer moving on. Maybe it was time for him to move on, too. He certainly would never have another horse like this. "Come on, Daddy, let's go get you something to eat," Murray murmured, knowing that his days in charge of the horse's care had dwindled to a precious few.

Two days later, there was a second farewell, as private as the first was public. As training hours began at Belmont, the Dancer was taken from stall 6 and loaded into a van outside Barn 20. Harold Walker led the horse away, with Murray too sad and emotional to take part. Arthur Daley captured the scene in a *New York Times* column that ran the next day: "In the ghostly half-light of yesterday's dawn . . . there were few to bid farewell to the king of the turf. A sad-eyed Winfrey watched him go. The 250-pound Harold Walker, the only groom strong enough to hold him, led him by the shank down the road to the van. The huge grey reared and bucked. Maybe he didn't want to quit the racing scene. At 5:51 A.M. he was in the van. It was his last post time."

A group of writers and photographers chronicled the horse's arrival at Sagamore Farm later that day. As he was being led off the van, the Dancer stopped, raised his head, and pricked his ears as he surveyed his surroundings, then nodded as he was led toward the barn where he would take up residence as America's most famous sire. Discovery, now a grand old man of twenty-one, had long occupied the first stall in the stallion barn, but he would move to the second stall to make room for his famous grandson. An arch would have to be cut into the doorway to enable the giant Dancer to pass back and forth without ducking his head.

A crew from *Omnibus,* a popular TV program, arrived at the farm within days. *Omnibus* was a serious-minded magazine-style show that aired on CBS on Sundays, featuring segments on a wide variety of topics. Don Hewitt, who later became famous as the executive producer of *60 Minutes,* headed the crew that came to Sagamore. On October 24, 1954, *Omnibus* began with the host, Alistair Cooke, detailing the episode's schedule. The first and last of the four segments would consist of one-act plays performed by a repertory theater company *Omnibus* was starting. In another segment, Allen Funt, the host of another popular CBS program, *Candid Camera,* would interview the young sons and daughters of United Nations delegates. In the third segment, Cooke said, viewers would meet "the famous American racehorse, now in retirement near Baltimore . . . Native Dancer."

The Dancer's segment opened with a shot of Ralph Kercheval, the manager of Sagamore, patting the famous grey in the stallion barn. "This is Native Dancer in the flesh," Kercheval said. Over the next fifteen minutes, Kercheval, Winfrey, and Guerin took turns walking around the barn and discussing the Dancer's breeding and racing career. Only one member of the horse's human "team" was missing. "Mr. Vanderbilt can't be here, unfortunately," Kercheval explained, "because he is in Africa working in conjunction with the World Veterans Federation."

Guerin, dressed in racing silks, gave a voice-over commentary as viewers watched a replay of the Metropolitan. "I get scared to death every time I see that film," said Guerin in his high-pitched Cajun accent. Winfrey, wearing a dark fedora and a white sports shirt with the collar open, replied, "You're not the only one—I haven't gotten over it yet." The trainer then ran his hands over the Dancer and offered a detailed physical description as a camera closed in: "Native Dancer is a big horse . . . his tremendous power is back here across the loins . . . very heavy and very strong . . . up here on his shoulder he's very thick and muscled . . . here you see a very heavy jowl— you'll never see a jowl much heavier than that on a thoroughbred . . . a beautiful head, wide between the eyes, with an alert expression."

Native Dancer stood calmly through the physical, nodding occasionally, as if he agreed with the compliments. Upon finishing, Winfrey turned to Guerin and said, "I think we're ready to give him a little go now, Eric, a little exercise." The trainer helped the jockey up, and Guerin rode the horse around a corner and into Sagamore's indoor training oval. Native Dancer jogged back and forth in front of the camera as Guerin spoke to him soothingly. "Hey, now . . . behave, boy . . . come on, let's go." The segment ended with Kercheval holding a microphone as Guerin dismounted behind him. "Native Dancer proved himself to be a champion on the racetrack, and we want to see if he'll continue to be a champion as a sire," Kercheval said. "That's what we want to know now."

With the departure of Hewitt and the *Omnibus* crew, the

Dancer's time in the public eye was over. The roar of the crowd and
the pomp of the winner's circle were giving way to the serenity and
abundance of a sire's life. The waiting line to breed to him had started
forming when he was two, and it was growing madly now. There was
a rumor that he might service fifty mares in his first year, with each
service costing $5,000. "The same indefinable genius that clings to
his races is even more pronounced as one imagines his future as a
stallion," Shipman wrote. "His masculinity is so pervading that if he
fails to stamp his [progeny] with authority, one's whole faith in the
meaning of individuality will be in question. He is a superb male animal."

Kercheval was in charge of him now. It was the farm manager's
job to remake the Dancer into an effective sire, essentially breaking
the horse again but teaching him to breed, not to race. Class was in
session through the winter of 1954 and spring of 1955 as the Dancer
was bred to his first book of mares. He had a lot to learn at first. "He
wanted to rush and dive at the mares," Kercheval recalled. Finally,
Kercheval took the shank from the groom one day as a breeding session was beginning and tugged hard as the Dancer started to lunge
again. The horse pulled back, reared, and flipped over backward,
crashing in a heap.

Kercheval was horrified. Horses that topple in such a manner
can land on their heads and suffer brain damage. "I could already see
the newspaper headline: 'Old Football Player Kills Great Racehorse,'"
Kercheval recalled. Native Dancer was motionless on the ground for
more heartbeats than Kercheval cared to count before finally stirring.
Kercheval stood back, afraid of what he had wrought. "And I'll be
damned," the farm manager recalled, "if that horse didn't get himself
up, take three or four steps over to me, and look me right in the eye.
I've never seen another horse respond like that. I thought, 'What, is
he gonna hit me or something?'"

Stunned and relieved, Kercheval led Native Dancer outside for a
lecture. "I said, 'Do you know how to do things properly now?'" the
farm manager recalled. "He went back in that breeding shed, walked
over to the mare, got himself ready to breed, and damn if he didn't
look right over at me, like he was getting ready to show me that he

had learned his lesson. I gave him a motion and said, 'Yes, go ahead,' and he went on and covered that mare perfectly, a beautiful job. It was like we had had a conversation. And I never had another moment's trouble with him after that."

Kercheval sat in his den in Lexington, Kentucky, as he recalled the moment. He was almost ninety now, able to reflect on a long and vigorous life that had included playing college and pro football and working with top thoroughbreds for decades. The fact that he had helped plan the mating that produced Native Dancer touched him with awe. "He was the strongest horse I ever saw," Kercheval recalled, "more like a big, powerful draft horse than a thoroughbred. He just had immense strength. And he was the smartest horse I was ever around, bar none. They say horses don't think, and I guess horses don't think, but some are able to reason within their wisdom, and a few operate on another level altogether. Native Dancer was that way. After that day that he flipped over, which, I believe, scared the hell out of both of us, if I ever pulled on the shank, he'd stop and look at me and say, 'Okay, boss, what's next?' It was amazing, the way that colt thought. God, what an animal he was."

# EPILOGUE

T he Dancer roamed Sagamore Farm's fields for thirteen years, maintaining his vigor and playfulness as his coat gradually turned a startling, distinguished white. "I was at a race at Laurel [in Maryland] in the early nineties, and a man came up to me and said, 'Was that your dad's farm?'" Alfred Vanderbilt III said. "I told him it was, and he said, 'Oh, I used to drive by there all the time and see Native Dancer in the field. It was like seeing Winston Churchill.'"

He was voted Horse of the Year for 1954 in every year-end poll of writers and racing officials, taking such honors for a second time even though he had raced only three times during the year.

Gradually, the Dancer grew accustomed to his new life as a stallion. A troublemaker at first, he bit a finger off one groom's hand, then bit the groom's replacement on the arm. A wily veteran groom named Joe Hall came to the rescue and developed a lasting bond with the Dancer similar to Lester Murray's relationship. "Joe Hall could walk into a stall and talk to a horse, and it was like a principal talking to a kid," recalled Laura Riley, a Maryland veterinarian who worked at Sagamore breaking yearlings in the 1970s. "When I met him, he was immensely proud of having been the big horse's groom. So proud to have been entrusted with the great horse. Also proud that he was the only one who could deal with him. Otherwise, the horse may not have gotten to stand stud."

The Dancer was never less than one of the world's foremost stallions, his stud fee starting at $5,000 in 1955 and rising over the years to $20,000, the highest advertised fee in the world. But money was no object to the horsemen who wanted their mares bred to the Grey Ghost. A succession of top mares from across America as well as from Canada and Europe made the trek to the Worthington Valley north of Baltimore. Harold Ferguson, hired as Sagamore's office manager in 1951, replaced Ralph Kercheval as the overall farm manager in 1958—Kercheval went back to training a stable—and carefully guided the Dancer's stallion career along with Vanderbilt, limiting the horse's bookings to between twenty-five and forty a year.

With the racing industry watching, the Dancer's sons and daughters began competing on tracks across America and Europe in 1958. The first crops were mildly disappointing, compiling respectable totals of wins and earnings but lacking horses of distinction. The Dancer's first champion was a filly named Hula Dancer who raced in Europe and was undefeated as a two-year-old in 1962. The first American-based star was a brilliant colt named Raise a Native who raced only four times but won the 1963 Futurity Stakes in a romp and set a track record for five furlongs at Aqueduct. Vanderbilt raised the Dancer's stud fee by $2,500 solely because of the furor the colt caused.

A bowed tendon prevented Raise a Native from running in the Kentucky Derby and possibly avenging his father's only defeat, but the Dancer's blood soon began to haunt Churchill Downs. In the same year Raise a Native was unable to run, one of the Dancer's grandsons, a small, fiery Canadian-bred colt named Northern Dancer, won the 1964 Derby. Foaled out of Natalma, a Native Dancer–sired mare, Northern Dancer also won the Preakness before finishing third in the Belmont in his bid to become the first Triple Crown winner since Citation. Two years later, a dark brown colt named Kauai King, sired by the Dancer himself, scored a front-running win as the 5–2 favorite in the 1966 Derby and also won the Preakness before faltering in the Belmont, finishing fourth in his Triple Crown bid.

Respect for the Dancer as a sire was on the rise. Forty-five

Dancer-sired horses won races in 1965, the total up sharply from thirty-one two years earlier. In 1966, with Kauai King leading the way, forty-three Dancer-breds combined to win one hundred races and $977,254, the second-highest total of the year for any sire, behind only Bold Ruler.

Another strong year was ending and the Dancer was already booked to breed to twenty-eight mares for the coming season when he refused to take a carrot from Joe Hall on the afternoon of November 14, 1967. Massive and white at age seventeen, he usually eagerly took a carrot in exchange for letting Hall put a shank on him. He refused the carrot again in his stall and glanced back at his sides several times, as if he were experiencing pain there. Hall suspected a mild case of colic; the groom had walked the Dancer through a bout with colic six years earlier and detected some of the same symptoms.

A farm superintendent phoned Dr. Irvin Frock, a local veterinarian. Colic medicine was administered and the Dancer's condition fluctuated through the night; he pawed the ground and was restless at times—traditional signs of intestinal distress—then seemed relieved. When his condition worsened the next day, Dr. Frock, fearing an intestinal blockage, advised that he be transferred to a clinic.

The Dancer was taken by van to the University of Pennsylvania's New Bolton Center in Kennett Square, Pennsylvania. Barely able to stand during loading, he was severely dehydrated and in shock by the time he arrived in the evening, his temperature and heart rate soaring. He was immediately sedated and wheeled into surgery, and when the surgeons opened him up, they found a tumor the size of an orange looping over the small intestine and "strangling" it. They also found other small tumors throughout the abdominal cavity.

Ten feet of intestine were removed during three hours of surgery. The Dancer was then taken to a recovery stall shortly after midnight, still under sedation. Hall, who had made the trip with the Dancer in the back of the van, recounted what happened next in an interview with turf writer Snowden Carter that appeared in the December 1967 issue of *Maryland Horse* magazine: "We all stand around and watch him as he comes to. Dancer tries a couple of times to get up, but he can't make it. All the time, I'm talking to him. I keep saying to myself, 'This ol' horse ain't gonna die.' But he does. About 5:30 [A.M.] I'm standing beside him. He draws a deep breath and then he don't breathe no more."

It was hard to imagine, but the mighty Dancer was dead.

"After a while they wheel him back to the van," Hall continued in his *Maryland Horse* interview. "We're bringing him home to bury him, but I still don't think that Dancer's dead. We get to the farm at about 11:30 in the morning and there's nobody around. I'm sitting up front with the driver. I tell him to blow his horn so they'll know we're here. He reaches up and pulls that cord to the horn. When I hear that horn, then all of a sudden I can't hold the water back to save my life. The water runs down my face. I don't know why the horn did that to me. It sounds so far away. I said to the driver, 'Man, don't blow that horn no more.'"

The Dancer was buried in a field at Sagamore Farm, his grave marked with a headstone alongside those of Discovery and some of Vanderbilt's other top horses. Vanderbilt was disconsolate. "He got letters from people from all over the world, and he didn't want to answer them," recalled his daughter Heidi. "I was surprised that he wasn't going to take that on himself. I don't know why. He could be very reticent about things that were painful. So I told him I would answer the letters. They were from people who remembered watching the horse on TV, or he'd won them some money. Some of them had followed his entire life and knew everything about him. They were heartbroken that he died. These were genuine letters of condolence. There were many. It took me a long time to answer them all, and they kept coming and coming. It was sad, but also wonderful that he had been such an important horse to so many."

The Dancer's success as a stallion was illustrated in his career production statistics. Of the 304 foals he sired in thirteen crops, 224 reached the races and 194 of those who raced won at least once; both figures were well above industry averages. Most significant, an exceptionally high 15 percent of his foals won stakes races, the ultimate barometer of class. Though generally regarded at the time as a mild disappointment when measured against what had been expected of him, the Dancer had passed along quality to the generation that followed him.

As if to honor him, one of his sons, Dancer's Image—a grey with tender ankles, no less—won the first Kentucky Derby run after his death, rallying from tenth on the second turn to win by a length and a half. Dancer's Image was later disqualified and placed last, in one of the Derby's greatest controversies, when his postrace drug test allegedly turned up traces of phenylbutazone, or "bute," a painkiller legal at some tracks but not Churchill Downs.

Still somewhat uncertain at the time of his death, the Dancer's influence on pedigrees soon became far more profound than anyone could have imagined. His son Raise a Native was an enormously successful stallion, siring Alydar and Mr. Prospector, two dominant American sires of the 1980s. And Northern Dancer, Native Dancer's grandson, surpassed them all as the most successful sire of the second half of the twentieth century, with many of his champion sons and daughters racing in Europe.

Through the greatness of Raise a Native, Alydar, Mr. Prospector, and Northern Dancer, Native Dancer's name emerged as one of the great and enduring markers of class in a pedigree. He was a great-grandfather of Affirmed, a Triple Crown winner in 1978. His descendants won many of the major races around the world, including the Breeders' Cup Classic, England's Epsom Derby, and France's Arc de Triomphe, and they dominated the Kentucky Derby. The Dancer was a great-grandfather of Derby winners Genuine Risk (1980), Alysheba (1987), Strike the Gold (1991), and Fusaichi Pegasus (2000); a great-great-grandfather of Ferdinand (1986), Unbridled (1990), Thunder Gulch (1995), Real Quiet (1998), and War Emblem (2002); and a great-great-great-grandfather of Sea Hero (1993), Grindstone (1996), Charismatic (1999), and Monarchos (2001). The latter, racing forty-eight years after the Dancer in the Derby, was a virtual clone of his famous forefather, a powerful grey.

With War Emblem's victory at Churchill Downs in 2002, five straight winners and seven of the past eight were traceable to the Dancer within four generations. To say the Grey Ghost was haunting America's greatest race would be an understatement. It was as if there was no end to the revenge to be exacted for his loss to Dark Star.

Remarkably, Vanderbilt wasn't among the many owners and breeders who won major races with horses that traced to the Dancer. Though he bred mares to the Dancer every year and certainly benefited in the 1950s and 1960s as the owner of such a sire, Vanderbilt himself never bred another horse of the same caliber. After Kauai King was purchased out of a sales ring and won the Kentucky Derby, Vanderbilt joked, "I guess I should be buying Native Dancers instead of trying to breed them."

He tried to breed another with the same sire and dam in the 1950s; once the Dancer's greatness was known, Geisha was never bred to any stallion other than Polynesian. They had five full brothers and sisters, all bred by Vanderbilt, but none had their famous brother's class. Only three made it to the races, and just one, Geisha's last foal, was able to win a race. "The full brothers and sisters were nice horses with that good conformation and vigor, but they didn't want to run like Native Dancer," Dan W. Scott told the *Thoroughbred Times* in 1998.

When Heidi Vanderbilt turned eleven in 1959, she received one of the full brothers as a present from her father. "His name was Noble Savage," Heidi recalled. "He had started on the track, but he was a terrible handful and not a good racehorse, and that combination got him demoted. He was a dappled gray, about 16.1 or 16.2 [hands tall], not as pretty as the Dancer. I was riding a lot and looking for a show horse, a hunting horse. It was not a great match. I was eleven and he was three. He was too much horse for me at that age. When I was fourteen or so, we sold him. He was a very, very good jumping horse. I went and saw him jump at Madison Square Garden. He went white-gray like his brother."

Vanderbilt's racing stable dwindled significantly after a phone call from Bill Winfrey, his trainer, in 1956, less than two years after the Dancer's retirement. Vanderbilt, Winfrey, and jockey Eric Guerin had continued to race and win in 1955 with a large stable including Social Outcast and Find, but then Winfrey, who had always eyed other professions somewhat enviously, abruptly decided to retire.

"As my father told the story years later, he was literally leaving the house to go on a trip to Africa and the phone rang," Alfred Vanderbilt III said. "It was Winfrey saying, 'I've raced the best for the best, I've had it, I'm through, I'm going to retire.' Dad said, 'All right, I'm leaving, too. I'm going to retire, too. Sell the horses.' It was a huge decision absolutely made on the spur of the moment."

Vanderbilt's marriage to Jeanne had collapsed—their divorce was finalized in December 1956—and he was traveling extensively as president of the World Veterans Fund, the money-raising arm of a federation of veterans' groups in twenty-nine countries. He had toured Asia through the first months of 1956 and was headed to Africa when Winfrey called. On May 21, 1956, a dispersal of Vanderbilt's racing stock was held at Belmont. Thirty-seven of his forty-two horses in training were sold, leaving only old-timers Social Outcast, Find, Beachcomber, First Glance, and Crash Dive to race in cerise and white. Winfrey continued to train the horses through 1957, fulfilling what he saw as his obligation to the stable before retiring. In the end, Find earned more than $800,000, Social Outcast earned almost $670,000, and Vanderbilt's foal crop of 1950 was regarded as one of the greatest in history.

In 1958, Winfrey moved to San Clemente, California, with his wife Elaine, "certain as anything can be certain that I'd never go back [East]," he told the *Blood-Horse* in 1985. Vanderbilt hired George Poole to train the stable—Poole had been John Gaver's assistant at Greentree—but the stable was no longer a powerhouse and Poole resigned in 1962. Vanderbilt continued to race a small stable through the years with other trainers such as Mike Freeman, Bobby Lake, Rick Violette, and Mary Eppler handling the stock. Vanderbilt "never stopped trying" to lure Winfrey back, according to Winfrey's son Carey.

After moving to California, Bill Winfrey took real estate classes and pondered a career change but always came back to the track. He spent most of the rest of his life in California, raising eight children. His family came first. "He felt that the separations caused by the nomadic life of a trainer had ruined his first marriage," Carey Winfrey said, "and by God, he wasn't going to let that ruin his second."

Winfrey did come back East in 1962 when Ogden Phipps asked him to replace retiring legend Sunny Jim Fitzsimmons as the trainer of the family's Phipps and Wheatley stables. "It was my ego, I guess, that took me back," Winfrey told the *Blood-Horse*. The job was the best in the country with Phipps-owned champion sire Bold Ruler filling the barn with talented homebreds, and Winfrey won $1.35 million in purses in 1964 to break the record for a trainer held since 1947 by Calumet's Jimmy Jones. That year, Winfrey had the champion two-year-old colt, Bold Lad, and also the champion two-year-old filly, Queen Empress. Bold Lad was a disappointment in the 1965 Kentucky Derby, finishing tenth as the 2–1 favorite, but another two-year-old star, Buckpasser, came along that year and Winfrey again earned more than $1 million, finishing second in the country to Hirsch Jacobs.

With many years of certain success ahead, Winfrey stunned the racing world by walking away from the Phipps job in December 1965. The Phippses were more hands-on than Vanderbilt, and while Winfrey told the *Blood-Horse* in 1985 that he was never second-guessed, he also said, "I just didn't have a feeling of freedom there." Carey Winfrey said, "He walked away on principle from the best job in the country." His replacement dominated the trainers' earnings list for the next three years, but Winfrey, ever the iconoclast, moved back to California and took his family to Europe for a year. Elected to the National Museum of Racing's Hall of Fame in 1971, he continued to train a few horses through the years. He died in 1994 of complications from Alzheimer's disease.

Unlike Winfrey, Eric Guerin had tasted victory in the Kentucky Derby, winning aboard Jet Pilot in 1947. He had three more chances after losing on the Dancer, finishing third in 1955 on Summer Tan, sixth in 1956 on Career Boy, and thirteenth in 1971 on Impetuosity. Although his career peaked during his association with Vanderbilt, which ended in the late 1950s, he continued to ride through the 1960s and early 1970s, finally retiring at age fifty-one. He was still active when elected to the Hall of Fame in 1972.

After retiring, he worked as a mutuels clerk in New York for three years in the late 1970s, then underwent heart surgery and, improbably, went back to the track and found work as an exercise rider, galloping horses for Hall of Fame trainers Allen Jerkens and Woody Stephens. "He did it because he loved horses and wanted to be around horses," said his nephew Frank Curry. "He was in his sixties and still doing stuff teenagers do, just so he could be around horses."

A costly divorce years earlier had lowered his lifestyle, but he re-married happily and spent more than thirty years with his second wife. "He wound up later in life not having that much money, but the nice thing was, he had none of the surliness that he might have had because he was winding up that way," Jerkens said. "He was just as nice and easygoing as when he was riding and winning. He was gal-loping horses for me, and he had the same wonderful patience with the horses that he'd had when he was on top."

After moving to Florida in 1989, Guerin worked as a mutuels clerk at Calder and Gulfstream, then became ill with a blood disorder and died of heart complications in 1993. He was sixty-eight. His obit-uaries pointed out that he had won 2,712 races over thirty-five years but would be remembered for losing the Derby in 1953: even in death, he couldn't escape that defeat. "Eric Guerin was a good man and a good rider, and he helped Native Dancer on numerous occa-sions," *Daily Racing Form* columnist Joe Hirsch said. " The worst thing that can be said about him is that maybe he didn't help that one time."

Guerin's final rites, held in the winner's circle at Gulfstream, were poignant. A musician played "The Lord's Prayer" on a harmon-ica, and Guerin's son, Ronnie—the youngster of "Hi, Ronnie" fame, now almost fifty—spread his ashes in the flower beds. Ronnie then turned to the small circle of mourners and said, "I would like to think that somewhere my father is riding Native Dancer right now—and Dark Star, you don't have a chance this time."

Vanderbilt remarried in 1957 to twenty-year-old Jean Harvey of Chicago. They had three children and traveled extensively, often with Broadway producer-director Harold Prince and Prince's wife, Judy. "Alfred loved to travel, to probe, to learn, and to have a good time," Prince recalled. "We went to the Greek islands together, the four of us, and stayed on Mrs. [Joan Whitney] Payson's boat. Then we went to Russia. That was fun. We arrived at the airport in Moscow, and the minute they saw his passport, they went nuts. It became clear that this was one of those names they had studied in their history books. But what they had been damning to hell, the capitalist Vanderbilts, they also were duly impressed by. It was like the czar was coming back. They saw Vanderbilt and decided I wasn't Harold Prince, I was Prince Harold. We got on the coattails of that. We stayed a block from Red Square. They gave Alfred and Jean the Lenin Suite."

Ultimately, Vanderbilt's third marriage also ended in divorce amid rumors that Vanderbilt, at sixty-two, was personally and professionally fond of Robyn Smith, a twenty-nine-year-old female jockey. (Smith later married Vanderbilt's friend Fred Astaire, after Vanderbilt had introduced them.) Years later, Vanderbilt's daughter, Victoria, said that when she had asked her father about his life, he replied, "It's pretty simple. I went to the races, got married, got divorced. Went to the races, got married, got divorced. Went to the races, got married, got divorced. Went to the races."

Although his racing stable never ranked among the national leaders after the 1956 dispersal, he remained prominent in the industry. He made the cover of *Sports Illustrated* in 1963, the headline reading, "Alfred G. Vanderbilt Rebels Against Racing's Establishment." In the article, written by Alfred Wright, Jimmy Kilroe, the director of racing at Santa Anita, said, "Looking at it from the standpoint of racing officials, owners, breeders, trainers, jockeys and the racing press, I would have to say Vanderbilt is the most respected man in racing today."

Through the years, he remained involved in the industry as a Jockey Club member, president of the Thoroughbred Owners and Breeders Association, and chairman of the New York Racing Association for four years in the early 1970s. He was honored with the Eclipse Award of Merit, for lifetime contributions to the sport, in 1994. The New York Turf Writers voted him the Man Who Has Done the Most for Racing four times.

"Racing was his heart and soul," his daughter Victoria said at a memorial service after his death. "Sure, he loved pretty girls and travel, his kids, his books and music, chicken hash at the '21' Club and a good game of charades. But none of that could compare to his passion for the sport of kings."

It remained the constant in his life even as his travels around the world took him away for months at a time every year. He always came back to the races and his beloved morning routine. "Even as he got older he continued to go to the track every single morning," Heidi Vanderbilt said. "He just loved the horses, the sport, the people. He loved watching the horses. He loved the casual conversation that's really what the track is all about. He would go and talk and watch. That was his breakfast."

Gradually, the way of life he had been born into—the life he had always known—ceased to exist. Louis Cheri, his valet and confidant, died. Sagamore Farm was sold to a developer in 1986. "He was a witness to huge changes in lifestyle," Harold Prince said. "Things that had been taken for granted started to just go away. But I never heard him call attention to it."

Society changed profoundly around him, with generations of "new money" surpassing the old and its world of understated manners. "He still had a lot of money, but he didn't have billions, and he had devoted his life to a sport you don't make money in," Alfred Vanderbilt III said. "I think his expectation was, 'I'm still going to be Alfred Vanderbilt tomorrow,' and that would be a constant. But it wasn't. Things turned on their head in a lot of ways in the sixties. After the Beatles went on *Ed Sullivan,* what had been high [society] practically made you a pariah. All of our parents were baffled by what was happening and why, and he was no different."

But he still had his friends and family, his books and music, his dry wit and nonconformist's outlook. "I interviewed him late in life, and he didn't look down on new things, like so many older people do," Tim Capps said. "There was a traditional part of him that wished racing could be like it was, when you drew 40,000 fans and everyone wore a coat and tie, but he knew the world had changed. That told me, 'Here's a guy who has lived his life as a progressive, always a little ahead of other people.'"

There was sorrow later in his life. His eldest son from his third marriage, Nicholas, was reported missing on a climbing expedition in British Columbia, Canada, in 1984, and never found. Then, sadly, the onset of macular degeneration robbed him of much of his sight. "His life was filled with joy until the unfortunate latter days," Clyde Roche said.

Though virtually blind, he still went to Belmont almost every morning, then returned in the afternoon for the races. "I would talk to him every day by the rail," Allen Jerkens said. "His chauffeur would bring him, and he would bring cookies for the people he liked, people who rode the ponies and such. They'd come up to him and say, 'Mr. V., where's my cookie?' A lady made them for him. Sometimes he'd be a little tired and go home early. He couldn't see well. He'd go by voices mostly. But he still came."

Harold Prince and Vanderbilt had lost touch after Vanderbilt's third divorce, but they reconnected one day at Belmont in the early 1990s. A mutual friend, Tommy Volano, a music publisher and horse owner, brought them together. "Tommy said to me, 'I want you to come to Belmont with me. I've got a reason,'" Prince recalled. "I said, 'Great.' He had cooked up a lunch with Alfred, who could no longer see. Alfred would sit under the TV monitor and listen to the races. Sit there all day. He couldn't see the races, but he could hear them, and he so wanted to be there. It was wonderful to see him again. And it was the last time I saw him."

Vanderbilt was still racing a small stable, with his horses now trained by Maryland-based Mary Eppler. She won some stakes races for him, and then Vanderbilt, at age eighty-three, sent her to a 1996 Florida sale of unraced two-year-olds with orders to find a Kentucky Derby prospect. She delivered. A colt named Traitor, purchased for $102,000, won the Futurity—the same race for juveniles that Native Dancer had won in 1952—and finished second in the Champagne Stakes. He was considered a top contender for the Kentucky Derby the next spring.

"Traitor looked like another great horse, and Dad was very excited," Heidi Vanderbilt said. "It brought back memories of Dancer. Dad thought he could get to the big races again with Traitor."

The Dancer's Derby loss had become a painful memory for

Vanderbilt through the years. He had never entered another horse in the race and didn't even return to Louisville for years. Then his passion was rekindled when Traitor came along. "Before Mary bought Traitor, I told her that I was getting pretty damn old, and that if I'm ever going to win a Derby, I'd better do it soon," Vanderbilt told *Los Angeles Times* racing writer Bill Christine one morning at Hialeah in March 1997.

It didn't happen. Traitor had surgery to remove chips in his right knee in the fall of his two-year-old year, then missed two weeks of training the next spring when he lunged into a fence after a workout at Hialeah. He was declared out of the Kentucky Derby, then was permanently retired when he tore a ligament in his left foreleg during a gallop at Pimlico before the Preakness.

Vanderbilt was devastated.

"It was a huge disappointment," Heidi Vanderbilt said. "He'd had this wonderful career in racing, with this gap of one race, and when Traitor couldn't go, Dad realized that he wasn't going to have that race. There was no way to make it okay. You couldn't say, 'Well, I'll get it later.' If he hadn't been blind, this might not have become an issue. It wasn't like he talked about it. He rarely referred to it. But I knew what happened. When Traitor got injured and he was so upset about it, it had to do with Dancer losing the Derby. He was upset about Traitor, but also about Dancer. I think it's common as you get older to choose the things you didn't have and reflect, and that certainly happened with Dad and the Derby. He never put on a grand opera about it. He never spoke in these terms. But not winning the Derby was very important to him. That loss in 1953 was a very big sadness and a very big sorrow."

On November 12, 1999, Vanderbilt spent the early morning at Belmont, then returned to his home near Mill Neck, on Long Island, and went to his bedroom to take a nap. He never awakened. "My father went to the track this morning," Alfred Vanderbilt III poignantly told reporters who called within hours, working on obituaries. In death, at age eighty-seven, he was recalled as a racing man without peer, an owner, breeder, track operator, and industry leader, and, perhaps, the last great sportsman.

A memorial service was held, appropriately, in the clubhouse at Aqueduct, and hundreds of mourners came to pay their respects on a foggy, misty morning. Harold Prince, Clyde Roche, and Vanderbilt's daughter Victoria were among those who spoke, and at the end of the service, the mourners were asked to turn to the track. A filly ridden by a jockey wearing Vanderbilt's cerise and white silks came out of the mist and raced through the stretch as the crowd applauded. It was the last ride for Vanderbilt's colors.

In one of his last interviews, Vanderbilt told turf writer Tom Keyser of the *Baltimore Sun,* "I'm interested in what happens in racing because it's been my whole life, but it ain't what it used to be."

No one could argue. Racing had fallen far from the high of the early 1950s, when crowds of 50,000 routinely attended major events and the sport was deeply ingrained in the public's awareness. Although still a multibillion-dollar industry with its share of intense fans, and still popular in Kentucky, Southern California, and across the country during the Triple Crown, racing was no longer regarded as a major sport in America by the end of the century. It had been passed and lapped many times by pro football, pro basketball, hockey, golf, and even stock car racing.

The biggest blow, unmistakably, was the rise of other forms of gambling, beginning in the 1960s. Racing no longer had the betting market cornered once gamblers were able to go to Las Vegas or buy a lottery ticket to scratch their itch. The sport's concurrent decline in popularity was not a coincidence. Although the rise of off-track betting and simulcasting increased betting totals, fans were discouraged from going to the races, thus emptying grandstands and ruining the atmosphere.

"In their anxiety to get more betting, they took the people out of it," Allen Jerkens said. "In the fifties, people would bring fifty dollars to the track, and if they blew it, they blew it. Now there are all these gimmick bets, and so many races to bet. How much does the public have to bet? In the old days, you would go to the paddock, look at the animals, make a decision, and bet. Now you're too busy betting on a simulcast race, betting numbers, betting gimmicks. It's taken away the horse part of the game. A lot of the younger people aren't interested in the animals themselves. That hurts racing."

Industry infighting and numerous political missteps were also ruinous, as was the sport's inability to connect with a younger crowd. Fabled champions such as Secretariat and Seattle Slew resonated beyond the sport's boundaries, but overall, racing failed to maintain even a semblance of the vast constituency it had gripped in Native Dancer's day. In the end, critically, it failed to use television correctly, stubbornly clinging to the outdated notion that the medium might ruin attendance as other sports, most notably pro football, used it to catapult to spectacular prominence.

"The people in racing have only themselves to blame," Joe Tannenbaum said. "They continued to see TV as a nemesis, and the sport virtually dropped off the screen, except for the major events. And that was very, very damaging." Added Tommy Roberts, "It's just incredible, looking back and knowing what you know about the power of TV. You say, 'How could they be so blind?' But they were."

The sport still had a wondrous past and a sizable following, however, and as the century ended, there was a rush to put the chronicle of American racing history in order. A panel of racing experts convened by the Associated Press was asked to select the best horses of the century. Native Dancer tied for third with Citation, behind Man O' War and Secretariat and ahead of Triple Crown winners such as Seattle Slew and Affirmed. One could only wonder what Eddie Arcaro, who died in 1996, would have said about a tie between the Dancer and Citation. A similar panel commissioned by the *Blood-Horse* placed the Dancer seventh.

"He's never really received the acclaim he should," said Tommy Trotter, a panelist in the end-of-the-century voting. "Secretariat was beaten once as a two-year-old. Native Dancer was unbeaten. Secretariat was beaten three times as a three-year-old. Native Dancer lost once by a head. Secretariat didn't race as a four-year-old. Native Dancer didn't race much, but he carried 130 pounds and 137 pounds and won and was voted Horse of the Year. It might be that people don't think of him because he seldom won easily, but his record speaks for itself."

Joe Hirsch said, "He was one of the unluckiest horses of all time. He had a remarkable record, winning twenty-one of twenty-two. To win them all wouldn't have been human. But if not for those inches that cost him the Derby, he would have gone undefeated. And while they talk about a Triple Crown being rare, an undefeated career is really rare. Colin went undefeated in 1905. So did Personal Ensign eighty years later. That's it, two in history. And Native Dancer was almost the third. If he'd won the Derby, somehow made up those final inches on Dark Star, there's no telling what people would think of him now."

# ACKNOWLEDGMENTS

Thanks to the many people who donated their time and their memories of racing's golden age. Here are those who were interviewed or helped in any way: Claude Appley, Mary Appley, Ted Atkinson, Dale Austin, William Boniface, Tim Capps, Costy Caras, Frank Chirkinian, Bill Christine, Frank Curry, John Derr, Judy Ohl Deubler, Leonard Dorfman, Dominick Dunne, Dorothy Everson, Clem Florio, Bob Fortus, Jackie Gibson, Tom Gilcoyne, Beth Guerin, Dr. Alex Harthill, Joe Hickey, Allen Jerkens, Joe Kelly, Blanche Kercheval, Ralph Kercheval, Tom Keyser, Leonard Koppett, Chick Lang, Charles Ray Leblanc, Jinx McCrary, Jim McKay, J. C. Mergler, Mervin Muniz, William Passmore, Lulu Pate, Pete Pedersen, Joe Pons, Harold Prince, Laura Riley, Tommy Roberts, Dr. Jack Robinson, Clyde Roche, Chris Schenkel, Dan W. Scott, Dan W. Scott III, Bayard Sharp, Bill Shoemaker, Bert Sugar, Joe Tannenbaum, Tommy Trotter, Alfred Vanderbilt III, Heidi Vanderbilt, Jeanne Vanderbilt, Carey Winfrey, Elaine Winfrey, Vic Ziegel.

The Maryland Jockey Club, Churchill Downs, Alfred Vanderbilt III, Carey Winfrey, Claude and Mary Appley, the Library of Congress, the *Baltimore Sun*, the Enoch Pratt Free Library in Baltimore, the New York City Public Library, the Keeneland Library, and the Maryland Horse Breeders Association provided microfilm and/or hard copies of old newspapers and magazines, or other research tools. Ray

Paulick of the *Blood-Horse* was kind to grant access to his magazine's incredibly comprehensive morgue files. Books that helped provide background and understanding included *Their Turf,* by Bernard Livingston; *The Fireside Book of Horse Racing,* edited by David F. Woods; *The Tumult and the Shouting,* by Grantland Rice; *The Best Sports Stories of 1954,* by Arno Press; *The Thoroughbred,* by E. S. Montgomery; *This Was Racing,* by Joe H. Palmer; *The Fifties,* by David Halberstam; *The Fifties: The Way We Really Were,* by Douglas T. Miller and Marion Nowak; and *The American Dream: The 50s,* by the editors of Time-Life Books. Gerry Strine's superb 1985 interview with Bill Winfrey, published in the *Blood-Horse,* was invaluable, as evidenced by the credit it receives throughout the text. Also helpful, not to mention inspiring, were John McNulty's classic 1953 *New Yorker* article, "A Room at the Barn," Marshall Smith's 1953 *Life* feature on the Dancer, and the turf writing of columnist Evan Shipman and others from the long-defunct *Morning Telegraph.* Those were the days.

Special thanks to my agent, Scott Waxman, for helping make the book a reality; Les Pockell at Warner Books, whose suggestions for the manuscript were insightful; Alfred Vanderbilt III, who took a keen interest in the project and helped in countless ways; Olive Cooney, who provided origins of inspiration, a stack of research material, and lots of enthusiasm; Beverly Bridger at Sagamore Lodge, who helped me understand the Vanderbilts; the editors of the *Baltimore Sun,* who gave me a year off to write; Steve Proctor of the *Sun,* who read the manuscript and made helpful suggestions; and Jean Eisenberg, who read every version of the manuscript as it progressed. Most important, I'm grateful to my wife, Mary Wynne, and my children, Anna and Wick, for their patience, understanding, and love. This book is for them.

# INDEX